With a Merry Heart

Also by Janet Gillespie

A Joyful Noise

With a Merry Heart

JANET GILLESPIE

Harper & Row, Publishers
New York, Hagerstown, San Francisco, London

FIRST EDITION

Designed by C. Linda Dingler

Library of Congress Cataloging in Publication Data

Gillespie, Janet.
   With a merry heart.
   1. Gillespie, Janet. 2. Wicks, Robert Russell,
1882–   3. Wickes family. 4. Presbyterian Church
—Biography. I. Title.
BX9225.G49A34 1976   974'.04'0924 [B]   76–5125
ISBN 0–06–011537–8

76 77 78 79 80 10 9 8 7 6 5 4 3 2 1

To Muddie ("Mum"), who has a merry heart, with much love and thanks

A merry heart maketh a cheerful countenance.

Proverbs: XIV, 13

With a Merry Heart

❧ 1 ❧

Mornings in Summer

When I look back at my beginnings it is always a sunny morning at Snowdon, our summer house, and people are laughing and running up and down stairs with their arms full of clean sheets and diapers. Pop in a woman's apron is upstairs emptying slop jars into a tin pail and sluicing out chamber pots. I am sitting with my brother Aldie in the sun by the front door waiting for our Uncle Tink to come down the hill and play with us. The sun is hot and the scent of honeysuckle from the vine outside pours in with the warmth.

Then there's another vignette of Pop standing on the sideboard flapping his arms and crowing like a rooster while Aldie screamed in his highchair below. This somewhat bizarre behavior was commonplace in those days and was an attempt on Pop's part to distract his son's attention so Mum could get some cereal into his mouth. Aldie was from birth a fussy eater; in fact, he seemed to be against all food except milk. As a result his mealtimes were bedlam, with Pop climbing over and under the furniture, bellowing like a bull, mooing like a cow, or combining the roles of dog and cat in an ear-splitting fight. He would even come up under the tray of the highchair and allow Mum to feed him oatmeal out of Aldie's spoon—an act of heroism that impressed me a good deal.

The sideboard at Snowdon was not something you forgot easily.

It was a massive affair of golden oak surmounted by a large mirror with gargoyles on each side. On top of this was a shelf and on top of that was a hideous bearded face holding the ends of two garlands in its mouth. The very thought of this face and the sideboard brings back to me the blissful feeling of summer mornings on the hill when the house was new and smelled sweetly of pine boards and kerosene lamps. The faint clamor of gulls floated through the open windows all day long, and the breeze sang in the screens as it did nowhere else. On that sideboard used to stand cut-glass bowls full of strawberries or sliced peaches and bunches of field flowers stuffed into Dundee marmalade jars. The latter were my contributions—buttercups, daisies and red clover that grew in the long grass all over the hill.

The house was finished when Aldie was six months old, so this must have been its first summer and Aldie's too. It follows that it was my third. I had been born in July of my first summer and didn't get to the Point until August. My second summer is a bit vague in my mind, but there is a historic photograph of me in the ancestral baby carriage overseeing the planting of the Scotch pines that bordered the road to the hill. Baba, my grandmother, believed in celebrating all anniversaries with some significant act, and on my first birthday she set out one hundred little trees to mark the event. They were *Scotch* pines because of our Scottish heritage and, as Baba often said, we would always remember that year because of me—her first grandchild.

There were other events that made that year memorable but I was unaware of them at the time. It was 1914.

The road was called Scotch Pine Lane after this. In that era it ran from the main road up over the top of our hill and down the other side to the shore of the West River—a distance of about half a mile. It was a dirt road with a strip of grass down the middle where Gyp, the family horse, left hoof marks and piles of manure.

Synton, Baba's big Victorian house, stood on top of the hill facing the sea, and when I was born it was the only structure on the property. My grandfather built it in 1888, two whole years before even Mum was born. It was a nineteenth-century "summer cottage"—a huge square house with brown shingles, a roof like a

Chinese straw hat and a veranda all around, where old silvery rocking chairs sat waiting in the sun. There were enormous linden trees near one corner, and when they were in bloom the veranda and the whole house smelled of honey.

The view from Synton was spectacular. The sea filled the whole horizon to the south, and on the west was the tidal river running four miles inland between wooded banks. You could look right across the Massachusetts border into Rhode Island, a feat that seemed amazing to us, but Pop told us that he could spit from Massachusetts into Rhode Island, and once he took us over to Adamsville and did it. So did we. Of course, Baba was not told of this vulgar affair.

Baba lived at Synton the year round with Aunt K., Mum's older sister, and Tink, her youngest brother, who was our beloved playmate and one of our favorite human beings. He was about twenty but he had never grown older than three inside, so his interests and ours were identical. Every summer morning opened up a prospect of enchanted hours in his company, as except for meals and sleeping he spent all day with us. Like Aldie and me, he was under the rule of grownups and nursemaids. His own nurse, Lizzie, was a formidable character who had been with the family ever since Baba was married, but by our time she was so old that she never left the house, and Tink was relatively free once he came down the hill to us. Together we formed a triumvirate against the regiment of women and spent a lot of time giggling and whispering together in our hammock.

No one in the whole world was like Tink, with his rosy button nose, impish grin and dumpy, pear-shaped figure. He had a special nice smell like hay and freshly ironed shirts, and everything about him was cosy and comforting. When we cried he patted us like puppies, soothing us with tender words and promises of future joys.

Tink came down to play with us the minute he finished breakfast and would have moved in with us if he could. But we were within megaphone distance of Synton so Baba was able to summon him at mealtimes.

Our land was west of Synton, about halfway down the hill to

the river, and the house was built on the brink of a great well of green leaves and blue water. On the west side we were above the treetops and so high above the river that the sailboats down there looked like toys.

On the east side, though, the house seemed to hug the hillside, snuggled down among the junipers and bayberry bushes like a partridge on a nest. I always think of it buried in pink roses and honeysuckle and sunk to the windows in Pop's barberry hedge, but I suppose in the first year it stood alone on the grass, with only the big flat doorstone in front of the little porch.

Pop had no money outside his minister's salary, so he had been able to build only a basic shelter—four shingled walls with a gambrel roof and a woodshed containing a privy. By Baba's standards it was a very primitive affair.

I loved the house then. It was so light and airy it hardly seemed like a real house at all—more like a barn. Compared to our house in the city it was just a shell of new lumber, with unsheathed walls of pine from which the resin still oozed in sticky drops. We used to pry these off and chew them in our leisure moments. You could also push knots out of the partitions and peek into other rooms.

Between the studs were little shelves and cubbyholes where people left shells, birds' nests, fishing lines, hairpins and other odds and ends on their way somewhere else. There was very little furniture in the empty golden rooms, and the floors were clean and bare, with a few bright rag or braided rugs scattered about. What furniture there was had come from Synton's attic or Pop's old home in Utica. There was a little Franklin stove in the living room, a central table with a long felt cloth on it and a kerosene lamp in the middle. Most of the chairs had been picked up for a few dollars at local auctions—antique rockers or old ladderback chairs that Baba had bought for the maids' rooms. To fill up space Baba had sent down two spinning wheels and some bright red-and-black scrolls from Japan. I remember particularly a little rug made of gaily colored scraps of wool all on end like flower petals.

There were sea chests to keep sweaters and things in and some old pine bureaus upstairs, but there were no closets, and clothes were hung in corners behind curtains of flowered cretonne.

4

Living in that house was almost like being outdoors, it was so light and uncluttered. I loved it from the first minute I walked in the door.

The privy alone was an experience to one raised with real bathrooms. Ours was at the back of the woodshed beside the tool closet, and to get to it you had to go out the kitchen door, past the icebox and through all the stuff they kept in the woodshed— kerosene, potatoes, onions, the lawn mower, a lot of empty cartons and, of course, wood. Pop said he didn't see why in Sam Hill somebody couldn't throw away something or at least keep the onions and potatoes from rolling all over the floor. This was after he'd eaten a potato soaked in kerosene and nearly been sick.

"Well, what did you eat it for?" asked Mum, when she had stopped laughing.

"Because I thought you all had done it for a joke, dad-gast it. Eye Guy, I'll taste that potato as long as I live." (Pop, being a minister, had to invent his own swear words.)

Kerosene was a major item in the household economy, and we had a large galvanized tin can of it on a greasy shelf in the woodshed. There was a kerosene stove in the kitchen, and kerosene lamps were our only source of light besides candles. Mum had a collection of old lamps she had bought at auctions, each with its own idiosyncrasies. Most of these were squat vessels of thick glass with curly handles, but there were two on stalks, and then there was the big nickel-plated lamp on the parlor table. This had a milk-glass shade, but the others had only tottering glass chimneys that were always falling off and breaking or getting smoked up the side. We used to watch the grownups trimming the wicks, but one side of the flame was inevitably higher than the other and would send a tail of fire up inside the chimney. Presently black smoke would begin to pour out the top, flakes of smut rained down on people's books and the cry went up.

"The lamp's smoking! Turn it down!"

The nickel-plated one in the living room would sink down until there was nothing but a red coal on the wick. Someone would shake it and say it was empty, and then Pop would get up and take it out to the woodshed to be filled. When the kerosene can itself was empty Pop took it down to Whalen's on the town wharf for refilling. New lamp chimneys, as I remember, came from Manchester's store in Adamsville, where they were displayed on wooden pegs overhead.

Although the light cast by kerosene lamps was, in our opinion, hopelessly inadequate, the whole business of the lamps and the smell of kerosene were part of summer and consequently magic.

In the same way the drawbacks of a plumbing system built around bedroom china and a privy came to be cherished because we experienced them only at the Point. The smell of chloride of lime had as much power to evoke summer as the smell of kerosene.

On those summer mornings the house woke up with the clank of the first slop-jar lid. This was followed by the surreptitious sounds of toothbrushing, and eventually the kitchen pump began to bray like a donkey, a signal that the cook had started breakfast.

Aldie and I had usually been awake since sunrise, as our room was on the east side of the house and the sun woke us like a burglar training a flashlight on our faces. We slept at the time in a room called the Babies' Room, which had no real entrance except through our parents' bedroom. However it was connected with the maid's room by a pitch-black tunnel under the eaves. This space had a triangular opening at each end, inadequately covered by a bit of curtain, and it was used as a two-way closet and an emergency entrance to our room. The maid hung her clothes at the far end and ours were supposedly hung at our end, but the midsection and eventually the entire closet became congested with junk—old sails, piles of *Geographics,* boxes of books and a thousand twangling wire coat hangers. Anyone fighting his way through it in the dark, as Buffy, our nurse, often did, was apt to measure his length among the sails and rubber boots, bringing down armfuls of clothes and coat hangers in the process. Nobody could creep up on you in silence, but we were afraid of the closet just the same. It was bliss to wake up to sunlight and the sounds of human activity among the washbowls and pitchers.

I remember sitting up in my crib and looking over at Aldie, who slept in a carved rosewood crib once used by Tink. Aldie had to have his crib against the wall because he was sure that a fox in a red cap would come out of the closet and bite him in the head. We had also invented a witch called Exzizzable who scared us nearly to death. The closet was just the kind of place Exzizzable liked, but Buffy didn't take her seriously.

"Stuff and nonsense," she'd say. "She isn't real. You made her up."

Buffy was a very comforting person to have around, and we adored her. She was only about twenty, but to us she was quite old. She was not pretty, her hair was all screwed up in a little knot at the back of her head and she wore glasses, but she was beautiful inside, loving, merry and beautiful.

As soon as Aldie was awake I'd get into his bed and we'd start giggling. We were like twins, blond and blue-eyed with round pink faces like babies. I thought we were a single entity—*us.*

We'd listen to the house waking up and snicker wickedly if we heard somebody trying to use a thundermug quietly. These vessels had the resonance of some kind of musical instrument. All the pieces of bedroom china were of enormous size fit only for giants. Even Pop had difficulty lifting the huge water pitchers or dumping the washbowls and often overshot the slop jars, flooding the floor with soapy water. Everything anyone did in connection with bedroom china was broadcast through the house as through a loudspeaker. The lids of the slop jars and thundermugs rang like gongs and were as much a part of the happy sounds of summer mornings as the crowing of Aunt K.'s roosters up the hill or the stutter of fishing boats going down the channel to the sea.

We could hear Buffy in her room clanking things together at her washstand, and presently she would come stumbling through the closet to catch Aldie before he wet his bed. As I remember he was in the process of being housebroken when we slept in the Babies' Room and was always being snatched up and rushed off to his pot or taken behind trees outdoors.

I used to run into my parents' room and hurl myself shrieking upon their prostrate forms. Their big double bed, a golden oak relative of the sideboard with a headboard as high as a wall, seemed to me a joyous landscape of white hills and hollows arranged expressly for my pleasure. Pop used to make a mountain of his knees for me to scale and collapse it when I reached the peak. He often told Mum his dreams during this exercise, and she would go into gales of laughter. Most of his dreams were about finding himself in the pulpit in his underwear or going to a funeral naked —minister dreams.

Their room smelled delightfully of Hind's Honey and Almond Cream and Pop's shaving soap. Their washstand had a gilt-edged set covered with morning glories, the same blue as Mum's Japanese kimono. There were curtains of blue-and-white Japanese toweling at the windows, and each one framed a piece of blue sky and blue water.

After Aldie had been potted he came racing in and took a flying leap into the bed. A terrific roughhouse ensued, with Mum tickling anybody she could get hold of. This lasted until she started in on Pop, and we helped her by sitting on him. Pop would hoot and howl for mercy, and then the whole bed would be heaved up in an earthquake of blankets and sheets, and he'd shoot out in his nightshirt whooping with laughter.

"Eye-Guy," he'd say. "Three against one. Call that fair?"

In the mornings Pop's blond hair stuck up in a crest and his blue eyes looked naked without his glasses. He was not tall but broad-shouldered and lean, with an athlete's build. At this time he was about thirty-three.

Mum was nine years younger, slim waisted, but bosomy like a brown-eyed thrush. She sang like a thrush too, and you could hear her all over the house. In the mornings in her blue kimono with her soft brown hair loose she looked like a girl, rosy and as pretty as a peach. Pop loved her so much he could hardly pass her without giving her a kiss.

Mum used to stand in front of her bureau brushing her hair while Pop stood by the window checking up on tide and weather, which he'd report to us.

"Northeast wind. Looks like a weather breeder," he'd say, or "Not a breath. Going to be a scorcher."

Buffy used to come in then and remove us to be dressed. Later we'd be allowed to return and watch Pop shave, something we did every day of our lives.

At the Point Pop used a Victorian shaving stand—a peculiar little mahogany box on a stalk with a fancy mirror and a little drawer where he kept his razors. We stood on chairs on each side of him, and every now and then he'd dart at one of us with his shaving brush and dab lather on our noses.

Then we'd all go down to breakfast, and the eternal battle over oatmeal would begin. Pop used to distract us by telling us stories about the Old Farm in upstate New York where he had spent his boyhood summers. Sometimes we'd eat all our oatmeal before we knew what we were doing.

Tink used to appear at the front door at a very early hour, and there were times when the drone of his approaching mouth organ could be heard during morning prayers, a family ritual that followed immediately after breakfast. First Pop read aloud from the Bible, then everybody turned around and knelt in front of their chairs while he said a prayer. Aldie and I used to peek through our fingers at the assembled bottoms and snicker. The whole business seemed to go on forever, and we got very fidgety during the Lord's Prayer. At the final Amen we made a break for freedom but were always caught and rushed off to the privy in the woodshed. This was a grownup obsession that was very tiresome, as our own wishes were never consulted. We sat there until we were "finished," and for years I thought "finished" was a dirty word.

Mornings in summer followed a rigid pattern, and after Pop had done his washstand duties he had to drive to The Milk in the Artful Dodger, the family car. The Artful Dodger was a 1916 Dodge with great personality and much the same status in the home as a horse or dog. He was a tall, rangy touring car with a canvas hood and black button-tufted seats—a glorious vehicle, beloved by all. We never missed a chance to go for a drive, and of course Tink was in seventh heaven as Synton was still in the horse-and-buggy age. Baba was against what she called "motorcars"—horrid noisy things and very dangerous.

Pop drove the Artful Dodger with a flair, like a man driving a chariot. He used to yodel at the wheel and yell out the lines of hymns or psalms that were of a joyful nature. Driving to The Milk meant going to the end of our lane to collect the milk cans that had been left behind the stone wall the night before. A farmer filled these at dawn with fresh unpasteurized milk, and it was important to get them early before the sun moved around the wall and soured the milk. The state of the milk was a daily issue at meals, as Aldie and I refused to drink milk that had "turned." Sometimes it was just on the turn and loud arguments followed. If it really curdled the cook would hang it in a pointed cheesecloth bag, and the whey dripped into a bowl underneath. The result was cottage cheese. It seems to me that there was always a cheesecloth bag dripping in Synton's pantry or in our kitchen. I will say here that the thought of Little Miss Muffet on her tuffet, whatever that was, "eating her curds and whey" was repulsive in the extreme to anyone who had ever smelled or seen cottage cheese in the making. However, driving to The Milk was a lovely start to the day, and it still makes me happy just to think of it.

In early summer the lane was bordered with freshly opened wild roses, and festoons of honeysuckle filled the air with sweetness. Baby rabbits bounced ahead of us down the ruts. There was a cool place in the valley where the lane ran through the woods, and here we always stopped to listen for the wood thrush, whose bell-like notes reminded Pop of the woods near the Old Farm of his childhood.

We stopped on the way back in front of Synton, for this was the hour when Baba held court. Her drawing room served as a clearing house for family news as well as any little tidbit of gossip someone had picked up at the post office or at the library.

There were three granite steps set in the side of the terrace at Synton, and here Baba had planted some Scotch harebells the summer I was born. They were my flower (we all had birthday flowers), and in July their powder-blue bells were all out, trembling on thin, wiry stems. As we climbed these steps and the broad wooden steps of the veranda we could hear the gabble of women's voices from inside the house.

"They're at it, hammer and tongs," Pop would say as we went through the screen door into the special smell of Baba's front hall. It was a bouquet composed of sweet geraniums and damp earth from the conservatory, the incense of wood fires, kerosene lamps, leather bindings, fresh flowers and Yardley's lavender. I supposed mixed in there was Pear's soap, an oval amber soap imported from England, which we saw only in Synton's bathrooms.

Baba always sat facing the door in her rosewood armchair, and when we came in she would stop talking and hold out her ringed hand in a welcoming gesture like a queen receiving ambassadors from a foreign land.

"Well, Robert," she'd say. "What is your plan for the day?"

Baba was small and straight-backed with hooded brown eyes like a hawk. At that time she must have been in her fifties and her hair was still brown, her cheeks as rosy as her daughters'. She had a way of tossing her head and smiling that was charming. We, of course, thought of her as very old, and she always dressed in grandmother clothes; violet Liberty prints, purple silk and black, with amethyst brooches and pendants. She was a true matriarch as well as a fascinating and delightful grandmother.

Mum was usually perched on the blue plush window seat, but Aunt K. would be standing up with the tools of her next mission in her hands. It might be the flat garden basket with her English trowel in it, or a bunch of flowers she had picked for a shut-in or a round basket of eggs for Mum. Aunt K. was always on her way somewhere else, but she couldn't resist the morning report. She was taller than Mum and wore her golden-brown hair in a heavy coil on the back of her head. Like Mum she had the vivid coloring of Baba's family: glowing pink cheeks and bright brown eyes. Since graduating from Wellesley she had remained at home, like a dutiful Victorian daughter, to care for Baba and Tink. As the servants grew older she did more and more of the work but she was a born country woman and much preferred gardening to garden parties and raising animals to paying formal calls. It was hard to catch her indoors as she loved to be in old clothes out in the garden or off driving Gyp about the countryside.

"I'm just leaving," she would say automatically, but she stayed on.

Aldie and I sat on the floor, where we were given a silver box of tiny animals to play with. In summer the red oriental rug was replaced with one of pale cream with medallions of Chinese blues and pinks. The long room was crowded with furniture whose rosewood and mahogany legs stood up above our heads. Sunlight poured unhindered through the big windows and glowed in the green showers of the maidenhair ferns. There were no draperies or curtains in Baba's rooms, as they would have interfered with The View and her carefully planned vignettes of gardens and trees. Also her plants needed the sun. Plants stood in front of all the south and west windows, on little plant tables, on antique candle stands and on the huge mahogany case containing the Japanese armor. When I think of Synton I am always visited by a sort of vision of bright spangled sunlight falling through a tanle of green leaves and vines, and in the midst of it a golden bird singing piercingly.

This was Pretty-Pretty, the canary that had a private apartment in the conservatory off the dining room. From our place on the floor in front of the fireplace we could look through the two wide doorways right into the conservatory's green jungle of overgrown plants and vines.

Tink sat with us on the floor eavesdropping. He was a human tape recorder and never missed a word. Later he would play it back to interested parties, and in this way kept us all informed of the latest scandals and secrets.

Every now and then the ladies' voices would lower to a murmur and you'd hear a strange word like "divorce."

"Hear that, dear Jan?" Tink would say. "Divorce. Call that pretty? No, I do not. Siskusty."

"Theodore," said Baba.

Then they'd tell us to just run upstairs and play in Tink's room.

"B.Y.C." Tink would say to us as we toiled up the big oak staircase. B.Y.C. was his way of describing the grownup habit of spelling out words they didn't want us to hear.

"Divorce" was a B.Y.C. word.

We didn't mind playing in Tink's room as he had a pile of *London Newses* dating back to the Crimean War or some such ancient conflict. He also had terrific pictures: three of large workhorses in full color, another of kittens in a basket and Landseer's "Dignity and Impudence," an engraving of a large bloodhound with a tiny terrier.

We used to climb up into his huge antique four-poster and look at *London Newses:* sepia double-page spreads of men fighting with swords, battleships sinking and kings and queens in court dress. I can still see those pages of little oval photographs.

When the B.Y.C. session was over we were called downstairs and said good-bye in the front hall over the earsplitting trills of Pretty-Pretty in the conservatory.

Pretty-Pretty sang almost all the time, and along with him you could hear the thick measured ticking of the grandfather clock, a heartbeat that never stopped. At Synton, though, time never seemed to pass. Nothing much had changed there since Mum herself was a child. Baba chose her own period to live in and had stopped time in its tracks at about the date of Queen Victoria's Diamond Jubilee, which she had attended. The house was lit by kerosene lamps and candles, and the only transportation was Gypsy, the bay mare, who added an air of incredible glamour to the most ordinary excursion. There was still a privy out back at the extreme end of a long latticed runway, but this was only used in emergencies as Baba had finally accepted the invention of the watercloset. She also had a telephone, very inconveniently located on the wall of the butler's pantry. However, she refused to recognize the internal-combustion engine, and this gave life at Synton a special charm. It had its drawbacks, of course. There were times when it would have been nice to drive to the village without having to capture and harness up a large animal. This is what Aunt K. had to do every day to go down and get The Mail, but in the summers she sometimes went with us in the car. This gave her time to go down to the river for the family swim, which followed the morning report at Synton. Baba had given up swimming, but she often came down to observe the sport.

Ours was a tidal river full of saltmarshes and mudflats and the shallow water was so rich in eelgrass plantations that at low tide our cove looked like a hayfield. The beach was nothing but stones, very rough on the feet, and at the water's edge there was a fine crop of rockweed, so slippery that people often fell on their hands and knees, sustaining painful lacerations from the barnacles and periwinkles underneath. Even when you reached the water it was necessary to wallow several yards through mud and eelgrass before it was deep enough to swim. The eelgrass jungles were infested with crabs and eels, and guests, shrieking and staggering through the shallows, were an amusing sight to old hands. However, members of Mum's family had swum at the river since 1888 and preferred it to the ocean beach where the "summer people" went. The morning swim was a family occasion. There, besides the Synton and Snowdon contingents, were Mum's older brother Uncle B. and his wife, and a mixed group of guests.

There were no bathhouses in Synton's boathouse, so the ladies of the party undressed inside, draping their intimate garments on the East Indian catamaran that filled most of the space. The men undressed around the bend in the path, and we were undressed by Buffy behind the boathouse, where we couldn't by any chance catch a glimpse of a grownup body. One memorable day, though, an unexpected bevy of guests came down the path and caused a stampede of semi-nude males to burst from the underbrush—a fascinating sight. For weeks afterward we used to re-enact this episode with Tink behind the boathouse. As usual, we went too far, and Aunt K. and Buffy surprised us while we were erupting stark naked from a viburnum bush. The repercussions were awful.

At noon we drove to The Mail. The post office with its array of varnished little boxes was at the back of the country store down in the village. While the grownups waited for the mail to be sorted we pressed our noses against the glass show case, where licorice whips, candy bananas, all-day suckers and gum were displayed. No one ever bought us any of these delicacies because cheap candy was bad for our teeth. Gum, of course, was out of the question, as Baba said it was vulgar. Only cheap "horrid" people chewed gum, so it was forbidden on the hill. Pop, though, sometimes treated us to a package of Wrigley's Spearmint and happily chewed it with us.

"Just remember to spit it out before we get home," he said, "or my name is mud."

Summer afternoons were long and lazy and included naps. After naps we went sailing, regardless of the wind or tide. We were all so used to climbing overboard and pushing boats through mud that it hardly mattered whether there was much water in the river or any wind to fill the sails.

These were the idyllic summer days before the War (I) and before Dave, our next brother, was born. Twice in this pre-Dave era Aldie and I were left behind at Synton after Labor Day, summer's official end, but summer kept right on going in an endless succession of blue days. This was surprising to me, as I had thought summer stopped as soon as we went back to Holyoke. After that I decided that summer lived at the Point the year round, just like Baba.

Those visits at Synton have merged in my mind so that they seem to have been continuous. The second one, on the occasion of Dave's birth, was of major significance. It was the last time Aldie and I would be the only grandchildren; the last time we were called "the Babies"; the last time we were really alone together, a perfect sexless unit, with no need for anyone else.

During those Synton visits, we lived in the Garden of Eden but like Adam and Eve we behaved very badly.

✵ 2 ✵

Carry Me Back
to the Horse and Buggy

Of those two visits to Synton the only specific events I recall involved wicked behavior on our part. As far as I'm concerned our sojourn there was just one long series of crimes, some involuntary but most knowingly concocted by us in cooperation with Tink. This state of affairs did not bother us much and an aura of enchantment lies over the whole period. We lived at the slow and dreamy pace of the horse and carriage, and our days were shaped to the peaceful round of Aunt K.'s tasks in kitchen, garden and barn. Aunt K. and Buffy were almost never cross and Aunt K. was so tender-hearted that she was unable to discipline even her own dogs. The worst punishment we ever had was a scolding and as there were three of us, we usually ended up in fits of giggles.

Our first visit, they tell me, came to an abrupt end when Aldie rolled off Baba's big double bed and broke his collarbone. I remember nothing of this minor affair but I can recall every detail of the cherry tomato fight on the Sunday afternoon Mrs. Southard came to tea. Tink, usually our fellow conspirator, was not involved in this, as he did not indulge in criminal behavior on the Sabbath day.

Mrs. Southard was a regal old lady, a neighbor of Baba's, who always seemed to dress in black lace, with one of those bead collars around her throat. Very unwisely, Buffy dressed us early in our

Sunday clothes and sent us out into the garden to play until the guests arrived. As I remember we were both in white from head to foot, Aldie in a sailor suit with a black silk tie, I in a dress with pink smocking and a pink butterfly hair ribbon. In no time flat we had crawled in under Aunt K.'s tomato vines and started eating cherry tomatoes. Almost instantly one exploded in my hand, and it occurred to me that it would be funny to squirt one at Aldie. It hit him in the eye and a hilarious battle followed. When Mrs. Southard's limousine rolled up to the front door and Buffy came to get us we were a horrible sight.

Of course, they wouldn't let us come to tea but that didn't upset us at all, nor did we feel in the least guilty. The cherry-tomato fight had been terrific, and I remembered it with simple joy. It had been wonderful down in our secret place under the tomato vines, an aromatic green cave full of blobs of sunlight. The golden afternoon outside throbbed with cricket song and we were happy, intoxicated by the obvious havoc we were causing. I knew perfectly well we were being naughty but I also knew with calm certainty that we were naughty only in grownup terms. Since all the really interesting and original things we did were labeled "naughty" by the adult world, I didn't mind being naughty at all. I liked it and so did Aldie. We were not interested in goodness; it was too boring.

I don't know whether you've ever noticed but in the children's books of the Victorian era the only individuals who had any fun were the bad ones. Having been told not to do something they did it and had a lot of wonderful adventures. Look at Peter Rabbit. Instead of staying home and picking blackberries like those good little milksops Flopsy, Mopsy and Cottontail, he ran away to Mr. McGregor's garden, where all sorts of things happened to him. Disobedience, in Beatrix Potter's books, was obviously the road to romance.

Good children in these old books were usually sick in bed of some nameless disease, and the more angelic they were the sicker they got. The really saintly ones always died. Even dogs and horses that were too good ended up dead.

Baba occasionally read us a frightful book called *Slovenly Peter* about naughty children who for minor sins like nail biting were rewarded by mutilation, torture, grotesque malformation or even death. One poor character who wouldn't get his hair cut ended up with hair that never stopped growing, and the nail-biter's fingernails turned into things like scythes. This vile book was translated from the German and could have been written by the Kaiser. I don't know why Baba read it to us but possibly it was to get across the message that we were not being as *good* as we should be.

Baba had never had much to do with small children, even her own, and had no intention of starting at this late date. In her own nursery the grosser aspects of child culture had been tended to by Lizzie. While we were visiting, Buffy and Aunt K. took all the responsibility for our care and feeding. Baba turned over her quarters to us and moved downstairs to the guest room at the other end of the house.

It was pretty awesome sleeping in what was virtually the royal suite. The furniture in Baba's bedroom was on a gigantic scale and the major pieces were of mahogany. In spite of the existence of a bathroom, Baba had retained her mahogany washstand, with its gray-and-white china set. There were a towering Empire bureau and a double bed to match. Here Buffy slept in solitary grandeur. I slept on the chaise longue, a hard wooden couch thinly covered by a lumpy cushion, probably the most uncomfortable accommodation I have ever experienced. Aldie, fighting every inch of the way, was ensconced in an antique walnut crib in Baba's dressing room. We had never slept in separate rooms before, and it took the combined efforts of Buffy, Aunt K. and Tink to persuade us to go to bed at all.

You have no idea how little light one candle gives unless you have tried it in a Victorian house full of dark woodwork and mahogany furniture. We had to use candles upstairs because kerosene lamps were too dangerous to carry around. Synton's candlesticks were like saucers with curly handles, and they stood in the butler's pantry during the day. A box of safety matches sat in the saucer but Baba supplemented these luxuries with pointed "spills," or lighters, made of rolled-up newspaper. Some of the Sunday papers had comic sections—"horrid vulgar things"—

which we weren't allowed to read, and these were quickly made into pretty-colored spills, which were kept in jars on the various mantelpieces.

Everybody had his or her special candlestick, and if you had to go to the bathroom you carried it in with you.

As for getting up in the night to go to the bathroom, the less said the better. At the first cry of "I have to go pee-pee," Buffy would plunge out of bed, stub her toe on Baba's Quaker rocker, yelp with anguish and grope her way to the bureau, where she usually knocked over several items before finding the matches. In Aldie's precarious condition it was vital to get to him immediately, or she had to go through the dismal business of changing sheets.

On our first night at Synton we were picked up at ten to go to the bathroom, and there in the hall was Baba in a nightgown with her hair in a pigtail. I was absolutely appalled, and Aldie shrieked like a banshee. Baba's purple dresses and hairpins were, we had thought, part of her body. As far as we were concerned she had been born wearing them. To see her in a pigtail and nightgown shook the very foundations of our world. The next morning, though, the sun was out and everything seemed normal again. As soon as we awoke we used to climb into the big bed with Buffy and make her tell us stories, but she kept falling asleep in the middle of a sentence and we'd have to hit her to wake her up.

Baba's room had windows to the east and south, so it was bright with morning sun. I used to lie and look at the flower paintings my grandfather had given her: wood violets on a piece of mossy bark, a watercolor of wild roses and a big one over the washstand of Scotch thistles, Mum's flower.

Buffy stood us on her bed to dress us, and we could see all the way to the islands on the rim of Buzzard's Bay. They were blue and mysterious with distance. Sometimes there was a schooner out there leaning to an invisible breeze, and in the clarity of that September air we could count the masts. A four-master was a prize.

When we were dressed, Buffy took us out the back door of the dressing room into the servant's wing and down the back stairs, at the foot of which was a pitch-black labyrinth of passages and storerooms to be traversed in order to get to the kitchen. Buffy said to us, "Run like a lamplighter," and off we'd go, scampering and squealing until we reached the kitchen door and fell through it. On the other side was a blaze of sunlight and clouds of golden steam with Aunt K. in the middle of it, getting the day going. Oh, the bliss of it! The big black stove snapped and crackled, the double boiler of oatmeal hissed and rattled, the dog, Gelert, jumped all over us in welcome and everything was merry and noisy.

Aunt K.'s kitchen was, in our eyes, the best room at Synton, and we spent most of our indoor time there.

Victorian children did not eat with the grownups, so we were relegated to the kitchen for our meals, a great treat for us, as we were never allowed in our own kitchen, the lair of the cook, who drove us out with Irish shrieks if we so much as poked our noses in the door. Synton's kitchen, it's true, still contained servants—Lizzie, and at intervals Bessie, the ancient cook, now retired, but both of these figures were waited on hand and foot by Aunt K., who did all the work of the nonexistent staff. The kitchen had become her special province.

It was a Victorian kitchen, a large, square brown room with counters and cupboards of varnished wood, whose rich patina was the result of years of use. There were windows on three sides, and between the two east windows stood the great coal range, a noble object with nickel-plated trim and all sorts of little shelves and warming ovens. It had the luster of a good rubber boot, as Aunt K. kept it well blacked and polished.

The windows on each side of it were full of flower pots and dripping with green vines. Plants flourished in the warm, steamy atmosphere and so did animals. There was usually a cage of guinea pigs or a carton with kittens in it or even a baby rabbit. Wherever Aunt K. was there were always plants and animals of various species so the kitchen had gradually become a kind of greenhouse-zoo.

The sink with its black pump was over in one corner, and there was a couch under a sunny window for Lizzie to rest on. Her Boston rocker stood by the serving hatch to the butler's pantry, but she was never there in the early mornings as she and Bessie had breakfast in bed, served by Aunt K.

Next to the sink was a sunken counter where Aunt K. beat up cakes and made bread. Nearby was a high shelf with a clock on it, and behind the hall door hung a roller towel with red edges.

The icebox was out back somewhere—in the laundry, I believe. The servants' sitting room was out back too, but they never sat in it. Everybody sat in the kitchen, everybody except Baba, of course.

Against the inner wall stood the old-fashioned kitchen table with real kitchen chairs around it, the varnished ones with hooped backs. There was always a fringed red damask cloth on the table, with the kitchen sugar bowl in the center of it. We were so small that our chins were on a level with the table; in fact, they had to put us on top of large encyclopedias so we could see our food.

What with the stove and the sun the kitchen was wonderfully warm and snug and smelled of good things—spices, geraniums, wood smoke, dogs and fresh bread, hot from the oven. Something was always going on: soap suds were whisked up in the blue enamel dishpan, bread was kneaded, potatoes were peeled, dogs fed, cookies cut out, eggs beaten, cream whipped. Onions burned in frying pans, oatmeal boiled over to the accompaniment of shrieks of laughter from Aunt K. and Buffy. Everything was always all right in this delightful new world where food was cooked. When Aunt K. made bread she gave us each a bit of dough to knead into tiny loaves that she baked in brown custard cups. We sat on the counter while she beat up cakes; we stuck our fingers in batter, licked frosting spoons and eggbeaters—liberties undreamed-of at home.

"Oh, what a day!" Aunt K. always said happily. The early mornings were her time; she rose with the sun every day so as not to miss anything and to get her housework out of the way and spend the rest of the time outdoors. Sometimes when we came downstairs we would find her putting her bread to rise, patting the white dough into loaves and cuddling them into their pans like a mother bedding down a baby. Some days she had made gingerbread and the kitchen was spicy with its fragrance. On other mornings she was in the conservatory watering plants or feeding the canary, whose golden screaming made our ears buzz.

The first ritual of the day for us was, of course, oatmeal at the kitchen table. While we were choking it down, Tink appeared through the door of the butler's pantry, for, like Baba, he would never use the servants' staircase. At the sink he took down his blue enamel cup, pumped it full of water and drank deeply. Then he turned, beaming, and came over and joined us around the table. I'm sorry to say that our conversations at meals were apt to be on a very low level and often consisted entirely of making faces, giggling and belching. We achieved this latter effect by swallowing quantities of air. All this ceased abruptly the moment Lizzie opened the door.

I don't suppose Lizzie could have been seven feet tall but she seemed so to us in her Victorian uniforms, unchanged since the nineties. She wore black alpaca dresses with high lace collars and huge starched aprons, blue-and-white-checked for morning, white for afternoon and evening. She also had a kind of fatigue uniform of some black material with a woolen shawl around her shoulders and felt boots on her feet to ease her corns. It was in this garb that she usually appeared first—a towering figure with eyes as blue as Canton teacups and hair like milkweed silk.

"Well, Master Theodore!" was usually her first remark, and Tink was at once transformed into a model of propriety. Lizzie creaked her way over to her Boston rocker, where she stayed grumbling and ordering people about for the rest of the morning. Luckily, as soon as we got Tink outside he was open to any suggestion, however subversive. I regret to report that during our second visit our crimes were on a grander scale, as we were a year older and Aldie was able to contribute more to the action. Tink was far from being an innocent bystander and was often the architect of these operations, although he was never blamed for them; I was. Tink was an artist with a talent for mischief, and when his genius spoke a special impish expression appeared on his face. As the idea flowered in his mind a beatific grin would spread over his features and he would begin to giggle. Then he would bring forth his plan. It was always inspired, a truly great thing like letting all the chickens out or throwing eggs at the barn door. One of his specialties was running away and hiding, so we tried this once, but as Tink's *modus operandi* was to sit behind a bush indefinitely we found it boring. Also the reactions of our keepers were so violent that it was hardly worth it.

Once we went into the barn and spit in Gyp's face, causing her to snort and kick around in a very gratifying way. This too provoked retaliations out of all proportion to the event. The Age of the Horse was very much alive on the hill, and the nineteenth-century attitude toward these sacred animals still prevailed. It seems to me in retrospect that the major part of Aunt K.'s day was spent ministering to Gyp: feeding her, watering her, grooming her, cleaning her boudoir, catching her in the paddock, harnessing or unharnessing her or trying to persuade her to take us somewhere in the buggy or buckboard. Tink and Buffy assisted Aunt K., and we were allowed to help in minor ways. We were seldom out of range of the smell of horse; our clothes and hair were always full of hayseed, and Buffy dumped piles of it out of our shoes every night. The day began in the barn with chores—a series of rites involving hay, water, grain and manure, with a special feature called "Getting the Eggs."

Every morning Aunt K. took the garbage pail—"gibbige" as Baba would say, "garbage" being too earthy a word—and we all set out for the barn. There was a narrow crunchy path, surfaced with coal ashes from the stove, that went from the kitchen door to the barn. The very texture of this path was precious to me because it meant we were going out to do the chores. On the way we passed the clothes yard and then went along the edge of the big vegetable and flower garden that filled about half an acre of sunny field behind Synton's back terrace. This garden was separated from the farmyard section by a long sweeping shrub border, where Baba had planted all the old-fashioned flowering shrubs: forsythia, bridal wreath, weigela, snowball bush and a lot of rugosa roses that had suckered out into a prickly jungle.

The path went through an opening in this border into the working part of the estate. On the left were a little orchard, the cold frames where Baba's sweet violets and seedlings were, the raspberry patch, and beyond that Gyp's paddock. On the other side was the chicken yard, where the hens had made dust baths and craters under a spreading crabapple.

The path ended at the barn. There was an old red cedar in the center of the barnyard, and under it was grass like green plush, very soft and silky. The sun in this sheltered enclosure always seemed warmer than anywhere else, and the crooning of the chickens nearby enhanced rather than disturbed the peace of the place. In summer it smelled of raspberries from the big patch by the barn, but in September it was sweet with the sticky scent of sunflowers and the fragrance of ripe grapes from the arbor. Crickets sang in the long grass; yellow butterflies spun patterns in the sunlight.

At chore time this peace was temporarily shattered by the squawks and shrieks of the hens sighting Aunt K. and the garbage pail. Necks and wings outstretched, they came running from all directions like club women catching a bus.

"Good morning, ladies," Aunt K. said, dumping her pail over the fence and smiling benignly down on the revolting scrum below.

Gyp would hear us out there and whinny impatiently from the barn.

In those days Synton's barn and carriage house were in their pristine Victorian state, just as the last groom or man had left them. In the carriage house the buggy and buckboard stood with their shafts resting on the floor. A privy called "the men's outhouse" was in one corner, and somewhere was a bench with cans of axle grease, sponges, pails and other paraphernalia used in the care of the carriages.

Next door was the stable where Gyp lived in her box stall. There was a harness closet with everything hung neatly on wooden pegs, the leather well oiled, the bits and buckles shining like silver. The grain closet was under the stairs, and there was a black pump with a pail on a shelf below it. Upstairs was the hayloft where a mother cat lived and where Aunt K. put setting hens or "broodies," hens trying to set, who had to be isolated to make them go back to work.

When we rolled back the barn door, Gyp nickered in welcome, stretching her neck out for her carrot or sugar lump.

"Hello, old girl," Aunt K. said and kissed her on her velvet nose. Tink followed suit, but we declined the honor as Gyp had a way of tossing up her head and giving you a stunning blow in the face.

The stable was warm from her big body and smelled of horse and manure, hay and grain—the authentic smell of happiness and of summer. For the next hour we waited on Gyp like slaves on a queen. Aunt K. pumped water and held up a pail for her to drink. Then she took a measure of oats and dumped it in the manger. We went up in the hayloft and shoved hay down the wooden chute, while Tink swept the barn floor. Gyp consumed her breakfast with a noise like a stone crusher, and finally Aunt K. sent her out into the paddock with a brisk slap on the rump. Then she went out to feed the hens and get the eggs while we helped Tink muck out Gyp's stall and make her bed—a delightful, malodorous job performed by Tink with hoe and pitchfork. The old bedding, reeking of ammonia, was piled in a wheelbarrow and transferred to the manure pile outside.

"Dressing, dear Jan," Tink used to say in explanation. Nobody ever said "manure" up at Synton; it was "dressing" for the gardens —wonderful stuff whose origin was never mentioned by ladies and gentlemen. Bodies, whether of animals or people, were an unfortunate reality, but no decent person discussed their functions.

It always seemed silly to me for Aunt K. to let Gyp loose, as it was such a frightful job to catch her again. Gyp's one aim in life was to eat, either in her stall or out in the paddock. Pulling a lot of people in a carriage was no part of her plan. Aunt K., on the contrary, was young and merry and wanted to go gypsying around the countryside whenever the weather was fair. Every day at mail time there was a battle of wills out in the paddock.

Of course, the relationship between Aunt K. and Gyp may have been unusual. Gyp was to Aunt K. a kind of giant pet, and like all Aunt K.'s pets, Gyp knew instinctively that she could get away with anything. At Synton dogs had to be stalked and captured under blankets to get them into the house. Sometimes trails of dog biscuits would be laid across the lawn up the steps and into the kitchen. With Gyp things were even harder, as she was so enormous and powerful. Aunt K. would try to coax her with an apple and gentle persuasion, but Gyp only galloped around the paddock like a wild mustang, snorting and kicking up her heels. Then Aunt K. would leave a measure of oats on the ground and hide just inside the barn, waiting to pounce out. Often she was forced to enlist the help of Buffy and Tink, and they would fan out and chase Gyp up and into the barn. She came at full gallop and plunged through the door, slipping and clattering to where Aunt K. stood with upraised arms. Sometimes Gyp dodged around her and thundered into her stall, where she stood blowing stertorously through distended nostrils. Usually, though, Aunt K. grabbed her halter and put her on the crosstie.

We stood on the stairs during this contest, as the noise was terrific and Gyp's rolling eyes and yellow teeth were far from reassuring.

It's hard to believe now but Aunt K. and Buffy performed these athletic feats wearing ankle-length skirts, shirtwaists, and peculiar hard black shoes. Their hair was wound into buns or rolled over their ears and fastened with masses of tortoiseshell and wire hairpins. In Buffy's case these were constantly falling out, and the small doughnut at the back of her head used to unwind and collapse down her back. Hairpins were much in evidence in those days; there were always some on the floor, on shelves and in little dishes on bureaus. Catching Gyp involved a perfect rain of hairpins, and once they got her on the crosstie both Aunt K. and Buffy stood and twisted up their locks, their mouths full of pins.

Gyp's capture was only the beginning; there followed currycombing, brushing and harnessing-up. Gyp seemed to have as much dust in her as an old rug. The process of harnessing-up and inserting the bit between her teeth was an invigorating affair. I can still see Aunt K. forcing Gyp's mouth open, getting all covered with green foam and horse spit. Eventually Gyp was led out, trailing her harness, and backed between the shafts of the buckboard. This vehicle had one seat facing forward and one backward. They were of blue upholstery, button-tufted, with curly iron armrests. The body of the buckboard was painted dark blue picked out with light blue, and it had carriage lamps fixed to each side.

Tink held Gyp's head while we all climbed in, using a little step like an iron pancake turner. Then he heaved himself up beside us, and the carriage rocked like a ship at sea.

"All set?" Aunt K. called, then flapped the reins on Gyp's back, clucked to her and we were off. By that time the morning was half over but nobody cared.

I remember how quiet it was in our lane. You could hear the cricket song in the grass and smell the sweet fern beside the road. Gyp held back in the shafts, easing her way down the steep hill; then in the valley she broke into a trot, her hoofbeats muffled by the sandy track. In our back-facing seat we could see the sand spin off the wheels and the green central ribbon of grass unroll backward. Down the middle of the green strip the grass was worn and cut up with Gyp's hoof prints and liberally decorated with piles of manure. When we turned into the main road Gyp's hoofs clip-clopped merrily on the macadam.

We made dooryard calls all the way down the road, but we seldom got out of the carriage. We would drive into the yard, and presently the lady of the house would look out the kitchen window and come out, drying her hands on her apron or holding them up covered with flour. She would stand a while by the front wheel visiting, and often she and Aunt K. exchanged slips of plants, eggs or surplus vegetables. Sometimes we anchored Gyp with an iron weight and went into the kitchens of the silvery little Cape Cod houses to inspect a batch of kittens or a new plant. These kitchens had black iron ranges polished to an ebony gloss and on them pots bubbled and kettles steamed. There were plants on the window sills and comfortable chairs around a central table where the lady of the house usually kept her work basket. It seems to me there was always a cat curled up somewhere. We were given kittens to hold or cookies out of brown crocks to eat while Aunt K. and her friend discussed the affairs of the day.

"I declare, Katherine," I'd hear them say, "I haven't yet got out to the dunes to pick my beach plums. I've been so busy putting up beans." And Aunt K. would tell how many jars of wild grape Baba had done and then they'd go on to items of local interest.

"My land, there goes the stage," the housewife would say,

looking over her geraniums, "and I haven't put my bread in yet."

"The stage" was the Model T Ford driven by Fred Manchester, who brought the mail from Lincoln Park, delivered packages, picked up passengers and took the mail bag up again to Lincoln Park every day. It wasn't for years that I realized that "stage" stood for "stagecoach."

There were special days—blue and gold September mornings—when we set out early and drove all the way to Adamsville, and once we went beyond Adamsville to the blacksmith's to have Gyp shod. This drive was so long that we had to stop at a watering place near an ice pond to give Gyp a drink. In the Age of the Horse there were turnoffs wherever there was a brook: brown pools surrounded by ferns and jewelweed, where water striders skated about and dragonflies crackled past on glassy wings. Aunt K. drove the wagon right in up to its hubs; Gyp lowered her great head and sucked up the water with a kissing sound. We could hear it sloshing around in her interior like water being pumped into a pail—very interesting.

Horses seemed to have incredibly noisy insides, and our drives were often accompanied by sounds like crockery being tumbled about in dishpans or the explosive reports of escaping wind. I'm sorry to say that the latter used to send Tink and us into gales of giggles. On the rare occasions that Baba was present these episodes were treated as nonexistent, and she would quickly call our attention to some roadside flower or bird. Aunt K. would look at us sideways but she didn't dare laugh.

Mr. Simmons, the blacksmith, had his smithy out in the barn, and inside it was shadowy, lit by the flames from the forge. All over the floor were the bluish shavings from horses' hoofs, bent nails, old horseshoes and other incredibly desirable treasures. Mr. Simmons always seemed to me a great man, brave and handsome. He had black hair and bright blue eyes and wore a leather apron on which he held Gyp's hoof upside down for paring and shoeing. First he took off the old shoe, then, with a draw-shave, cut off all the dirty rough bottom of the hoof, leaving it smooth and blue. After this he pumped up the forge and heated a new shoe red-hot and glowing. This he pounded out on the anvil and doused in a tank of water. When it was right, but still red-hot, he applied it to Gyp's hoof, and a frightful smell of burning filled the air along with a lot of acrid blue smoke. Then he *nailed* the shoe right into Gyp's foot, a terrible sight. We loved Mr. Simmons, but I always pictured Hell as located in his barn.

After one of these long drives we felt very short when we once more stood on the grass of the barnyard. It was an awful comedown to see the world again from our low level around people's knees and the legs of tables.

Baba would hear us come up the back steps, and she'd hurry to the door of the butler's pantry to greet us and lure Aunt K. and Buffy and the mail into her part of the house.

Baba never came into the kitchen at all except in late summer to make her jellies and preserves. Ladies, she said, did not sit around in kitchens gossiping with the servants. She intimated to us that for Aunt K. cooking was merely a hobby, a pleasant diversion like needlepoint, quite suitable for a lady to do. Baba by sheer force of character was able to maintain the illusion that a whole staff of servants still operated behind the door to the butler's pantry. Aunt K. preserved this fantasy by rising at dawn and getting most of the cooking and baking done before breakfast.

Our visit with Baba came at teatime, when she entertained us in various ways and read to us out of one of the little green Beatrix Potter books. Each day she taught us something new. I remember when she lifted down the celadon green vase with the goldfish on it and put it into my hands.

"This is cloisonné," said Baba. "Japanese. A very valuable example."

She made me repeat the word "cloisonné" and pointed out the exquisite work on the goldfish, where every scale was as glittering and perfect as on a real fish.

She let us play with the ancient bronze elephants, gifts from maharajahs in India, and showed us the pictures in some of the special books. Aldie's favorite was *The Comic History of Rome*, which had in it a lot of wonderful cartoons. The one we liked best showed two men in togas, and underneath were the words: "Caesar and Pompey, very much alike, especially Pompey."

This delighted us as we saw the joke.

Following our lesson we had our story and were led off to supper, baths and bed.

I'm sorry to say that the end of this visit at Synton was distinguished by one of our worst crimes—the great manure fight. I don't know who started it; it was more like spontaneous combustion. We were out in the paddock (forbidden), surrounded by piles of manure in various stages of desiccation, and suddenly the inspiration struck all three of us at the same time. Missiles flew thick and fast, and we were staggering with laughter when Tink scored a bull's-eye right in Aldie's mouth. Aldie began to howl and headed back to the house, while Tink and I slunk after him, snickering nervously. All hell broke loose in the kitchen, and they put Aldie in the sink and washed out his mouth with soap. Everybody, including Lizzie, lectured Tink and me on our evil ways. Tink hung his head in shame, but I shook with unseemly giggles, utterly unrepentant. There was something about horse manure that was exquisitely humorous.

Luckily for everybody Dave entered the world shortly after this disgraceful episode. Pop telephoned while we were having our supper, and the house echoed with the shrieks of women. The next thing I remember is climbing the stairs of our city house with a row of grinning faces peering down at us over the bannister.

❧ 3 ❧

His Tribe Increases

The house where we lived in winter was on a steep elm-shaded street in an old residential section of Holyoke in Massachusetts. The houses were all of Victorian vintage, period pieces in brownstone or fancy shingles with front porches draped in Dutchman's-pipe vines or wisteria, with pink hydrangea bushes on each side of the steps. Each one had a granite mounting block by the curb and a black iron hitching post shaped like a horse's head with a ring in its mouth. There were no garages on our street and we were one block below the carriage-house district, so cars were parked by the mounting block with front wheels turned in. I think people must still have thought in terms of horses that would stand when left, but ours was a steep street and somebody's car was always getting loose and rolling majestically downhill into a snowbank or, even better, crashing into a telephone pole and breaking the headlights.

Our street was Oak Street and our house was number 231. It was a wonderful house of classic Victorian design, with a pepper-pot tower on one side and a big curved veranda whose balustrades and columns were locked in a death grip with wisteria vines like boa constrictors. Other vines smothered the pillars on either side of the veranda steps, and Boston ivy clothed the Elizabethan chimney on the south side. The house had scalloped cream-colored shingles on the top half and maroon clapboards on the bottom, but the unpruned luxuriance of the vines hid most of the maroon part and gave the place a pleasant look, disheveled but comfortable.

The yard was as wildly overgrown as the house, for we had no gardener and Pop made no attempt whatever to control the vegetation. The old lilacs and syringas were as tall as the second-story windows and had trunks big enough to climb. The borders had grown up to saplings, rank weeds and runaway vines, a green tangle where birds nested and wildflowers sprang up. There were a lot of birch trees and a great cherry with a frivolous circular summerhouse under it. This whole glorious conglomeration stood at the top of a steep bank, the best place to coast in the whole block.

It's hard to remember which of our many arrivals at 231 was the one in 1917 when we came home to meet Dave, but it really doesn't matter because they all felt the same. Every time we turned the corner at the top of Oak Street and rolled downhill under the elms, we were amazed to see people still going about their daily business just as though nothing had happened. As far as we were concerned all life had ground to a stop on the day when we left for the Point in June. We knew some peculiar people stayed in the city all summer, but we didn't expect them to act normal when we weren't there.

"All ashore that's going ashore!" Pop used to shout, and we'd climb out onto the mounting block. I remember standing there with my clothes all twisted around listening to the city. My ears felt as though they were stuffed with cotton through which came the muffled sounds of screen doors closing, lawnmowers whirring dreamily and the whine of trolley cars downtown. There was a warm sweet smell of cut grass and tar, and after the clear salty air of our hill this air seemed too thick to breathe.

The approach to the house was up a long flight of red sandstone steps. At the top was a cracked macadam walk that led between the big bridal wreath and the hydrangea bush to the veranda steps. These wooden steps and the porch itself had a special resonance like drums, the sound of coming home, of Pop coming home at night, of us coming back to Mum after playing. In warm weather the front door was always open, and we went in through the screen door into the dark, rich, fruitcake atmosphere of the front hall. The veranda roof and all those wisteria leaves successfully excluded all light and air from the living room beyond, and as the woodwork was varnished walnut and the walls were covered with something like blue burlap, you had to stand still for a minute until your eyes became accustomed to the dimness.

On the left rose the great Tudor staircase, with its tall mullioned windows, its two landings and massive oak bannisters. The afternoon sun used to slant through those leaded glass casements in long shafts of light, where golden dust motes whirled in an endless dance. The prisms of the chandelier threw little rainbows on the wall, and we thought these were all fairies.

I can't pretend that I remember all this from the September of Dave's debut. All that remains of that occasion is our entry into Mum's room, which seemed to be congested with people, including a strange female dressed in crackling white with a small white cap on her head. Baba was there—peculiar, because she didn't belong in that house. Mum was there in bed wearing a pink bed jacket with her hair in a braid. Even Delia-Pelia, the Irish cook, was there, and everybody was beaming down on us, waiting to see what we'd do.

I stood by the bedpost feeling shy, with Aldie close beside me. He had the hiccups and kept chirping like a bird. Presently Pop told me to hold out my arms. I did this and he lowered into them a large, warm baby with a big head.

"This is your baby brother, Dave," he said in a croaking voice, and the baby stared at me sternly out of round dark-blue eyes.

"Put your hand under his head," said all the women in chorus.

Then somebody took him away and pretended to let Aldie hold him.

After that we climbed up on the bed to hug Mum, although it was clear the white lady didn't approve of our doing so.

Mum explained that this individual was a nurse and her name was Miss Sharkey. Miss Sharkey was so clean it was hard to believe she was real. Mum told her to bring the baby over, which she did reluctantly, and then we unwrapped him and looked at his little pink feet clamped tight to his bottom. Mum unfolded his hands and showed us all his fingers with their tissue-paper nails and let us put our fingers out so he could grab them. Then we touched his downy head, and Mum showed us the soft place on top where we could feel his heart beating. She then wrapped him all up again and let us kiss him on the back of his neck, where babies always smell sweet. This was too much for Sharkey, who said in her prim nurse voice that we were not "sterle." We found she was always talking about things being "sterle." It was some time before we knew what this was. We couldn't go near the baby unless we had washed our hands, because we weren't "sterle." Things dropped on the floor were not "sterle" and had to be taken away and boiled. It was very peculiar.

"What's 'sterle'?" I asked Mum, at last.

"Sterile," she said. "It means clean."

Sharkey was so "sterle" herself that she smelled of disinfectant, and her hands were red from constant scrubbing. When on duty she was very prim and proper, but we soon noticed that at intervals an amazing transformation took place. It usually coincided with a telephone call for her from a person called "the Five Cent Gent." This mysterious gentleman, we gathered, called from a pay telephone, so all his calls were preceded by the words "Five cents, please" and the sound of a bell. Buffy or Aunt K., who had replaced Baba as Synton's representative, would answer the telephone and cry out, "It's the Five Cent Gent, Sharkey!" whereupon Sharkey gave a coquettish shriek, turned bright pink and covered her face with her hands. Then she went out to the telephone and a whispered interview followed. Later on she would emerge from her room, dressed to kill, like a butterfly coming out of a cocoon. For the first time we saw a woman wearing rouge, lipstick, and powder, for the ladies in our family were innocent of makeup. Sharkey's hair was puffed out over her ears like ear muffs, the white cap had vanished, and instead of the crackling uniform she wore a blue dress of some slithery material and all kinds of glittering beads and bracelets. A cloud of powerful perfume came out with her.

While we all waited for the doorbell that would announce the

Five Cent Gent's arrival, the ladies teased Sharkey unmercifully and the air rang with her screams of protest, but it was clear she was the heroine of the hour and loved every minute of it. The next morning she would be as prim and starched as ever.

Sharkey kept the baby in her room, tucked up in a delectable little bed called a "bassinet." I was absolutely charmed with the bassinet—a hooded oval basket exquisitely dressed in crisp dotted-swiss muslin over pink silk. It was full-skirted as a ballerina, edged with lace ruffles and threaded with pink ribbons, with a big pink satin bow to finish it off. Inside was a lace-edged pillow, doll-sized sheets and sweet-smelling wool blankets, fine as cobwebs. Wrapped in a special flannel blanket, the baby would be tucked tight into this nest, where he lay with his fists on either side of his head, remote and mysterious. Sharkey kept the shades down in the room all the time and we were forbidden to go in there, but I did so whenever I thought it was safe. Then I stood with my chin on the lacy edge of the bassinet, watching the miniature face, where shadows of expression flickered, adoring the tiny hands that clenched and opened while he slept. Sometimes I stroked his head with my finger and touched the soft place in the center. These were my favorite moments with this little brother, when he and I were alone in the warm quiet.

Bath time was something else again, a public ceremony accompanied by the shrieks and howls of the victim. It took place in the Big Bathroom at nine o'clock each morning. Sharkey did not approve of an audience—so un-sterle—but the place was usually so crowded that there was standing room only.

The Big Bathroom was, to be accurate, the only full bathroom we had, our house having been planned when bathrooms were still slightly indecent, like privies, and so relegated to the back premises. The best bedrooms had built-in marble washstands, and Mum and Pop also had a bathroom with a tub but no toilet facilities, so the Big Bathroom was used by everyone, including the maids. It was a period piece of great charm, large and square with pale blue walls, white-painted cupboards and a floor paved with small octagonal marble tiles that often came loose. The wide marble washstand and enormous claw-footed tub gave the place the sumptuous look of a Roman bath, but the toilet lowered the tone considerably, being a collector's item with a brown varnished seat and a tank operated by a greenish metal chain. At bath time Sharkey plugged in a round electric heater and focused it on the rocking chair where she would sit with Dave in her lap. In an almost religious silence she set up the folding rubber bathtub with crossed walnut legs, a family heirloom from Mum's clan. On a chair beside it she laid out towels and diapers and the baby basket, a beribboned affair like a tiny bassinet filled with baby equipment —cotton, castile soap, Merck's baby powder, boric acid, lanolin and other fascinating items that we now saw for the first time.

After Sharkey had filled the tub and tested its temperature with a bared elbow, she brought in the baby, and we all stood back to allow her to make her way to the white rocking chair in front of the tub. The ranks then closed again and the ritual began. Aldie and I as the shortest members of the audience stood in the front row, Buffy and Aunt K. and sometimes Pop stood behind us, and the maids craned their necks by the door.

We watched spellbound the unwrapping of the baby, layer by layer, until he was revealed, red and scrawny as a plucked chicken. We did not blame him for screaming then, as all manner of liberties were taken with his person. Swabs of cotton, suppositories, were applied to every orifice; he was placed on the scales and the bathroom reverberated to his yells. Finally he was lowered into the tub, his hair soaped and a small washcloth laid modestly over his private parts. Once, before Sharkey could do this, he managed to hit her in the eye with a magnificent fountain. She was not amused by this tour de force, but it caused a sensation in the audience.

I loved best to see Dave wrapped cozily in the big white towel, pink as a damp rosebud and as sweet-smelling. It took quite a while to dry, powder and reassemble him, for in that era babies were incredibly overdressed. First Sharkey did something about "the cord," as she called it, a shocking sore place where we had our belly buttons. A small bandage with gunk on it was laid over this, then a flannel binder was wrapped firmly around Dave's middle and pinned in three places. Next came the short-sleeved silk-and-wool shirt and the three-cornered diaper of the original "diapered" bird's-eye cotton. These were pinned where the points met with a large safety pin and at the sides with two smaller safety pins. Over the diaper went the rubber pants, which were, I think, made of yellow rubberized silk. Now came the long-sleeved silk-and-wool shirt, a long flannel petticoat, a white petticoat delicately embroidered with a lace edge, and finally the dress—a delicious confection of filmy batiste, hand-sewn with invisible stitches, tucked, embroidered, lace-edged, with little puffed sleeves. Even baby boys used to be done up like valentines. On top of the dress went a sweater, and wool booties were pulled over his bare feet. By this time the top of his head would be dewed with perspiration, but this didn't deter Sharkey from wrapping him in a wool blanket, one of a large collection. He was now dressed for his ten-o'clock feeding, and we all trooped after Sharkey to Mum's room to observe the amazing process known as "nursing." Dave, at this point, was trying to eat his own fingers, snuffling and whimpering like a puppy, but he had to wait while Sharkey swabbed out his mouth with boric acid, a practice now obsolete. Mum was generously endowed, to say the least; in fact, she was absolutely spectacular, and I remember asking if I could lay my head on one of her "pillows," it looked so white and soft. This request outraged Sharkey, who, when not in the Five Cent Gent mood, was excessively modest.

Babies, in that era, were kept on a rigid four-hour schedule and were only fed on the exact dot of six, ten, two or whatever. Even if Dave howled—which he did—he was not allowed to come in to Mum until feeding time, but to calm him Sharkey used to rock him in her darkened room, singing a droning song of extreme monotony, almost a dirge.

Following the feeding Dave was removed, and Sharkey brought Mum what she called the Patient's Nourishment. This consisted of a glass of milk and two hot bran muffins with butter. Nothing before or since has ever looked so good as the nourishment. Sometimes Mum allowed us each to have a small piece of buttered muffin as a treat.

During the period of Sharkey's reign Mum's room was the center of all life in the house. It was a big sunny room with a round bay in one corner, where Pop had his Morris chair and Mum kept her sewing table. Unlike the downstairs the atmosphere was light and cheerful, with white-painted woodwork, pale wallpaper and curtains with pink peacocks on them. Set into an alcove in one wall was the marble washstand, with a mirror over it and a sort of wooden lace frill above the opening. The gigantic double bed and bureaus were of mahogany, heavy and as richly polished as horse chestnuts, but the sun and the white counterpane on the bed gave even these articles of furniture a bright and cheerful aspect. This room was really the only room in the house where anybody sat in the daytime, as it got the most sun. Now, with Mum enthroned there all the time, it was the hub of the universe, the very source of life. Except for naptime and the hour when Sharkey gave Mum a bed bath, the room was crowded with people, mostly women, laughing and talking.

In the early mornings while Pop shaved we stood inside the alcove on each side of the washbowl watching his shaving faces and waiting tensely for him to dab us with lather. Mum sat like a queen among her pillows waiting for her breakfast tray, and it was all very merry.

At intervals the family doctor, whom Mum always referred to as Dear Old Doctor Hubbard, paid a visit with his black bag and sat in Pop's Morris chair, diverting us with the big gold watch that hung on his watch chain.

After what seemed like a year Sharkey departed, carried away by the Five Cent Gent, whom we all observed from the front windows. Dave's bassinet was then moved into Mum's room, Buffy moved back into her own room, where Sharkey had been, and Mum returned to the hurly-burly of family life. As far as I can remember, she spent almost every waking hour in the little white rocker by the radiator in her room, rocking or feeding Dave. Mum absolutely reveled in new babies, inventing a little language for each one as well as a whole series of pet names. During the rocking sessions she sang all kinds of songs in her clear sweet voice. Aldie and I played on the floor nearby. We used to plaster modeling clay against the radiator, a massive embossed affair painted gold that always had towels and baby gear drying on it. We also melted crayons on it, and the smell of clay, crayons and toasting towels mixed with the fragrance of baby powder became for me a kind of symbol of coziness and love, of home.

After Dave was weaned and put on a bottle we were permitted to suck the last drops of milk through the nipple. These always tasted especially sweet and were a great delicacy. We took turns at the dregs, thus exchanging whatever germs were around. However, that was fine with us. If one of us had a cold the other one wanted it too. Having a cold was so much fun in our house that we could hardly wait to have one.

Mum often let me give Dave his bottle, and so delightful was the whole baby business that my one ambition was to have a lot of babies of my own. For quite a while it never occurred to me that Dave would ever be anything but a baby, a permanent cuddly pink bundle in diapers, who drank out of bottles and didn't talk or walk. I expected him to sleep forever in the bassinet beside Mum's side of the bed, while Aldie and I lived in our room for eternity.

Our room was our refuge, our nest, our den, where we romped and tumbled like little foxes, safe and silly. It was the tower bedroom, so that one corner was circular, with windows on three sides and a splendid view of the treetops and the roofs of neighboring houses. In this round bay stood the round white supper table, our two little Windsor chairs, Gillie the rocking horse, and the Bang, a cretonne-covered chest where we kept our blocks. There were blue-and-white cretonne curtains at the windows, and the design of the cretonne was the same as the curtains in Mum's room except that our peacocks and flowers were blue instead of pink.

We slept in identical white iron cribs with large hollow brass balls on the corner posts and marble-sized brass balls all along the railings. Every one of these balls could be unscrewed, and we used to suck the small ones, which tasted awful, like tin.

Our bureau was a Victorian fantasy, with a towering mirror and two marble-topped wings, with a well between them where we kept our windup Victrola and our collection of battered records: one of the Sousa marches, Harry Lauder singing "Stop Your Ticklin', Jock" with "I Love a Lassie" on the other side, and "Listen to the Mocking Bird" with Alma Gluck.

Next to my bed was a small fireplace, an ornate affair of glazed taffy-colored brick with a mantel of carved oak. It was never used and I kept my doll's stove in it. Above the mantel was a colored picture of incredible beauty showing barn swallows over a pond full of water lilies.

The other pictures were those apparently considered suitable for young eyes: a sepia one of children wading, "The Age of Innocence," "The Broken Pitcher," Raphael's cherubs and a very depressing old print showing a group of weeping children carrying another child who seemed ill or dead, and escorted by a dog carrying a straw hat in his mouth.

In this room Aldie and I evolved a complete culture of our own with its myths and legends; we composed songs or chants of a very monotonous kind and invented games suitable for two players only. These were Lemon Candy, Wellesley Fudge Cake and Elephant Ruggaby. The first two were primitive to a degree and had been invented to pass the time while beds were being made. We would trudge from room to room carrying a pillow between us and chanting rhythmically either "Wellesley Fudge Cake" or "Lemon Candy." They were very dull, but after all we were just beginning our career as inventors of games.

Elephant Ruggaby was a terrific game, and I am proud to say that I thought up the name. Each of us would crawl under a small rug, then stand up and sway around the room, bumping into the furniture and saying "Elephant Ruggaby" at intervals, as its syllables refused to fit into a chant. When under the rugs, inhaling dust and the smell of dog hair, I felt exactly like an elephant, big, wrinkled and gray, swaying along on feet like tree stumps. We had observed elephants in circus parades, and it was clear to me how it must be, surging by in all that loose dusty skin.

Another diversion of ours was to put on "Stop Your Ticklin', Jock" and lie on the floor pretending to laugh until we really became hysterical. Once Aldie even threw up.

Every evening after our baths we were put into our bathrobes and Comfy slippers and planted at the supper table to wait until

Buffy brought up our tray. Our suppers were almost always the same, dull but safe because we were used to them. I had shredded wheat in my bowl with the chickens around it. Aldie's bowl had brown rabbits on it, and he always ate crackers and milk and considered all other cereal garbage. He had violent likes and dislikes and refused to taste things whose texture or color displeased him.

"It looks just like dog's upchuck," he'd say, or "poisoned manure" and then we'd go into gales of giggles. We used to blow bubbles in our milk, which we drank from our special silver cups, and I remember just how it felt laughing into milk and getting it all down my chin, soaking my bib.

"Stop that. That's very naughty," Buffy would say, but we were incorrigible, secure in our alliance against authority. We didn't bother to rebel often; we just retreated into private laughter and secret innuendos that grownups couldn't understand.

During our repast Mum would come in all dressed up for supper, and I remember how soft and silky her long dresses felt and how sweet she smelled. There was one dress I loved, of light floating silk the color of Mum's brown hair, and there were pink roses on it somewhere. She used to stay with us until Pop came upstairs and then we'd have our story: one of the little green Beatrix Potter books or a Thornton Burgess. We had complete sets of both of these great writers. Pop read to us if he was there; if not, Mum did. Then one or both of them would tuck us in and hear our prayers:

"Loving Jesus
Meekin mild,
Look upon a little child.
Make me gentle Azooart.
Come and live within my heart.
God bless Mum, Pop," and so on down the whole list of relatives.

What "Meekin mild" or "Azooart" meant I hadn't the remotest idea nor did I even wonder about them.

Mum and Pop said, "God protect you," as they put out our light, and then they closed the door. Our evening was about to begin.

As the golden crack of light disappeared and we heard the foot-steps going downstairs we started to laugh.

"I'll begin," one of us would say. "I've thought of something. Once upon a time . . ." and the latest installment of our private soap opera was on the way. Heaven knows what a psychiatrist would think of it but, frankly, I don't care. The series took place, most regrettably, down the hole in the john, a scatological version of *Alice in Wonderland.* Raggedy Ann was one of the characters but the heroine was the Blue Lady, a dim female so good she never had to go to the bathroom. The villain was a creature called the Whirly Grunt Man, whose very name caused us to explode into hysterical laughter. I'm sorry to say the Whirly Grunt Man has survived and is still diverting our children with his adventures. The Blue Lady, oddly enough, was a real person, a girl who worked in a building on the corner and who walked by the house every day. I hope she was not as disabled by virtue as we imagined.

If we knew Mum and Pop were having a party we used to sneak downstairs to the first landing and look through the bannisters at the grownups going in to dinner. We could see them in the living room standing in front of the fire and reflected in the mirror over the mantel. After they disappeared into the dining room we heard the murmur of voices, the subdued clatter of silver and china and the "whuff" of the swinging door as the maids went back and forth. If we heard anybody coming we scampered upstairs and back to our room, where we climbed into our white iron cribs and lay giggling and squeaking.

If we scared ourselves too much with our soap opera we'd call for drinks of water, but ordinarily we went to sleep right in the middle of a sentence. There was one terrible episode called "Aunt Ethel's Belly"—but I'd better not go into that.

Mornings in our room were always a lovely surprise. We even enjoyed rain, especially the pattering sound it made on the roof, but a sunny day was like a present. On spring mornings the sun shone through the baby leaves and the robins were singing from every treetop. In June and September the windows were full of green; in October they turned to gold; but I remember our win-dows best in winter, which went on so long it seemed the normal thing in Holyoke. On subzero mornings we would wake up to see a fierce orange glow behind the frost feathers on the glass. In those days of steaming radiators the frost landscapes on our windows were fantastic—ferns of pure ice, every frond perfect, constellations of snow stars and forests of crystal trees. Ours were unusually dazzling because the sun rose just behind them.

Our family believed in fresh air at night no matter what the temperature, and on winter mornings our room was so cold that our breath smoked. This made our cribs seem even cozier, like the fur-lined nests of baby rabbits. I loved to lie all curled up inside my flannel nightie and listen to the day begin.

After Dave graduated from his bassinet they moved my crib into Mum's room and gave it to him. I was given a real bed, but I felt very unsafe in a bed without *sides.* This was the first sign that Dave might not be a baby indefinitely. The next thing we knew he was sitting up, and all of a sudden he could creep. Mum used to pick him up early, change and feed him, and then bring him into our room, where she'd put him in Aldie's crib. Then she went back to bed. Dave sat and peered at us through the bars of the crib like a baby animal in a zoo, making gurgling noises and drooling.

We were charmed with him and instantly put our minds to work to fit him into the game picture. First we tried a game called "Parakeet," in which Dave was a parakeet in a cage and had to be fed. He was supposed to chirp and eat whatever we pushed through the bars, but after we'd forced him to eat a red crayon and he threw up, "Parakeet" was outlawed by the authorities.

We soon realized that to use Dave properly we had to get him out of the crib. This was hard but we managed it. We then experimented a bit and came up with a marvelous game called "Bye-low Froggie dear." This entailed spreading a blanket on the floor and placing Dave in the exact center. Each of us then took two corners of the blanket and marched around him in a circle, chanting "Bye-low Froggie dear." Presently we had twisted the blanket into a tight knot around the Froggie, who screeched horribly. However, at the first sound of adult rescuers we quickly unwound him and were able to say we had no idea why he was crying.

Dave was only about six months old when Pop went to the War, a permanent business that was going on in France. We were so used to hearing about the War, the Germans and the Kaiser that we accepted them as part of the cosmos. A lot of men kept going over to France to the War and now Pop was going too. It never entered our heads that there was any risk involved in this venture.

❧ 4 ❧

"Oh, Boy, Oh, Joy . . ."

Before Pop's departure for France the War had only touched our lives in minor ways. There were, for instance, the Starving Armenians and the Poor Belgians. These peculiar people apparently had an unnatural craving for things like cold, lumpy oatmeal, apple tapioca, Brown Betty and other repulsive dishes, which I, for one, would have been happy to send them.

"Now finish up that oatmeal," Buffy or somebody would say. "Think of the Starving Armenians and the Poor Belgians. They'd give anything to have it."

"Well, give it to them. I don't want it," I said, but nothing was ever done about this.

There was also oleomargarine—an unpleasant white substance that Delia-Pelia used to mix up with some yellow coloring in the pantry. We refused to eat it.

When Pop decided to go to the War he wanted us to understand the whole business, so he put us through an educational process.

First, he taught us to sing all the war songs, assisted by a record that had on it a picture of a white dog listening to a large trumpet. "His Master's Voice," it said under it, very confusing as we had acquired the idea at morning prayers that the Master was Jesus. In any case we played the record and sang after Pop until we were word perfect. Not that we knew what any of it meant—pure gibberish—but when did grownup songs ever mean anything? You had only to listen to the hymns we sang in church. The war songs were a lot better than those, and we played them incessantly, marching around the room, stamping our feet and banging on make-believe drums. The best one for this was "Tramp, Tramp, Tramp, the Boys Are Marching," although "Oh, Boy, Oh, Joy, Where Do We Go from Here?" was almost as good. The best part of this one was:

> "Slip a Pill to Kaiser Bill
> And make him shed a tear.
> And when you see the en-a-mee
> You shoot him in the RE-AR." etc.

The idea of shooting somebody in the rear end appealed to our low humor.

Other popular numbers were "It's a Long Way to Tipperary," "Over There," "Soldier Boy, Soldier Boy, Whe-ere Are You Going?," "Keep Your Head Down, Fritzie-Boy," "There's a Long, Long Trail a-Winding," "K-K-K-Katie" and "Lafayette, We Hear You Calling."

They were great songs full of rhythm and, oddly enough, joy, although "There's a Long, Long Trail" seemed to us dangerously close to a hymn.

Pop continued our indoctrination by taking us out to Camp Merritt, where we saw the soldier boys drilling and lining up for meals, their tin plates in their hands. They must have been homesick, for we soon had a crowd around us, and one boy gave us each a dime. Later on we watched the Yankee Division march off to war with bands playing and flags flying. War was a romantic business back in 1918, and every soldier was a hero. Holyoke had its own regiment and Pop wanted to go with them, but being a minister he wasn't supposed to fight, so he went with the Y.M.C.A. When he got his uniform, he was as excited as a small boy with a cowboy suit. He had a real officer's cap, a fatigue cap, a Sam Brown belt, a tunic and riding breeches of heavy khaki wool, army boots and leather puttees. He also had woolen puttees that wound around his legs like giant bandages. Our favorite item was a delightful camping kit with a folding frying pan, folding fork, knife and spoon, a tin cup and a khaki-covered water bottle called a canteen.

To prepare himself for going Over There Pop tried to learn some French, but all I remember him saying was "bonjour," "allons," "bon."

His accent was terrible, but he had mastered the French method of pronouncing the word "bon." To illustrate this properly he pinched his nose between his fingers and did the same with ours.

"Bong, bong, bong!" we would all cry explosively.

Pop's greatest triumph was learning and teaching us "The Marseillaise," the French equivalent, he explained, of "My Country 'Tis of Thee."

Word by word, line by line, we struggled through "The Marseillaise" until we had the whole thing by heart. I can safely say that I remember every word of our "Marseillaise" to this day and have since translated it into French with amazing ease—a tribute to Pop's meticulous coaching.

Aldie and I would shout this masterpiece, standing hand in hand on our supper table, and our performance was always followed by a storm of applause and a standing ovation.

In April, Pop drove us down to the Point where we were to stay at Synton until our house warmed up. He sailed from New York on the *Leviathan,* a ship whose name seemed to contain all that was romantic and mysterious about the sea. We only saw him sail from Fall River on the *Priscilla,* a ship of the old Fall River Line. We all went up to see him off, and he took Mum over behind a pile of lumber to kiss her goodbye. Then he picked us each up and hugged us, and the next thing I knew he was waving to us from the deck of the *Priscilla,* a soldier boy just like the rest.

April at the Point was bare and cool, but there were blue scillas scattered under the lindens and crocuses out in the gardens. All the sunny windows at Synton were full of flats of seedlings, which people were always moving around. We were not supposed to touch these tiny gardens because it would hurt the baby plants.

Spring was baby time on the hill. There were kittens in the hayloft, baby chicks in the orchard, baby ducks in a carton behind the stove, and everywhere baby leaves unfurling and bulbs pushing green spears up into the sunshine. Mum used to sit on the new green grass by the garden with Dave, the new baby, while Aunt K. planted her seeds. Little blue butterflies danced over the primroses, honey bees nuzzled in the crocuses and in the air was the dreamy dazzle of spring, the sweetness of April.

Baba, on these occasions, patrolled the garden looking for mustard, against which she waged perpetual war. She taught us to recognize its bright green rosettes and cry, "Up-by-the-roots!" as we jerked it out for her. In the garden she wore her purple wool dresses and a heavy coat sweater that buttoned down nearly to her knees. Her hat, as I remember, was like a large turban, and she had on gray gloves to keep her hands from freckling. Every now and then she would hold up one finger for silence and we'd stand quietly to listen to a bird.

"That's a song sparrow," she'd say as the silvery warble rang out in the clear air. Then we'd try to see the singer swaying on his twig, his beak open, his little throat vibrating as the notes poured out.

While the ladies were in the garden we were usually told to play in the Cottage, Synton's playhouse, which was unchanged since Mum and her brothers and sister were little. When we were in there with the door shut we were less apt to get into trouble, because opportunities for wickedness were so limited.

The Cottage was an exact copy of Synton, with a veranda all around and two rooms inside, each with a wooden fireplace. The rooms were furnished with dwarf antiques of great charm: tiny bentwood chairs, an oval mahogany table, a whatnot full of doll's china, a miniature bureau and two bewitching wicker rockers just the size for us. One room contained a tiny work bench that had belonged to Uncle B. The walls were hung with delightfully romantic pictures, and there were curtains of Indian muslin at the windows.

Once we had swept and dusted the two rooms and set the table for tea, there wasn't much you could do in the Cottage but have a make-believe tea party. Also, on a hot day the place was an inferno, as we were forbidden to open the windows. Still, it was our house and we adored it. I used to pick bunches of flowers for the table and arrange everything neatly, and then we'd sit there and wonder what to do next.

Tink, our dear playmate, was unable to give us all his time because in April he was still on his winter schedule. His main winter chore was filling the wood boxes and splitting wood out at the barn. Aldie and I followed him about, trying to lure him away from his chopping block, but it was quite impossible.

"No, no," he said impatiently. "Finish work first."

It was very irregular for us to be there in April, and he could not change his routine until June. Once Tink started on a job, nothing and no one could interrupt him. He was like some relentless machine that has been set going and cannot stop until the cycle is finished.

When Tink was free we used to go up in the hayloft and play with the kittens in their hole down behind the haymow. The hayloft was a charming place, part of which had once been my grandfather's study. The hay was piled high behind a neat wooden fence, while the remaining space was empty except for a setting hen, blown up the size of a hassock, in one corner. On the walls were colored pictures from the Christmas number of the *London News* as well as a picture of a thirty-mule team crossing Death Valley—an advertisement for Thirty-Mule Team Borax, whatever that was. I believed this to be an authentic portrait of the Valley of Death in the Twenty-third Psalm.

On sunny days the hayloft was like a great nest, warm and fragrant, where we were safe from interruption by grownups. The mother cat seemed to accept us as just three larger kittens and purred away like a small engine while the kittens sucked and kneaded her side with their paws. We each had a favorite kitten that we put inside our sweaters. Mine was a tiger with a little face like a pansy and paws as soft and pink as raspberries.

The setting hen was very irritable and used to squawk loudly whenever anyone came near her corner, but Aunt K. paid no attention and used to lift her up every day to check on the eggs. One morning we were present when the first chick pipped its shell and, after a while, shouldered its way out into the world and collapsed in a wet heap, closing its eyes in exhaustion. We were horrified and wanted to help him in his struggles to free himself from the shell, but Aunt K. said calmly that he was fine and we mustn't interfere or the hen might kill him.

This upset me a good deal, but later on, when I saw the hen clucking about the barnyard with her brood of butter-yellow puff-balls, I realized that things somehow worked out. This was our first exposure to what used to be called the birds and the bees, but it left me as innocent as before, as far as "the facts" were concerned.

The house at this season had a special coziness and smelled deliciously of wood smoke from the open fires that Baba kept burning in the drawing room and dining room. She was the fire builder and was always poking at the logs with her brass fire tools.

I remember the sun on those spring mornings—floods of pure gold pouring through the curtainless windows onto the oriental rugs and making warm places for us to play. In summer the leaves of the great trees outside blocked much of the sun, but now the bare twigs let it all come through, and the whole house glowed like a lantern. It was wonderful to come back to after a walk on the beach, where we sometimes went to gather sea clams for chowder. There were often men over there digging with clam rakes, but the big sea clams lay on top of the sand after a storm, something we never saw in summer. They were huge things—up to eight inches long and heavy as stones. Aunt K. used to grind them up and make succulent chowders for supper.

Another gastronomical feature of the season was fried eels. At night we could see the lanterns of the eelers moving about the river like fireflies. We bought eels at Whalen's at the foot of the village street, and the whole process of preparing and cooking them was exciting in a ghastly way. First they had to be de-slimed in wood ashes, then they were cleaned and cut into chunks, which Aunt K. dipped into cornmeal and fried in salt pork grease. The sections squirmed horribly in the black iron frying pan; the kitchen became blue with smoke and broiling hot from the stove. Everybody present shrieked with disgust, but the final product was very sweet and tender, rather like smelt.

Suppers were the jolliest affairs imaginable, with all of us gathered around the table in the circle of light spread by the chandelier. Aunt K. provided with a lavish hand, and the serving table at Baba's right was crowded with steaming casseroles, bowls of fruit, platters mounded with sliced meat and plates of cake or cookies. Baba often pointed out the convenience of having all the food put on at once, thus dispensing with the service of the waitress. We all knew that Synton had no waitress except Aunt K., but we agreed that it was a perfect arrangement.

It was a woman's world we lived in, singularly peaceful and uncomplicated. The only signs of the War were the things people kept knitting out of khaki wool, and Pop's letters from France. They came with queer stamps on the envelopes, and often the letters themselves were full of holes from the censor's scissors. Pop was driving an ambulance at one point and he spoke of throwing oranges, cigarettes and chocolate to soldier boys on trains bound for the front. Once Pop himself went up to the front with the Holyoke regiment and lay in the mud under little pup tents while the rain poured down on each side and the shells whistled by overhead. He was with the boys until they went "over the top" but I can't remember whether he told us this later or whether it was in the letters.

He sent loving messages to us and told us about little French children in Paris and asked us to be good and take care of Mum. Mum wrote to him every day, and we drew him pictures and put X's for kisses on them. We missed him a lot but I don't remember feeling sad. He said he'd be back soon, and we knew he always did what he promised. We never worried about his safety, as we were too small to know that "shells" were anything except what we found on the beach. As for guns we heard them all the time. During meals the silver and glasses would chatter and the whole house shudder under us. At night we woke up to hear a distant thunder and feel our beds shake. Every time this happened Mum would say comfortably, "It's all right. That's just the guns at Newport."

Newport was where the big naval base was. Sometimes when we were picked up at ten o'clock to go to the bathroom, Mum would take us to one of the west windows and point toward Newport.

"Look," she'd say. "The searchlights." And we'd see shafts of gold light like giant knitting needles probing the sky in great clusters, criss-crossing and separating in a mysterious dance.

"What are they doing?" we'd ask.

"Looking for airplanes."

"What for?"

"Oh, just practicing."

Then the guns would shake the windows in their frames, rumbling under the searchlights like big iron balls tumbling downstairs.

We weren't afraid of the guns and thought them exciting. Anyway, Mum was there, keeping us safe.

There were recruiting posters around the stores showing the Kaiser in a spiked helmet and I didn't like his looks at all. There was something about spiked helmets that filled me with cold terror. I sometimes had nightmares about Germans in those helmets coming across the huckleberry field to get me, and then I'd jump out of bed and climb in with Mum.

"Mmm?" she'd murmur.

"Gotta bad dream," I'd whisper, wriggling down into the warm nest beside her.

"Well, you stay right here," she'd say and pull me in against her soft bosom, wrapping me close in her arms.

"Comfy?" she'd ask, and almost before I could answer I was asleep.

When the weather warmed up we moved down to Snowdon, and Buffy appeared to keep Mum company. We had a cook at first —a strange female called Fishy-Fishy—but she left after a week or two, and Mum and Buffy were on their own. Mum had never learned to cook, so I can only assume Buffy had, as we continued to eat.

Aunt K. had given Mum a government pamphlet showing how to make bread out of graham flour and cakes with very little sugar and only one egg and similar wartime concoctions. Mum and Buffy used to go into the kitchen with this pamphlet and Fanny

Farmer's cookbook, and the howls of laughter that issued from there were so infectious that we would go and watch. In those early days at Snowdon the kitchen was a small sunny room containing a malignant kerosene stove. This horrid appliance had three burners and a glass vessel at one end that went "glug-glug" at intervals. When you lighted it you had to tip back a rusty tin cylinder and apply a match to the wick. The flame either petered out miserably or rose to the ceiling in a pillar of fire with black smoke pouring from the top, and a rain of black particles drifting downward, coating every surface. Sometimes a pan would boil over and put out the burner, or oatmeal would suddenly erupt like a volcano and go hissing down onto the flame, making a horrendous smell.

During these summer months Mum and Aunt K. wore twin outfits of khaki with sailor blouses and ties and long skirts that buttoned down the front. Tink wore khaki too. It was the color of the War. Every time the ladies sat down they took out their khaki knitting wool and made mufflers and heavy socks and sweaters to keep the soldier boys warm in the trenches. Nobody told us what trenches were, but it seems to me I had always known.

Baba talked to me often about war work. Even on the hill, she said, we were doing our part. Raising food was war work, and the spring planting that year was on an enormous scale. Aunt K. spent most of her time on her knees setting out little plants, sowing seeds and weeding. Tink, whose schedule was upset by our presence, consented to rake and pick up stones in the new potato patch. However, when we moved down to Snowdon, he realized it was summer and went on vacation. His contribution to the war effort was the composition of a private war song in hatred of the Kaiser. It was called "Missa Willema Kaiser yai-yow" and was intended to be sung in our hammock.

It was peculiar at Snowdon without Pop, but summer was the same. The wind sang in the screens, the gulls called dreamily from the river and the air had the same fragrance as ever. We swam and went out in the boats, and the days were warm and blue, full of sounds of water. Pop was not visible, but in a way he was still there.

In September we all went into the woods and picked wild grapes for jelly. Buffy got stuck in the top of a tree and became quite helpless with laughter. Later we went after beach plums, and for days our kitchen and Synton's were dim with steam and the pungent, syrupy smell of jelly boiling down.

At Synton the canning had gone on all summer, and every time we went up there we had to go out in the kitchen to see a new row of Mason jars cooling on the counter, or a trayful of jelly glasses waiting for their paraffin. Baba would pick up a glass and tilt it to see if it had jelled properly. There was always a saucer with pink scum on it for us to lick. At the end of the summer the pickling began, and the sharp vinegary smell met us right at Synton's front door.

Once I went in and found Baba sitting at the kitchen table fanning herself with her apron. I had never seen Baba seated in the kitchen before, and she immediately rose from her chair and straightened her back.

"Come with me," she said. "I want to show you something," and she led the way to the cellar door.

Synton's cellar had a dirt floor and smelled damp and earthy but nice, like the leaf mold I helped Baba bring up from the woods for her garden. Against one wall was the fruit cellar, which was really just a big closet with a lot of wooden shelves. Baba opened the door and we went in.

"There," she said, pulling on the light. "Look at that."

All the shelves were lined with Mason jars full of different kinds of fruits and vegetables as richly colored as a stained-glass window. There were shelves where the jellies stood in jeweled rows and others that were green and yellow with pickles. Every jar had on it a label inscribed in Baba's illegible angular writing with the name of the contents and the date.

"See," said Baba. "We are all snug for the winter just like the squirrels. We won't be taking food from our boys in France."

The war ended before that winter began and the boys began to come home. Pop came back sometime before the Armistice, when the purple asters were thick along the land and the leaves had turned scarlet and orange in the woods. I remember he was very thin and hollow-cheeked, but he was himself, the same as ever. I don't remember how he got to Synton, but he was there and Aldie and I ran into his arms. Dave, to our horror, didn't know him and screamed when Pop tried to pick him up.

"Never mind," said Pop. "Remember—I've been away half his life."

It was true. Dave had just had his first birthday. Still, he should have known. I was so afraid Pop would be hurt that I felt almost sick. Luckily, the next day he was tossing Dave around and everything was all right.

One morning in Baba's dining room Pop gave out the presents he'd brought—a bolt of white satin from Lyons for Aunt K., another of purple satin for Baba. There was a barrel of Limoge china for Mum, wooden shoes from Belgium for each of us, as well as a lot of other delightful things. Most wonderful of all he brought me a walking doll from Paris—a doll with a china head, long brown curls, brown eyes that closed, visible teeth and jointed arms. She walked when you pushed her by the shoulders. I named her Paris.

Pop was full of war stories. I was particularly struck by the fact that somebody called Big Bertha kept throwing shells at him in Paris. He brought back an enormous white book full of photographs of the War, and as he turned the pages he told us about trenches and dug outs and what it looked like in No Man's Land. France seemed to be just a mass of rubble, one ruined village after another, with soldiers standing around laughing.

"There's Wipers," said Pop smiling. ("Wipers" was Ypres.) "I was there."

We were hypnotized by the War Book. There were even pictures of dead bodies in it, rows of them. I know now that Pop wanted us to hate war forever, and he certainly achieved his purpose. I still have nightmares about the War Book.

Pop didn't seem to have learned to speak French, although he used to yell "Allons!" whenever we set out in the car. He also had learned a phrase that became part of his language ever afterward. This was "perfect-a-menta bien."

"Ah perfect-a-menta bien!" he would cry when he was pleased

about something or when another perfect day dawned. This was often, as during this happy time there came a series of Indian-summer days, so warm and still that we went for picnics nearly every noon. We had a curious round object like a black hassock called a "fireless cooker" and they would fill this with hot stew. Other items were packed in wicker hampers and in our picnic suitcase, which had oilcloth-lined cubbyholes for various foods, stacks of tin plates and cups and eating utensils in little slots in the lid. It weighed a ton, so we had to eat fairly close to the car. The ladies would select a sunny hollow in the sand dunes with a view out over the salt marshes and after some discussion spread out the steamer rugs. Baba would choose her place and they would plant Dave in the middle of one of the rugs. Then Pop and Tink struggled up with the fireless cooker, the picnic suitcase and whatever baskets or hampers the ladies had inserted into the car. A picnic was quite an operation when Baba was present, as there was always a complete dinner. Aunt K. put in some of her hot rolls or fresh gingerbread, and the only thing missing was a white damask tablecloth.

When we were back in Holyoke Pop arranged on top of his study bookcase the souvenirs he had picked up on the battlefield: a French helmet, an American helmet, a German dagger, some jagged pieces of shrapnel, a brass shell case and a hand grenade. These murderous items soon became as much part of the domestic scene as the Boston fern or the telephone.

The Armistice occurred shortly after Pop's return, but I don't remember anything of that. We had celebrated the end of our war with Pop at the Point.

❦ 5 ❦

Horse-Chestnut Time

The end of the War marked the end of a lot of other things too, our freedom to name but one. We were sent to school—not a real school, it's true, but a private kindergarten in somebody's living room. The high point of kindergarten in my memory was an occasion when we were making valentines and a little girl called Helen Cadden ate some of the paste, which had turned a delicious pink from the red paper hearts. She said afterward that it tasted quite good. There was another episode when somebody named Billy O'Connor was publicly disgraced for chewing pencils, and we were invited by the teacher to observe his toothmarks. Chewing pencils, biting your nails, wetting your pants or pulling somebody's hair were the major kindergarten sins and about all I remember of my first exposure to education.

It was difficult to take kindergarten seriously and we didn't. One day in spring, my friend Alice Newton and I were en route to school and we decided not to go. Instead we picked dandelions and collected the pink catkins off the poplar trees. I remember clearly the sticky smell of the latter and the softness of the air on that spring day. I was filled with joy and was amazed at the behavior of our teacher when we were finally captured and brought to trial. It was spring. We hadn't wished to attend school. Nothing they said persuaded me we had been wrong to stay outside in the lovely sunshine.

This same group of scholars was later transferred to the third floor of a large Victorian house, but eventually we all went to a private school at the other end of town. Pop had very little use for private school, being a public-school man himself. Mum, on the contrary, had not gone to school at all at our age, but had been tutored at home, taken for nature walks in New York's Central Park by tutors, and had a schoolroom right in the house just like little English children in books. As far as we could see she and Aunt K. and Uncle B. had lived an idyllic life and had been able to travel around the world or go to the Point any time the spirit moved them. Consequently, Mum didn't take our school very seriously either and used to persuade Pop to stay down at the Point after school opened or go down early in June.

"A week or two won't matter," she'd say. "They won't miss much."

"That's perfectly true," said Pop. "It's time they went to a real school and learned how the other half lives," but as all our friends went to private school he didn't insist and we were usually a week or more late every fall.

After the long, hot drive we would climb out into leftover summer, and for several days everything seemed overstuffed and padded. Oak Street was overstuffed with leaves; in the house the stair carpets and thick oriental rugs deadened our footsteps; the velvet curtains blocked the sunlight; the heavy doors swung to with a rich click instead of the shattering slam of the ones at Snowdon. It was almost like being in church, but I must admit the feeling of luxury was exciting, especially in the bathroom. Unless you've been dodging spiders in a privy, shoveling chloride of lime down the hole and struggling with washbowls and pitchers you have no idea of the Lucullan character of a real bathroom. Our period bathroom was especially sumptuous, with all that marble and the oversized tub with its claw feet. Instead of ordinary faucets it had one high, curving spout like the neck of a swan, and when turned on full force the stream had the impact of a fire hose. On those warm, sunny afternoons of fall the windows would be open so that the filmy white curtains puffed inward and floated back. The sound of traffic in that peaceful time was no louder than the murmur of bees in goldenrod.

When we came in hot from playing, Mum would fill the tub almost up to the rim with cool water that was supposed to be the same temperature as the Westport River. Then we would go for a swim, splashing thunderously and surging back and forth until the water broke in a tidal wave over the edge of the tub. These baths were called river baths, and after one of them the bathroom was awash from end to end.

Almost as glamorous as the bathroom was electric light. Although I missed the nostalgic reek of kerosene, I did not regret the lamps themselves.

When we first came back from the Point, Mum and Pop would forget we had electricity and start groping around for the matchbox. Then they would remember and exclaim over the wonder of electric light.

"Eye Guy," Pop would say. "Look at that. Just press a button."

In spite of these compensations it took me a weary time to get back to the city in spirit. While the hot weather continued, I was sick with longing for the Point, for blue salt water and wide horizons and the smell of the hill. I would get my barn sneakers out of the back of the closet and inhale the faint odor of manure from their soles. Then I would bring forth all my souvenirs of summer—a bit of marlin from the boathouse, some rockweed, dried black and crisp, and the powdered remnants of sweet fern and bayberry leaves—all of which were powerful agents in evoking the special air of our hilltop. Sometimes, when I was rearranging my shell collection, a silvery stream of sand poured out of one of the moon snails, authentic fragments of the beach where we had run barefoot on hot mornings.

School was anathema. To stay *indoors* on a blue day, wear good clothes and hard shoes and *study* was almost too much to bear.

Then the birches in our yard turned to gold, there was frost on the lawns in the early mornings and the fragrance of pickling spice and hot vinegar came up the back stairs. Miraculously, the Connecticut Valley became the right place to be. Autumn ripened slowly there in the shelter of the gentle mountains. The Holyoke range was not very high and you could see the scarlet and daffodil-yellow trees bunched like flowers on the ridges. All around the city were purring fields of goldenrod and asters, where crickets sang as though summer would never end. In the old villages the white houses reflected the blaze of sugar maples. Along the Connecticut River the tobacco barns were full, every other plank in the walls sprung open to air the leaves. The Polish farmers were harvesting their huge onion crops, and in the apple orchards the picking had begun. In the city itself the horse chestnuts were ripe, and those fortunate enough to own a tree rushed home every day to defend the crop.

Our tree was just outside the dining-room window, a towering giant filling a large section of sky like a mountain. We kept a daily check on the condition of the prickly green nuts until at last they began to crack open and the horse chestnuts, glossy and unflawed, were revealed. From then on they rattled down through the branches, day and night, hitting the ground in a series of little thuds. We had all we could do to keep up with the harvest and fight off trespassers.

The fact that the tree's roots happened to be in the yard below ours was, we felt, a minor technicality. We considered it our personal property. It was a magnificent climbing tree as well as a source of superior horse chestnuts, and we spent many hours in its topmost branches, swaying and dreaming in the violet afternoons of spring, or on crisp fall Saturdays shaking down the last nuts. I regret to report that we also spied on the amours of the young lady next door, who was in the process of getting engaged. From a certain level we had a clear view into a small sitting room and soon decided that a tree of such value was wasted on anyone who spent the bluest days kissing on sofas. Fortunately, the horse chestnut grew close to the retaining wall on the lower side of our yard, and we had a secret passage through the barberry hedge. It was a simple matter to creep through this tunnel, drop to the ground and, like chipmunks, scrabble around in the leaves for nuts. I remember the intense satisfaction of finding a double horse chestnut, still in its kid-lined husk, but best of all I loved extracting one of the big oval ones, with a luster like polished mahogany. I always carried one of these in my pocket and tried to keep it oily by rubbing it on the side of my nose. We all did this. That's what horse chestnuts were for.

Although we were outraged if anyone outside our circle of friends tried to collect any of our horse chestnuts, we had no qualms about stealing all we could get on the way home from school. Pop had not been able to put us in public school, but he insisted that we walk the two miles to school and back. Far from minding this safari, we enjoyed every minute of it and had many adventures.

The early-morning trip had to be brisk or we'd be late to school but in the afternoons there was room for loitering.

We walked home in a loosely organized pack composed of those individuals who lived in our area. We needed the protection of numbers because there were gangs of public-school kids who lay in wait for us and taunted us with our private-school status. One of them, a boy called Bissell Alderman, was, we were told, "out to get" Aldie, who had informed on him for smoking corn silk at a picnic. Aldie had done this out of a misguided sense of honor resulting from Pop's lectures on the evils of smoking "behind the barn." According to Pop, with his country boyhood, dreadful sins were committed behind barns, and we were on our honor not to join in such activities. By some curious coincidence, Bissell and his cohorts were actually behind a barn during the corn-silk episode, and this had triggered Aldie's reaction.

On our walk home the group divided into two sections: the girls, who picked up colored leaves, and the boys, who swaggered along, shuffling in all the leaf piles, shoving each other off the curb into the gutter, and throwing things. There were several well-known horse-chestnut trees along our route, but you had to be careful because some were in the territory of public-school kids, who naturally had to protect their rights. Others were in the yards of cross old ladies or angry retired characters, who sat on their front porches watching through the Dutchman's-pipe vines. It was all right to pick up any horse chestnuts that had rolled out onto the sidewalk, but it was more adventurous to dash into the yards and grab some. These forays, combined with the lurking menace of Bissell Alderman and the shouts of enraged rakers whose leaf piles we had violated, gave spice and interest to every homeward trek. We arrived back in our own territory, refreshed and invigorated, ready for the major work of jumping in our own leaf piles and harvesting our own horse chestnuts.

The houses on our block were mostly inhabited by elderly couples, spinsters, fierce old ladies or ministers whose children had flown the coop or were too old or too silly to play outdoors. As luck would have it, the house directly behind ours contained children our age, but they went to *public* school and hated us. This situation was aggravated by the topography of the area, which I might as well describe here.

Our block was built on a steep hillside and the houses stood one below the other, so that the yards were like steps in a flight of stairs, separated by retaining walls of varying heights. The garage of the house behind ours was on a level with our attic windows, and the children of that household were able to spit on the roof of our playhouse ten feet below. This made for a certain tension between the two families, but the underlying cause of the hostility was, of course, our separate schools.

We felt it a drawback that the enemy stronghold was above ours, as it gave them an advantage. Still we had the playhouse and plenty of allies to help us defend it from invasion. I think it is safe to say that never once did an enemy foot cross the threshold of this sanctuary.

The Little House, as it was called, was created by Pop out of two upright piano boxes put face-to-face. He cut windows on each side and a nice door in front and covered the whole thing with tarpaper. The result was a small gambrel-roofed residence. We furnished it with orange crates, which made excellent shelves, tables and benches as well as stove and icebox. Here Alice Newton and I "cooked" brews of mint leaves and water in tin cans and in winter made ice cream out of snow and squashed barberries. Not only was the Little House a perfect playhouse, it was also a clubhouse to keep other people out of. Sometimes it was a fort or a covered wagon besieged by Indians. Sometimes it was a house inside and a stagecoach outside, with the driver sitting over the front door holding the reins of Gillie, our rocking horse. Wars raged over and through it, and it wasn't always easy to maintain a peaceful homelike atmosphere for our dolls when somebody was crouching by the window firing snowballs at the enemy outside. Of course, it was a slum compared to the perfectly appointed Cottage at Synton, but it had more possibilities.

Besides the Little House we had a sandbox to end all sandboxes —six feet square with a waist-high platform all around, just the right height for making pies. It was delightfully situated on the sunny side of a fence of honeysuckle with a big Persian lilac nearby. Pop had brought in an enormous supply of real sea sand from the beach at the Point. This was deep enough tö make adequate holes and tunnels for trucks and cars, with plenty of surplus for pies and cakes. The boys could set up a complicated engineering project in one corner while my friends and I made neat rows of pies with dampened sand along another side. We had plenty of earth-moving equipment, also pails, cups, spoons and pudding molds. On a sunny Saturday morning in spring the sandbox was an enchanting place, warm and sweet with the scent of lilac and syringa from the big bush by the side porch. After Dave learned to walk, though, they put him in the sandbox, thus reducing it to the status of a playpen. He trampled on our tunnels, destroyed our pies and threw Aldie's trucks in the bushes. When we tried to control him, he bit us. Luckily, by that time we were not confined to the yard and spent our free time running with the pack, sliding down the bank or tearing down the sidewalk on various wheeled vehicles.

Our front yard was a good fifteen feet above the sidewalk on Oak Street, and the lawn ended in a magnificent grassy bank, the steepest in the neighborhood. You could look down on the heads of those on the sidewalk the way the knights of old could look down from their battlements on besieging forces and pour boiling oil on them or drop rocks as the case might be. The bank gave us a real advantage during snowball fights, but actually its main uses were peaceable. In winter all our friends came there to coast; in spring and fall we went down it on scooters, express wagons or bicycles. One winter when there was a bearing crust we went down on skates.

The sidewalk on our side of the street was almost too good to be true. It was like a roller-coaster track with a starting point on Linden Street above. We built up speed on the first stretch, then swept around onto Oak Street in a hazardous right-angle curve. This was called Miss Eaton's Corner after the shaky old lady who lived in the brown house there. The surface of our sidewalk was macadam, much cracked and heaved by tree roots, with hollows where puddles formed after a rain, and we had the privilege of half killing ourselves on it at all seasons—on roller skates and scooters in spring and fall, on sleds, toboggans and skis in the winter. The knees of our stockings were always in rags, our knees themselves scraped and scabbed, and people were always going home crying with split lips and bloody noses. They soon came back, though, because nobody anywhere around had a yard as good as ours.

The main reason our yard was so superior was that it had been turned over to us and to the forces of nature. While we had worn down most of the side lawn, the forces of nature had created a jungle of the borders and were, on the whole, ahead of the game. Pop mowed what lawn we left him and assisted the forces of nature to make a bird and wildflower sanctuary where we could go on bird walks before breakfast and pick flowers. He and Mum moved in more wild flowers and ferns so we had yellow and purple violets, Jack-in-the-pulpits and bloodroot in spring and purple asters in the fall. The prim black iron fence that ran through this wild garden was all but invisible. The other fences and arbors installed by some unknown Victorian gardener had collapsed under their load of vines. Two or three stalks of asparagus near the broken-down grape arbor, one yellow crocus in the clothes yard and some lilies of the valley by the outdoor faucet were the only vestiges of the old garden left. Pop had a small rose bed under his study windows, but the rest of the property was just a glorious playground. Even the summerhouse had been taken over by us. This frivolous structure was circular and had a conical roof like a Chinese hat, with a thing like an acorn on top. It was clearly meant for decorous tea parties on summer afternoons, but we used it as a trolley car. The passengers sat on the seats inside and the conductor walked around the rail to take up the fares. Pop had hung a red wooden swing in the doorway, thus rendering the summerhouse useless for any serious adult projects.

The maids fought a losing battle to maintain the sanctity of the clothes yard, but we cut the lines constantly for jump ropes, reins and other vital necessities, and Pop put a compost heap at one end and the Little House for us at the other.

Every Saturday afternoon in the fall the whole family piled into the Artful Dodger and drove out to the South Amherst Fruit Farm to buy the fruit for Mum's great preserving orgies. Out in the farm country the front yards were heaped with pumpkins and squashes, tomatoes were lined up to ripen on porch railings and the air smelled of apples. On these expeditions Pop's Old Farm blood took over completely, and he stopped the car all along the way to show us classic details of the harvest. There was one farm where the apple orchards stretched on both sides of the road, all the trees jeweled with fruit, and some so loaded they had wooden crutches to hold up the branches. Here Pop would put on the brakes, turn off the engine and tell us all to get out.

"Now," he'd say, "smell that air and listen to the silence!"

Then we'd pick up some drops from the grass under the roadside trees while Pop discoursed on the apples of his youth.

"Winesaps," he used to say, "were so juicy they'd explode all over your face, and there were big dark red apples called Greasy Pippins that Harry and I used to polish up on the seat of our pants until they shone."

Then he'd tell how they used to dig a nice deep hole in the hillside and line it with straw, and he and Harry Hurd, who was a sort of extra brother, would put in there the best apples, cover them with more straw and a board and later in the winter they could uncover them and they'd be as fresh as ever.

McIntoshes, Pop said, biting into one, were wonderful eating apples, but when he was a boy there were little apples called Snow Apples, bright red with pink-veined flesh, that were even better.

Pop's father used to keep a bowl of Northern Spies on the table where he could get at them. Pop was always trying to find a source for these old varieties.

The roadside stands in the valley had gallons of cider, red corn for popping, baskets of grapes and apples and mountains of squashes and pumpkins. Mum was faithful to the South Amherst Fruit Farm, but we always stopped at a special stand for a gallon of cider.

"Got any Winesaps or Northern Spies?" Pop would ask, and every now and then he found some.

At times we left the main highway and cut across country, following the back roads that wound through the hills, past farms and orchards where apple picking was in progress. On a bright, sunny hilltop with a view over the valley, we would stop and get out to listen to the cricket song and throw apples. Pop used to cut some long suckers off a wild apple tree and sharpen the points. Then he showed us how to impale an apple on the tip and with a quick whipping stroke send it far out over the valley, over the scarlet and yellow sugar maples and the dry, golden fields into the violet distance. Once we stopped by a grove of chestnuts and Pop helped us to pry open the needle-prickly burs to get at the nuts.

"When I was a boy," he'd keep saying. "When I was a boy . . ." and "Up at the Old Farm we'd do this and this."

Mum didn't bother to throw apples or gather chestnuts. She'd just perch on a stone wall among clumps of purple asters and goldenrod, drinking in the color.

"Look at that tree," she'd call, and she was the first person who showed us that the hills in their autumn color looked like oriental rugs poked up with sticks. She was a wonderful enjoyer, an appreciater, and she loved living just as she does now at eighty-four.

The South Amherst Fruit Farm was a real working farm, with barns, silos, corn cribs and a haymow, where we could jump to our hearts' content. The minute we got out of the car the farm collie came barking over to meet us, his plumed tail waving. While Mum picked out her fruits, Pop took us into the main barn, barely able to restrain his eagerness to get back into the Old Farm atmosphere. He always stopped outside to point out the brilliant little picture framed in the far door. There, in vivid contrast to the rich darkness inside, was a sunny green slope with apple trees on it and a blue hump of mountain beyond.

"Barn-door landscape," he said. Then we went in and he said, "Now just smell that!"

We stood still, rapturously breathing in the warm, rich odors of hay and manure, grain and animals. There was a bull in a box stall down below, and when he heard us he'd thump the floor and give a low, snoring growl like a man playing a tuba.

Pop had taught us the classic design of a barn, and it was rather like his church: the dim center aisle where the hay wains drove in, the great lofts overhead under the vaulted ceiling, and the side aisles where in fragrant darkness the cows rattled their stanchions and the horses hung their noble heads over like bishops.

"The harness closet's here," Pop would say, "and right here is the grain closet. Just feel that wood. Look at the width of that board on the old grain chest. First-growth pine, I'll bet a nickel."

Then he'd admire the pitchforks with their silver tines and silky handles and the manure forks, the wooden measures and all the appurtenances of farming that he so loved.

Pencils of dusty sunlight slanted through knotholes in the hay-loft, and square blocks of sun lay on the floor of the tie-up. The cows turned their velvet eyes on us and blew gusts of sweetness from soapy noses. The barn cat wound around our legs, and nearly always there were kittens, light as thistledown, bouncing out of the corners.

We climbed a vertical ladder up to the haymow, where Pop rigged a rope for us to swing out on and drop into the hay like trapeze artists into a net. We also jumped off the highest beams we could reach and soon had hayseed inside our clothes, hayseed in our hair and dust up our noses.

We always stayed to see the cows milked. The farmer's son came whistling into the tie-up, two or three big silver pails in each hand. Then he'd shove a milking stool in beside a cow's rear half, plant a pail under her udder and sit down with his forehead against her side. Seizing a teat in each hand he sent alternate jets of milk drumming into the empty pail. Soon the drumming was drowned in rising foam and changed to a rhythmic hissing that seemed to lull the cow into a kind of trance. Pop used to strike up long conversations with the young man, who cheerfully discoursed on the habits and milk records of the various cows.

The farmer himself walked down the center aisle, pitching fresh hay in front of each cow, and the son moved from one udder to another, with us surging after him. He set the frothing pails in a row by the wall, filled a saucer for the cat, and at Pop's request gave us each a drink of warm milk out of an enamel cup.

The sun was low over the mountains when we climbed into the car, now deliciously fragrant from the baskets of fruit that jammed the floor of the back seat. All the way home we breathed the essence of Concord grapes and apples and refreshed ourselves with grapes when it seemed safe.

In the towns the leaf fires of evening made a blue haze of smoke under the elms and filled the car with their incense.

When we got home and Pop had carried in Mum's baskets, he came out and began raking leaves himself. This was one of the best times of the day, when, as the sun set and the darkness gathered, he rolled up great piles of leaves and left them for us to jump in. The leaves on the upper level ended up in the compost heap; the ones down along the sidewalk went into long rustling piles in the gutter. By the time the stars winked out overhead, we were ready.

"Stand clear, men," Pop would say, and striking a match on the seat of his pants, he lit our bonfire. We watched while the little flame licked into the leaves, then suddenly burst out in great flapping banners of fire, roaring and crackling the whole length of the pile. Sparks streamed upward into the darkness and the orange light from the fire made a glowing cave under the trees where we stood, our faces lit from below.

When there was nothing left of the fire but a drift of ash, breathing red and orange at its heart, we went in to supper. Mum was upstairs in her room rocking whatever baby we had then, and everybody ran upstairs two at a time.

The golden rain of leaves went on for a long time, and it seemed as though the supply would never give out. Streets, sidewalks and yards were buried in color, and then one day we woke up and the trees were bare. The whole world looked empty and cold. Mum got our winter clothes out of the camphor trunk, and Pop took us back into the country to buy our pumpkins for Halloween.

❦ 6 ❦

First Snow

The only good thing about November was Thanksgiving, an island of white damask with the turkey on its huge Sheffield platter at Pop's end of the table. Gumpkie, Pop's father, came for Thanksgiving, and we used to drive down to Springfield to meet him at the station.

Gumpkie was a perfectly enchanting grandfather, the only one we had and a sort of exaggeration of Pop. He was shorter than Pop, balder than Pop and had a close-clipped gray mustache, but he had Pop's wonderful wheeze-laugh and Pop's sense of humor. Unlike anyone on Mum's side of the family, he was a businessman and wore a derby hat and a chesterfield coat and smoked cigars. In a word, he was "in trade."

When Gumpkie got off the train he was surrounded by friends he had made on the journey and spent a while shaking hands and introducing the various people to us.

"Eye Guy," he'd say just like Pop. "I sat next to the nicest fella from Syracuse. Has a wife and five children, works in a hardware store. Having a hard time making ends meet, so I gave him a little something."

He was always giving people a little something, and this generous, trusting spirit of his may have accounted for the fact that his business kept folding up.

After the friends departed, Gumpkie bent down and hugged us. I remember the smell of cigars and the scratchiness of his mustache. Then he'd say something about the Amir of Siam or the Jackal, the main characters in the two serial stories he had started when Pop was a little boy and which were still going on.

The Amir of Siam had a nose so long that he was able to use it in many interesting ways. The Jackal was a raffish creature rather like something out of Disney, and his adventures were so funny that even Gumpkie would become speechless with laughter when he tried to tell us about them.

When we got home Gumpkie produced an enormous box of chocolates of a special expensive brand with a coronet on the package. After he had brushed up in the spare room he came downstairs, and he and Pop talked while we sat in Gumpkie's lap. Later they'd share the evening paper. Gumpkie liked to tease Kelt, our dog, who used to sit and stare at him from a spot in front of his chair. Kelt was accustomed to sitting in that chair himself and would growl or yip in a disapproving way if anyone else used it. At these times Gumpkie would be very still. Suddenly, he'd tear a hole in the paper and yell "boo!" through it. Kelt used to give a shriek and rush from the room, his tail between his legs, while Gumpkie collapsed with his wheeze-laugh, tears running down his cheeks.

Every morning we ran in to the spare room and climbed into bed with Gumpkie. Usually, he was hiding under the covers, pretending to be asleep, but the minute we crept up onto the bed he'd erupt in a welter of blankets and scream "boo!" again, the way he did with the dog. You can see why we loved him so. Until everybody got up he'd tell us stories about the Amir and the Jackaal and the Old Farm where he'd grown up. His heart was really on the farm, not in the clothing business. We could understand that.

Gumpkie left after Thanksgiving and we headed for Christmas, the next milestone on our long journey back to summer. The year went uphill to Christmas, then it was downhill the rest of the way to spring vacation.

We always had snow for Christmas, although there were years when things got pretty tense. Sometimes the ground was bare right up to the middle of December, and Pop would say at breakfast that it was time Jack Frost tended to his job. He had once told us that Jack Frost lived under the honeysuckle bush in the back corner of our yard, a place visible from his chair at the dining-room table.

"Jack Frost is still asleep out there," he'd say, glancing out the window. "Come on, Jack, give us some snow. Christmas is practically here."

We asked him what Santa would do with his sleigh if there was no snow, and he said it was a problem but Santa would make it if he had to walk.

"He can't do that," we said, shocked.

"Well, go out and stir up Jack Frost then," he'd say, and I really did go out to the honeysuckle bush and poke under a stone with a stick. I could see in my mind Jack Frost, in his silvery brownie suit with the white fur trim and snowflake buttons, all curled up underground like a rabbit.

Sooner or later there would come one of those leaden mornings when everything seemed to stand still waiting. Pop, who had been brought up in the snow belt of upstate New York, was an authority on snow and used to look out the window at breakfast and say he'd bet a nickel today was the day.

"You watch," he said, "in fifteen minutes you'll see a snowflake. This morning when I let out the dog it smelled like a storm."

We'd shovel down our oatmeal with eyes fixed on the Alisons' horse chestnut tree—our weather station—and almost always Pop was right. First one or two flecks of white drifted aimlessly past the window, then four or five, and suddenly the air was full of them, seething and swirling until they settled down into a real snowstorm. All our windows were filled with lovely swaying curtains of snow that blurred the familiar houses and clothed all the treetops like whipped egg white. The birches in our yard bent lower and lower as their twigs thickened, and in the drifted street cars went skidding sideways with squealing brakes.

Sometimes it didn't start to snow until after dark. We'd hear it hissing against the window panes and look out through cupped hands to see the street lights swarming with flakes like white bees.

Pop would come home with snow all over him, stamp his feet on the porch and slam the front door with a great shout.

"Hey, it's snowing!" he'd yell and give his Swiss yodel.

We'd run downstairs in our bathrobes, and he'd sweep us up and give us a cold, fresh kiss, his cheeks wet from the storm. Before he took off his overcoat he'd go out again and catch us some flakes on his sleeve.

"Look at that," he'd say. "There's a beauty." And we'd peer down at the filmy lace stars that dissolved in our breath.

"It's really coming down out there," he used to say happily. "Ought to go on all night."

Some winters the first snow came secretly while we slept, floating down in perfect silence all night long to surprise us with a quilted world in the morning. We'd be waked up by the plow rumbling down our street and run to the window in ecstasy to see the team stamping past between the cottony trees—giant furry horses snorting clouds of steam and shaking their bells lustily. The plows were careful to sheer off only the top layer of snow like the meringue on a pie, leaving a smooth surface for sleighs. There were still a lot of horse-drawn sleighs around then, and the early mornings were merry with sleighbells as the farmers came in from the country with loads of wood or hay.

While we stood by the window, eating snow off the sill, we'd hear the whisper of chains as the first cars broke out into the velvet streets. The whickering rhythm of those old chains was one of the special winter sounds of the city, and there was always some car with a bit of loose chain clanking against the mudguard in a jolly syncopated beat. Then there were the people who had no chains and were stuck. You could hear them spinning their wheels somewhere off in the distance.

We always ran into Mum's room to share the joy. I remember one special morning standing on the side of Pop's marble washstand, across from Aldie, and looking out of the little alcove to the sunny room beyond. Mum was changing a baby on the bed, and I guess it was Dave or we wouldn't have been small enough to stand up in there. I can feel still the peculiar joy of that snowy morning, the whiteness everywhere—the big double bed with its fat pillows and turned-back sheets and the lather Pop whipped up with his shaving brush. All the trees outside looked as though they had been dipped in a big shaving mug.

The house on the morning after the first snowfall was like a great ship getting up steam. The reflected light from the white earth shone upward onto the ceilings the way sun quivers on the roof of a boat's cabin. Down in the engine room the crew seemed to be laying about them with iron tools, stoking their fires and slamming their iron doors.

In the kitchen, Kack, the cook, clattered her stove lids and poured coal out of the coal hod with a gritty roar. Pop shook down the furnace, and we heard the scraping of his big shovel on the floor of the coal bin. Shortly thereafter the pipes began to clank and all the radiators started hissing like teakettles.

Pop sometimes spoke of the furnace in bitter terms and I thought of it as a large and dangerous creature, like a rhinoceros, crouched at the foot of the cellar stairs. The big gold radiators with their embossed decorations and clawed feet were almost like pet animals, and lovely on cold mornings when we cuddled up to them, laying our hands against their flanks to test the heat and turning ourselves to warm different portions of our anatomy. Buffy dressed us beside the one in our room and warmed all our clothes on it, even our shoes. Sometimes she left our shoes on too long and the soles burned our feet like hot metal. Also if you put shoes on the radiator wet, they dried up and shrank. I can feel now the parched stiffness of those little dried-up brown oxfords.

We went down to breakfast, scuffing along the thick oriental rugs to work up the electricity and give each other shocks. There were days when we could make blue lightning crackle between our fingertips, a painful but triumphant exercise.

By breakfast time the first shovelers were out—fathers in fedora hats and ear muffs or hired men in caps. The scraping of shovels echoed up and down Oak Street, and pretty soon the doorbell began ringing as the free-lance shovelers applied for the job of doing our walks. However, they were sent away, for Pop did all our shoveling as soon as morning prayers were over. He tended to cut short his Bible reading on snowy days, and once he said grace instead of the Lord's Prayer because his mind was on shoveling. Of course, he sometimes said the Lord's Prayer instead of grace by mistake, so it all evened up.

He would put on his enormous arctics, his fedora hat and ear muffs and set forth, taking his big wooden snow shovel from the cellar where it had spent the summer. He started shoveling on the porch, went on down the wooden steps to the front walk and down the long flight of stone steps to the sidewalk, where he shoveled out the horse block and a path to the street. Then he went back up and shoveled the path to the back door.

When Aldie and I were still under nursemaid rule, it took us nearly a full hour to get out into the snow. First Buffy dragged us off to the bathroom, then she and Mum waded into the back of the hall closet to hunt for our arctics—an almost höpeless quest as the place was dark as night and knee-deep in equipment that had been hurled in there the spring before.

Finally, they set about inserting us into our snow gear, not a simple matter. Snowsuits did not exist then, but we had long black leggings with buttons down the side and elastics under our shoes. The dye in these leggings ran the instant they got wet, turning our stockings and long underwear a repulsive purple like a black eye.

Over our shoes went arctics with black cloth tops and rubber soles. These were fastened with metal buckles that were always coming undone. One of the vivid discomforts of winter was biting off your mitten and holding it in your teeth while you tried, with numb blue fingers, to rebuckle your arctics.

On top we had sweaters, and our mittens, connected by a cro-cheted string, were pulled on over our hands. There was usually some difficulty in getting our thumbs in place. Over the sweaters went our coats of dark blue nubbly wool, called "chinchilla." Knitted scarves were wound around our necks and buttoned inside our coats, and then our hats were put on and their wide elastics snapped under our chins. Aldie's was gray squirrel with "ear lappies," as we called them. Mine was beaver. By the time they got us assembled we were so hot we could hardly breathe and said so.

"No, you're not," Buffy or Mum said.

"Yes, I am. I'm boiling."

"Nonsense."

We gave up and waddled to the door like stuffed teddy bears and were let out.

The first thing we did was to eat snow. We'd scoop a couple of handfuls off the porch railing and stand at the top of the steps, squinting out at the dazzling street. Pop would stop his shoveling and make a beautiful round snowball for each of us, smoothing off all the lumps with his big leather mittens.

After that we lay down on the pure unmarked field of the front lawn and made angels. The dog, excited by the snow, snatched mouthfuls of it, yapped crazily, ran in circles and then solemnly left his mark on the corner of a drift.

Having performed these rites, we all three climbed into the path to watch Pop shovel.

Pop was a great shoveler to watch because he had a theory about snow shoveling like everything else. Instead of going at it bull-headed he had method.

"You cut it like a cake," he said, "the way the Eskimos cut it for igloos," and then he'd chop out a dazzling white block and lift it out whole. His paths were always straight-sided and neat, of uniform width.

"You can tell a man by the kind of path he shovels," he once said.

While Pop shoveled he told us stories about the great snows of his boyhood in the Mohawk Valley, where the drifts were often so deep you could walk over the top of an apple orchard. If he had time, after the walks were done, he'd shovel us out a quick fort with walls like giant sugar lumps.

"Don't you pee on that," he'd say to the dog, frowning, and Kelt would drop his ears and apologize for the idea. "Worthless as a pee hole in the snow," was one of Pop's Old Farm sayings that he only used when he was alone with us, and we knew just what he meant. We were so short that those yellow notes left by the neighborhood animals were right on a level with our eyes and spoiled the clean snowbanks in the first few hours after a storm.

Finally, Pop made a little path to the top of the bank, then brought out our barrel-stave sleds and waxed the bottoms with candle ends. These sleds were replicas of some he'd used as a boy and were unique in our block. Nobody else's father had even heard of barrel-stave sleds. Ours were made out of two barrel staves with a seat at one end and a bar at the other to brace your feet against. They could be used on fresh snow just like baby toboggans and made a track like skis. They were just right for breaking out the bank, and before long we would have a wide smooth track ending in a snowbank.

Our real sleds were wooden with curved runners. Mine was green with a decal of a little girl on it, Aldie's red with some sort of elf.

After a morning in the snow, we'd be literally soaked to the skin below the waist, and our mittens were sodden lumps. Buffy used to peel off the wet leggings and drape them over the hall radiator, then shake the icy bits off our mittens and lay them on top. Our black and blue underwear had to be changed too, and our shoes were put on or under our radiator to dry. The whole house smelled of steaming wool, and for an hour after we came in our faces would feel burning hot from the snow.

One of the ceremonies of the first snowfall was putting the side curtains on the Artful Dodger. The side curtains were made of a material, now happily obsolete, which was supposed to look like leather but had something of the appearance of a diseased alligator hide. The lozenge-shaped windows of cracked celluloid were yellow and opaque from years of being folded up under the back seat. Pop used to drag them out and spread them on the ground to see which one went where. Then he'd bribe us to help him snap them on. His bribes were always the same.

"I'll give you a million dollars someday," he'd say, "if you'll help me put these dad-gasted things on."

Of course, we always agreed because it was fun to do things with Pop. When we got older, one of us might say, "What about ten cents right now?" but Pop stuck to his guns.

"A million dollars later on," he said firmly.

For the benefit of those too young to remember side curtains I must explain that there were little gadgets on the curtains that snapped onto similar gadgets on the car. To get these to meet when your bare fingers were stiff with cold was almost impossible. In a high wind the curtains slatted about our heads like the wings of giant bats. However, putting on the chains was even worse. Pop did this alone.

The chains were huge things made of steel links that had to be fitted on the tires like sweaters. In order to do this Pop laid them out flat on the road and then tried to back the car over them. After that he pulled them up and fastened them with some sort of snap. You couldn't put the chains on *before* it snowed because the bare pavements would wear them out, and anyway the noise was horrendous. As Pop usually waited until the middle of a snowstorm to do the job the chains would disappear as soon as he laid them out on the ground. He couldn't see through the falling snow to back up very well, so he had to have Mum or one of us out there shouting directions, which he couldn't hear over the noise of the engine. At intervals he'd climb out and go down on his hands and knees to see if he had backed over the chains at the correct angle.

Even when he did get the chains on there always seemed to be something wrong. One of the chains would be too loose or a link would break and slug against the mudguard with a sound like machine-gun fire.

When the Artful Dodger was under way in winter you could hardly hear yourself speak, what with the dizzy syncopated rhythm of the chains and the flapping and roaring of the side curtains. Besides the noise it was so cold in the car that we nearly froze to death in the back seat. Nobody drove in winter unless they had to. We all walked everywhere, and Dave was pushed in a little red sleigh with curly runners. There was a fur carriage robe to keep him warm, and if one of us got tired we sat on his feet and rode for a while. When we went downtown Christmas shopping, the return trip was all uphill, and sometimes both Aldie and I plus the Christmas packages were piled onto the sleigh, Dave screaming on the bottom.

At the end of the day just before our supper Pop would take us down to fix the furnace. The cellar stairs were the scariest place in the house and Pop admitted that he himself disliked the cellar.

It was pitch dark except for the place around the furnace, which, fortunately, stood right near the foot of the stairs. Off around the corner was the fruit cellar, where all Mum's preserve jars were and the stoneware crocks full of eggs in waterglass. As far as I was concerned the fruit cellar was the hiding place of murderers, but Pop said he doubted if there were any there.

"Rats, yes," he said, "and someday I'm going to get the big one that knocks over the jars and eats my apples."

He would open the iron door of the furnace and a great gush of heat came out. We would look in and see little blue flames dancing over a field of fire. The coals seemed to breathe, turning from brilliant orange to pure light and back to red. First Pop shook down the fire and rooted around with the great iron poker to break up any clinkers. Then he shoveled on more coal, opened the drafts and slammed the door shut with a clang. After that we'd sit on the stairs for a while listening to the furnace hissing and sputtering while it began eating the coal. We had interesting talks about all kinds of things during these sessions.

The first big snowstorm used to arrive around Mum's birthday —December thirteenth—when the farmers in their pungs came in from the country with fresh-cut Christmas trees and greens. The wreath man's sledge jingled up Oak Street, its runners squeaking on the packed snow and the shaggy horse steaming like an engine. The wreath man was ruddy and almost as furry as his horse. He brought with him a resinous odor of fir and pine mixed with tobacco reek and a whiff of manure—a glorious smell. On his arms the wreath man had threaded samples of his wares, all of which he had made himself. We always bought holly wreaths for all the downstairs windows, and then the man took off his huge mittens and counted out the change, blowing clouds of tobaccoy vapor as he named the coins.

Pop got a hammer and nails to hang the wreaths, a prickly and painful operation, during which he yelled a lot and danced around sucking his fingers.

When the wreaths were all up, their sharp-pointed leaves squeaked against the glass, an authentic Christmas sound. We all went out on the porch to see how they looked from outside, and they looked perfect, the clusters of red berries shining among the dark, lustrous leaves and the scarlet bows tied as neatly as my Sunday hair ribbons.

"There you are," Pop used to say. "Now Christmas can come any time it wants to."

⁂ 7 ⁂

Christmas

The first Christmas I remember was my second although no one will believe me as I was only eighteen months old at the time. Two days before Aldie was born Mum played the part of the Virgin Mary in the pageant at the church, and I was present in the audience, standing on a pew with Baba clutching the back of my dress. I remember the blue robe Mum wore and the way the light shone upward onto her face from the manger. As this was her only appearance in the role of Mary, I think that clinches it.

I don't remember Aldie's arrival but they tell me he was born in the middle of Pop's Christmas sermon, and Mr. Weber—one of the deacons—who had been glued to the telephone in the office, came out in front of the pulpit and mouthed the words "It's a boy!"—a piece of news that Pop passed on to the congregation as soon as he recovered the power of speech. Pop's emotional nature made him lose his voice at the mention of anything to do with the home, motherhood, the family, the country or for that matter any subject even remotely touching or poignant. How he managed to announce the birth of his first son to a large congregation at Christmastime will forever remain a mystery, as of course Mum was not present to report.

We saw the Christmas pageant every year, and somehow I've always felt I've been in Bethlehem with the shepherds, the kings and everybody else, standing in wonder before the stable where the light shone.

The Christmas season in Holyoke began officially when they decorated the downtown streets with garlands and lighted Christmas trees, and Childs' shoe store gave away tiny red cotton Santa Clauses when you bought a new pair of shoes. Childs' always gave us presents with new shoes and they varied according to the time of year. You could tell when spring came because we got cotton Easter rabbits with pink glass eyes, but the Santas were the best. It was usually new arctics or Comfy slippers we bought at Christmas. Mr. Provo in the children's section would dip into a shoebox, after we were fitted, and hand us our Santas. Then Mr. Childs, who was one of the pillars of Pop's church and a dear friend, came over and wished us all a Merry Christmas.

Out on Main Street in those late afternoons the sidewalk was slippery with melting snow and reflected the blues, greens and reds of the lights. People jostled each other in front of the store windows, and the tall glittering buildings seemed to reach up to the stars. The city after dark was as exciting to us as an enormous Christmas tree, and we stumbled along the jeweled pavements lost in wonder. We hardly ever saw the downtown streets at night except at Christmastime when Mum and Pop took us shopping, so to us they were as glamorous as Paris or Rome. Above the royal clangor of trolley cars and the endless swish of car chains we heard the bells of Christmas ringing, merry and clear. The bellringers, though, seemed far from merry.

Wispy-bearded Santa Clauses stood on the corners wagging brass handbells; Salvation Army ladies in bonnets were there too, shaking tambourines beside iron kettles full of nickles, dimes and pennies. The Santas often had runny noses, and their eyes looked sad and lonely. They were clearly impostors but disturbing ones, with dirty cotton borders to their red suits and ordinary arctics like Pop's on their feet. Who the Salvation Army ladies were we had no idea.

Besides Childs' Shoe Store we went to a toy store so glorious that all I can remember are dolls in starched organdy dresses standing in cardboard boxes, fire engines, doll carriages and shiny tricycles that we rode down the aisles. I think these were test visits as nothing was ever actually purchased during our sessions among the toys.

As Christmas approached, packages came in the mail and were rushed upstairs and hidden in the guest-room closet. Mum came home from shopping trips with her arms full of parcels and her eyes bright and mischievous.

"Never you mind what I have here," she'd say and tell us to turn our backs while she smuggled upstairs lumpy bundles in brown paper to join the packages in the guest-room closet. We would have died rather than peek at the contents of that closet. We wanted to be surprised and, almost more, to surprise.

Our own Christmas shopping caused us hours of anguished speculation and worry. We were given two dollars each to spend, a princely sum to us whose allowance was a nickel a week. We did almost all our shopping at the church bazaar, which took place in the parish-house auditorium, a vast room two stories high with floors polished like glass, superb for sliding.

People think ministers' children have a dull life but, believe me, the Christmas season in Pop's church was just one long festival, beginning with this bazaar. In retrospect we seem to have reeled from orgy to orgy, stuffing ourselves on candy and ice cream and the cakes made by the ladies of the parish. The bazaar came first so people could get their shopping done early, and we were there from start to finish, as were all our friends.

The hall was decorated with looped garlands and wreaths, and a towering Christmas tree, scintillating with glass ornaments, tinsel and strings of lights, stood at the far end. All around the sides of the hall were long tables, spread with damask cloths, where the ladies of the church displayed things for sale. There was a food table covered with fat frosted cakes, piles of homemade cookies, pies and pans of fudge—lovely to smell but not, in our opinion, worth paying good money for. Next to the food was a table of fancywork: crocheted pot holders, aprons, baby clothes and other items not so easily identified. We passed this by too, because beyond it were the toy table, the doll table and the white-elephant table. On these three was set forth the most desirable merchandise ever conceived by the human mind. The dolls were exquisitely dressed by the church ladies in clothes that were perfect confections of ruffles, smocking, lace and ribbons.

The bazaar I remember most vividly is the year of the Real Baby doll and the grape tray. It was the first year we were turned loose at the bazaar to do our own shopping, and I went fiercely alone, my small wash-leather change purse clenched in my hand. As soon as the doors of the parish hall were opened I headed straight for the white-elephant table to beat the stampede and grab the best treasure for Mum. On the way, though, I sneaked a look at the doll table and skidded to a stop. In the place of honor they had a baby doll that surpassed anything I'd ever seen. It was one of the so-called Real Baby dolls with a delicately tinted china head, supposedly modeled from that of a newborn child. The small face was squashed-looking, with just the remote, mysterious expression of a new baby. The eyes were brown and opened and closed, the hair faintly brown on the round little head. Some genius had dressed this doll in real baby clothes: a filmy embroidered dress of the finest batiste, tucked and lace-edged, and underneath all the correct things right down to the flannel belly band. To top it off the doll had a woolen sacque edged with pink ribbon, a knitted cap and booties and a pink blanket. I wanted this doll more than I had ever wanted anything in my short life. My longing was so intense it was really painful because I knew it was hopeless.

I stood with my chin resting on the table edge, transfixed with wonder, and presently Mrs. Childs, wife of Mr. Childs at the shoestore, stopped beside me.

"Do you like that doll?" she asked kindly.

"It's thirty-five dollars," I said, hoarse with emotion. Thirty-five dollars was like three hundred dollars—an impossible sum.

Mrs. Childs was one of the best grownups we knew. She lived with her family in a wonderful big house on the block above ours and was the sort of person who would buy half-dead flowers, repulsive Christmas cards, cans of leaf mold or anything children happened to be peddling in order to make ends meet.

"Maybe Santa will bring it to you," she said now, and I smiled politely. Grownups were notoriously unrealistic.

"Santa hasn't got thirty-five dollars," I said. I had learned this when we had examined an electric train in the toy store.

Mrs. Childs patted my shoulder in her kind way and said you never know. We parted and I went on to the white-elephant table, where I at once saw *the* present for Mum—a present of such extreme beauty that I could hardly believe my luck. It was a round tray with a tiny fence around it of a material that looked like lead. There were two handles on each side made of the same metal, and framed under glass on the bottom was a piece of wallpaper featuring a bunch of grapes—brilliant blue with acid green leaves—a gorgeous object. An old lady was examining it and I waited, holding my breath, while she turned it over to see the price. For a horrible moment she considered it, then put it down and moved on. I ducked under somebody's arm and reached.

"How much is this?" I asked.

"Fifty cents," said the aproned lady behind the table.

"I'll buy it," I said recklessly.

Fifty cents! It was a lot of money but I bravely handed over the big silver coin and carried off the tray wrapped in a wrinkled paper bag.

Next I went to the secondhand-book table, for I had to find a book for Pop. Until a few days earlier I had been in despair about a present for him as my ideals were of the highest, my available funds correspondingly low. All the presents I thought of—axes for his woodchopping, tools for his shop, binoculars for his bird watching—were right out of sight in price. When I consulted with Mum she said she was having a hard time herself but was giving him a flannel shirt and pajamas. One evening down in the cellar Pop said that the thing he loved best about Christmas Day was reading his new books in the afternoon. New books! He was only getting a shirt and pajamas. My heart really ached with sorrow for him and I promised myself he would have a book every Christmas from then on. Picking out a book on the secondhand-book table at the bazaar was far from easy. I couldn't take anyone else's suggestions because it had to be *my* choice. The selection at the bazaar was limited. There were titles like *V. V.'s Eyes, Pure as Ice, Chaste as Snow* and *Behind the Bonnie Briar Bush* that something told me Pop would not like. I hoped for a heavy book—one that weighed a lot. At last I found one that weighed a ton and had the word "Wisdom" in the title. Pop often spoke of "wisdom," whatever it was, and I got him that.

The toy table provided nothing that I considered good enough for the boys and I felt the old Christmas panic. However, Mum came to the rescue and later on took me downtown to Fringelins', a combined stationery and toy store, where I was electrified by a display of British lead soldiers in the uniforms of various regiments. Those busbies, scarlet coats, silver sabers and *kilts* enchanted both Mum and me. I couldn't afford the Cameron Highlanders—kilts were extra, as were sets with horses like the Household Cavalry or those with musical instruments like the kilted bagpipers. I settled for the Royal Guardsmen, who were seventy-five cents a box. As we trudged back up Essex Street in a sifting snowfall, I felt free at last, and Christmas seemed to open up before me and flower in a thousand jeweled lights.

Back in my room I set forth my purchases on the bed and gloated over them. They were so magnificent that I had to share them with someone, so I brought in members of the family one by one, after carefully hiding their own presents in advance. Mum said the book was about the heaviest she'd ever picked up and "wisdom" was just what Pop liked. He was always talking about it in sermons. Aldie agreed that it was gratifyingly heavy and said the grape tray was a terrific find. Pop, in his visit of inspection, said he doubted if such a beautiful tray had ever existed before. He wished he himself could think of something to give Mum half as good. He invited me to come down cellar with him for a consultation.

After Pop had shaken down the furnace and shoveled on some coal we sat on the cellar stairs and he began.

"There's just no way I can find out what she wants," he said. "All she says is that she doesn't need anything. Now you are a girl, you ought to have some idea what a female of the species wants."

I confessed that my mind was a blank.

"I thought of gloves," said Pop, "but she has gloves. Now your mother loves to walk, doesn't she? Well, what do you think of a pair of real hiking boots?"

I thought hiking boots were a terrible idea and had a sinking feeling Mum would too, but rather than hurt Pop I lied.

"I think she'd love them," I said.

Pop was delighted and said he'd go down and get Tom Childs to pick out the best pair he had.

"That's a load off my mind," he said. "You're a good girl to help your old man."

Although we thought about presents all the time during the days before Christmas, the magic of Christmas itself was so overwhelming that the actual presents were almost irrelevant. It was the loving agony of choosing and the limitless possibilities of anticipation that gave those lumpy brown parcels such mysterious power. Santa Claus to us was a real person like Gumpkie, whom we loved, but there was more to Christmas than Santa and his reindeer. There were the falling snow, the Christmas lights in the blue dusk, the strong green fragrance of our tree out on the porch waiting for its time to come. Central to it all was Jesus, the new baby, rosy and sweet, lying in the hay with the gentle farm animals around. I thought of it happening in Synton's barn in Gyp's stall at night, and I knew just how the stable smelled and how the hay rustled and the horse blew through his nose and whinnied.

The shepherds were like Tink and us, standing humbly in the shadows by the grain closet watching the kings come in out of the darkness like walking Christmas trees in their splendor. I pictured them kneeling in their velvet robes right down in the manure and straw of Gyp's stall and holding up their gold, frankincense and myrrh for the baby to grab at.

The Christmas pageant at the church did not interfere with my manger scene but fitted right in. We sat with Mum in the vast, whispering darkness of the nave, looking up at the chancel and at Pop in his gown reading the second chapter of Luke. The spicy sweetness of balsam firs filled the church, for they were massed against the walls and all around the chancel steps. We didn't have to understand the words of the King James version but every one had the power to evoke Christmas, a living wonder, there all around us. I think the most spine-tingling line for me was the statement "There went out a decree from Caesar Augustus that all the world should be taxed." That was *it, Christmas*—although I had no idea who Caesar Augustus was or what being taxed involved. Or, for that matter, "being great with child," a curious condition.

The angels, the shepherds and the stable appeared as Pop spoke the beautiful words. Light, apparently from the star, revealed them in turn.

The moment we all waited for was when Mr. Hammond at the organ broke into his famous "March of the Magi," which had the very sound of camels humping across the desert. He kept his finger on one high, silvery note the whole time to indicate the star, and down past our pew came the three kings, so close I could hear them clear their throats preparatory to growling out "We three Kings of Orien-TAR."

We all, including Pop, thought Mr. Hammond's business with the star in the "March of the Magi" was a stroke of genius unique in the history of music.

After supper we wrapped our presents in white tissue paper and tied them with red ribbon. The paper tore a lot and had to be repaired with Christmas stickers. We helped each other, holding our fingers on the knots. I crayoned my own cards with the classic Christmas trees—saw-edged triangles with a candle or ball on each branch tip; wreaths with red bows, and fireplaces of red brick with stockings hung on them. Carefully, we carried our packages downstairs and put them on the window seat in the bay, where the tree would be. Then we sat on the oriental rug in front of the fire and Pop read "The Night Before Christmas" with appropriate sound effects. He pranced and pawed for the reindeer, ran to the window and threw up the sash, he came down the chimney with a *bound* that shook the house, held the stump of a pipe in his teeth and talked through it (it was his thumb) and later put his two fingers in his mouth and gave an ear-splitting whistle. He shouted "On Comet, On Cupid, On *Donder* and Blitzen" in a way that made my hair prickle and at the end called "Merry Christmas to all and to all a Good Night!" with his voice breaking on the words. We were all shaken with emotion afterward and went off to bed in a quivering state. Aldie and I both believed that the most beautiful line in the English language was "The moon on the breast of the new-fallen snow" and we saw it in our yard when the angels woke us from sleep on what was surely a midnight clear. The angels were members of the church choir singing carols at the foot of our steps, but to us in our beds the sound of those pure voices ringing out in the frozen stillness was the sound the shepherds heard on the hills outside of Bethlehem. We ran to the window and saw only the snow, blue in the moonlight, and stars over the bare trees, but "Joy, to the World" filled the night and nobody thought to tell us that it was not angels but only Tillie Meahan, Fred Hunt, Mary Louise Parsons and the others out of sight behind the big bridal wreath.

The next minute it was morning with a red slit in the east where the sun was. We ran to Mum's room and tried to yell "Merry Christmas" before they did, but they were always right inside the door and we all shouted it together. Then we had to put on our bathrobes and slippers and wait while they put on theirs. Dave, being the smallest, went downstairs first, and we followed, descending into the darkness that smelled as sweet as pine woods from the tree. There in the corner we could see the top half of it, glimmering with colored glass bubbles and sparks of tinsel, magic as it never would be again above the white sheet that concealed the presents on the floor.

There were our three stockings, gloriously lumpy and deformed, and there were Santa's big ashy footprints all over the rug. He had knocked over the andirons, drunk the milk, eaten the cookie and left a scrawled note well smeared with wood ashes.

"Thank you for the milk and the nice cookie. Better get somebody to clean that chimney. Love, Santa," or something like that.

We each had our places where we opened the stockings. Mine was in one corner of the rosewood sofa, Aldie's was in Pop's green chair and Dave's under the library table. As we opened the little presents the mystery began to give way to reality. Pretty soon the stockings were just empty stockings again, slightly sordid, as mine was an old ribbed wool one with a darn in the toe. (It was the longest I owned.)

Each of us carried one present to breakfast to gloat over until the time for "opening the tree." Santa Claus, with great foresight, always provided special presents too big to fit into our stockings, which he placed on the floor underneath. This was fortunate as, unlike our friends, we had to wait until Pop had been to his Christmas service at ten o'clock. During this frustrating interlude we played with our new toys on the floor near the hidden tree and even poked the corners and lumps that pushed out the sheet in mysterious shapes.

For stocking presents the boys always had little iron trucks and cars; I always had a tiny doll and small animals for my collection, as well as new furnishings for my large antique doll house. There were tops for each of us and an assortment of "crawly bugs," made out of colored metal with a spool-like gadget underneath that you activated by wiping the bugs rapidly back and forth on the rug. I believe some thick gum was involved but don't ask me to explain further. If you were raised on crawly bugs you know what I mean. There were scarlet ladybugs, striped potato bugs and other insectivora—handsome objects the size of an egg with trembling rubber feelers. Mum let us have a table leaf to run them on and to race the iron trucks and cars. There was a special smell to crawly bugs, produced by the gunk underneath, the very memory of which makes me feel about five years old.

Finally, Pop came stamping up the front steps and the front door banged behind him. We all ran out squealing to watch him hang up his hat and coat. He looked at us sternly.

"What's all the excitement?" he'd say.

"The tree! The tree!" we'd yell.

"Tree, what tree?" and so forth.

Then Mum appeared and they sent us into Pop's study to wait while they unveiled the tree and arranged the major presents, unwrapped, in strategic positions. There were always special features that dazzled the eye on first view. One had been Gillie, the rocking horse Gumpkie had given us in the early days; another had been the doll's house for me and matching barn and silo for Aldie, built to scale by Pop. Once he made me a doll's cradle. There had been our wooden sleds and Dave's tricycle. The year of the grape tray it was the Real Baby doll. When the moment came and we walked, owl-eyed, into the tree's glittering presence, I saw her in her pink blanket lying there waiting for me. Mrs. Childs had done it. Even now the thing seems like a miracle. I don't remember being able to speak at all. I simply clutched my baby to me in ecstasy. She smelled as sweet as a real baby, for the genius who had dressed her had somehow scented her clothes. It was very like birth. I was a mother, no doubt about it.

Mum did very well over the hiking boots, and she really let herself go over the grape tray. You could see she could hardly believe her eyes, and when I told her it had cost fifty cents she was amazed. A fortune had been spent on her. Even so, she said it was a bargain. It is a measure of her nobility as a mother that she kept the grape tray propped up on top of the china cupboard for years and even called attention to its beauty when we had company.

As for Pop, he was dumbfounded by the book.

"If there's one thing I need," he said, "it's a book about wisdom. Now your old man won't act like such a knucklehead. How did you ever know exactly what I wanted?"

The boys really loved the soldiers; I could tell because they wouldn't let anyone else touch them.

Then it was all over. The room was strewn with crumpled papers of red and green and white. The Christmas tree was just a tree with things hung on it, and all secrets were known. Now was the time for gloating, for savoring, for taking possession of our treasures. Each of us sat in his or her place examining minutely each present in turn, reading the directions of games and instructions for putting together the various objects the boys usually got from relatives. Some presents were difficult to identify. Certain old ladies tended to give curious things for removing stones from cherries, for threading needles or unscrewing covers from jars. No one could ever figure out how they worked.

During this period of digestion, so to speak, we shared the trials and triumphs of Christmas shopping. I described again the miraculous discovery of the grape tray and extracted the last drop of wonder from Mum, the lucky owner. We revealed to the last penny how much everything had cost and how hard we'd searched for each item. I forced myself to explain to the boys that I hadn't had enough money for the Household Cavalry or the kilted bagpipers.

Mum told about Mrs. Childs and the Real Baby doll. Pop enlarged on the peculiar virtues of the hiking boots, and I urged him again and again to tell how he loved to read his new books on Christmas.

"That's a long book. It will take ages to read it," I said.

"Never in my whole life have I had a longer book," he said.

When these rites were completed everybody rose and thanked everybody else all over again. We all kissed Mum and Pop and were thoroughly hugged. Then Mum said we'd better go out and get some fresh air, and Pop said he needed some exercise to work up an appetite for that goose.

Out in the snow we stayed together, making a snowman, sliding or building a fort. Christmas morning was a family time and playing with friends was not done until afternoon.

At noon we changed into Sunday clothes and went in to Christmas dinner, where on shining damask the furnishings of festivity were set forth: silver dishes of salted nuts, cut-glass dishes of celery and currant jelly and special silver baskets of Christmas candy people had given us. Often some lone individuals without families were asked to share the feast. In came the goose, crisp and brown as mahogany, and Pop, standing up, plunged his fork into its breast and quoted Bob Cratchit, saying, "There never was such a goose!"

We were merry together just like the Cratchits, only instead of plum pudding we had one of Kack's masterpieces—Bavarian cream or chocolate mousse with sweetened whipped cream, and maybe her devil's food cake that had fluffy white frosting with a thin brittle layer of bitter chocolate over the top of it—a real killer.

After Christmas dinner one's faculties were somewhat dulled; in fact, we could hardly move. Later on we went out into the cold, blue afternoon, where already the sun was far down the sky. Time was all mixed up on Christmas. Now we met our friends out with their sleds and we all boasted of our presents. I remember one friend of mine often got new underwear for Christmas. Underwear! Never at any time did we get anything so dismal. Our presents were frivolous, wonderful, for joy only.

On Christmas night Pop built a fire in his study and we ate our supper there. Pop's study was one of the best rooms in the house, with bookcases all around and green velvet curtains edged with bands of leather. The wallpaper was some sort of clipped green velvet, and the cushions on the window seats were of button-tufted green plush. Pop's Victorian "gentleman's chair" was upholstered in green plush too, so the room had something of the feeling of a mossy glen in the forest, deep and shadowy with the bright fire at its heart.

Mum made something in a chafing dish on the desk. We toasted marshmallows and Pop told stories about the Old Farm or the Jackaal or the Young Man of Sprightly Nature (Pop himself). The Young Man of Sprightly Nature had many real adventures, but the best one was driving in a stagecoach through a forest fire in the Yosemite Valley.

"Tell about the forest fire," we'd say, and on Christmas night he would.

Mum told about her Christmases in New York in the glamorous time when horses and carriages were the only traffic on Fifth Avenue.

After supper Pop read aloud Dulce Domum from *The Wind in the Willows* about Mole and Ratty on Christmas Eve.

We had reached the peak of the winter season, the top of the mountain on the other side of which were spring and eventually summer. From here on it was all downhill.

❊ 8 ❊

A Room of One's Own

There were five whole years between Dave and the next baby, and we took it for granted the family was complete. Dave had grown up very fast. Aldie and I often felt that he got far more attention than he deserved. He was a picture-book baby, blue-eyed and rosy-cheeked like an advertisement for Mellen's Food, the pablum of that era. All females made cooing sounds when he appeared, and Mum used to talk baby talk to him, and to our deep disgust inquire if he was his mummy's "Ludgepin." I have no idea what a Ludgepin was, but Dave at these moments would push out his upper lip in a pout of self-conscious cuteness that was almost more than decent people could stand. This was known as the "Ludgepin Face" and was a signal for one of us to tip him over or take away his zwieback, a revolting form of infant toast that he used to suck and reduce to pulp.

By the time he was three he was so good that he nearly measured up to one of the angelic children in books, and like them he got sick. One terrible night he developed a high fever and became delirious, yelling for Mum to save him from a man with a "yacht face." He was all better the next day, but the man with a yacht face became part of the family legend. We asked Dave later about him, and he said that his face was just like the bow of a yacht, what did we expect? Because of the man with a yacht face Dave's heart temporarily did something, so they kept him out of school for a whole year, a piece of favoritism we resented deeply. The only effect this vacation seemed to have on Dave was that he became quite self-sufficient, unlike Aldie and me, who had always lived as a team. He carried on long conversations with himself, invented solitary games and didn't seem to need anybody else. Later, of course, he had plenty of real playmates, but during his year's leave he became an individual and even developed an eccentricity all his own. He wore hats; not just hat hats but character hats. The first one was a miniature sailor hat, which he wore every waking hour.

One spring before the man with a yacht face Mum had been sick in bed again. Both Sharkey and Baba turned up but nothing else happened. No one told us, naturally, that she had had a miscarriage, but this was the reason why there were five years between Dave and Bobsie.

When Dave got so big that he could climb out of his crib and jump all over Mum and Pop in bed, they moved him and his crib into our room, and I was given Buffy's old room next door, a big square room with windows looking right into the Alisons' horse-chestnut tree. It had two closets, a white iron bed, a washstand alcove like the one in Mum's room and long filmy white curtains at the windows. It was a wonderful room, but I had no intention of moving.

"Why can't Dave sleep in there?" I asked when Mum tried to explain the situation.

"Because he's a boy like Aldie. You're a girl and you should have a nice room of your own."

"I want to sleep in our room with Aldie," I wailed. "Why can't girls sleep with boys? We're just the same."

"Now come on," Mum said firmly. "What's the difference between boys and girls?"

"Girls wear dresses. Boys wear pants," I said.

"Yes, well, you know you and Aldie are different when you take baths—"

"Oh, *that,*" I said. "But why can't I sleep in our room? I do now."

Pop took me in hand after he came home.

"Why can't girls and boys sleep together?" I began at once.

"That's a good question," said Pop. "Let's see."

Then he said boys and girls were made differently.

"I know *that,*" I said. "But why—"

"Girls play with dolls—" Pop began.

"Aldie plays with a doll, too," I said.

This was true. Aldie had a boy doll called Keith Falconer after some heroic child whose achievements escape me.

"All right," said Pop, defeated in this round. "There's another reason that you'll find out about later. Now let's talk about something else. I think it's time that we started reading *Little Women.*"

From then on every afternoon we sat by Pop's fire and had a nice talk, and then he read me some of *Little Women.* The boys were not allowed in, and for the first time I felt like a separate person and a girl.

Shortly after this Mum told me that I was old enough to eat supper downstairs. Every evening, she said, before Pop came home she and I would dress for supper the way all ladies did. Instead of putting on my nightie and wrapper and eating shredded wheat out of my dish with chickens around it, I put on a Sunday dress and went downstairs to wait for Pop. Mum used to brush my hair until it crackled and tie my hair ribbon in a butterfly bow.

"Now you can go and ask Kack for a hot biscuit and read a little by yourself until Pop comes home," she said.

Kack was a voluptuous redhead with a firecracker temper. She had apparently been briefed ahead of time, for instead of driving me out of the kitchen she gave me a hot biscuit lavishly buttered, and I took it in to Pop's big chair, where I curled up with my book. The new lovely private feeling that came of being a girl and dressed for supper was enhanced by the fact that I was sitting in the living room *all alone.* On late winter afternoons with the lamps on it had the rich, luxurious look that only a Victorian drawing room possesses. Like Baba's drawing room it was furnished in mahogany and rosewood with a lot of green plush and acres of oriental rug. The sofa and its little matching chairs had rosewood grapes carved into the frames and were deeply button-tufted. There was stuff like crimson burlap on the walls, and right across from me was a vast picture of a Highland shepherd and his flock with a mountain in the background.

Because of the tower the room had a round bay like ours upstairs, but this one had window seats all around, with red plush cushions on them. We liked to sit there sometimes and look at the *London News* or *Punch.* Mum's desk stood in the bay and so did the Boston fern on its high pedestal. I loved this end of the room and the fireplace part, where I sat, but not the other end. Down there by the dining-room door was the parlor organ, where we sang hymns on Sunday afternoons, and the piano, where I practiced Czerny exercises. The whole area was gloomy because of "Nearer My God to Thee" and the boredom of practicing.

From the green plush depths of Pop's chair I could see between the Corinthian columns of the wide doorway into the front hall, where the crystal chandelier was lighted. I nibbled my biscuit in tiny little bites to make it last and read my book, which it seems to me was one of the *Anne of Green Gables* series. It was a luxurious interlude in the day and came to an end when Pop's footsteps pounded up the porch steps, across the veranda and into the hall. He always slammed the front door with a thunderous crash, stamped the snow off on the oriental rug and gave his Swiss yodel to announce his arrival.

I used to run out to be hugged and watch while Pop scaled his hat at the hatrack to see if he could hit one of the pegs. (He never did.) After he had kicked off his galoshes and thrown his coat on the love seat he ran upstairs two at a time to kiss Mum. She was always in her room rocking Dave and reading to Aldie. When Pop had reported on his day he came down again and we had our read of *Little Women* by his study fire.

Suppers in the dining room under the Tiffany glass chandelier were just as glamorous as they had sounded. We would have casseroles or something made by Mum in a chafing dish from the raw materials provided by the kitchen. There might be creamed oysters, dried beef or hard-boiled eggs served up on toast made in a sort of Model T toaster. We also had more hot buttered toast with Roquefort cheese on it—a specialty of Pop's. Mum poured us cups of tea and I had mine with a lot of milk and sugar to make cambric tea. This was the mysterious supper food we had imagined when we knelt on the stairs, each hand clutching a bannister.

From where I sat at Pop's right I could see the reflection of the dining room in the big plate-glass window opposite. Instead of the usual view of the Alisons' horse-chestnut tree, there was the round island of the lighted table with the chandelier above it and the three of us in our places, eating and talking. It looked even cozier out there than it did from inside, but I knew that there was really nothing beyond the glass but the winter night and the great cold city, the mountains and the stars. Every time I taste Roquefort cheese I remember those peaceful suppers. They didn't last very long as Aldie was right behind me in age, but in that brief period I evolved a tradition of my own.

After I had dressed for supper I sat at the desk and made fancy place cards for Mum and Pop. I decorated them with seasonal motifs: snowflakes and snowmen in winter, hearts and bluebirds for Valentine's Day, pussy willows for spring, daffodils and baby chicks for Easter. I colored them with my crayons, and inside each one I printed "I love you." They were, in a way, daily valentines and had a gratifying reception. After Aldie came downstairs I stopped making them.

Thursday was Kack's night out and we ate in the kitchen, which like all Victorian kitchens was part of "servant country," sealed off from the rest of the house by heavy varnished doors and dark halls floored with dung-colored linoleum and wainscoted in varnished matched boarding.

The kitchen itself was a large square room painted an unlovely mustard tan, with woodwork the color of molasses, a linoleum rug in the same shades and a central table covered with white oilcloth. Over the midpoint of the table hung a light bulb with a shade of frosted glass shaped like a canterbury bell. The sink was black soapstone with zinc drainboards and brass faucets that turned green. The only spot of color was the calendar provided by the milkman at Christmas. All the kitchens in our experience had the same color scheme; it was supposed to be practical and wouldn't "show the dirt." Luckily ours was on the south side of the house, so in spite of its drab décor it was a cozy and comforting place to be in the daytime. The sun poured in both windows, and the big black stove always had a steaming kettle on it purring away like a great cat. The stove made the kitchen alive. It was a beauty, decorated with curlicues and nickel-plated trim, and had warming ovens, little extra shelves and an array of fancy tools to go with it. The name GLENWOOD was printed in raised letters on the door.

On Thursday nights the stove was out, and in the stark glare of the central bulb the kitchen looked very dismal. On Sunday night we had a cold supper—shredded wheat, cornflakes or crackers-and-milk (Aldie). As part of my new grownup role I was given a job to do in preparing the feast. This was to make an eggnog for Pop.

Mum showed me how to break an egg into a bowl and beat it to a froth with the eggbeater. Then I poured it into a tall glass, filled this up with milk, added sugar and grated some nutmeg on top. Pop said it was the best eggnog he'd ever had, and sometimes there was so much froth on top it went right up to his nose. This culinary triumph made me feel almost as old as Mum.

In spite of my advanced age I still played with dolls and kept my baby doll tucked up in Dave's old bassinet beside my bed. Then one day Mum took away the bassinet, saying that it needed to be recovered.

All the old skirts and petticoats were removed and fresh new ones sewed on by hand. Crisp pink ribbons were threaded around the edges, the lace washed and starched. Pop got out the baby's bathtub and put fresh rubber sheeting on it. As if this were not enough Mum began knitting tiny garments of pink wool. Did we suspect anything? Certainly not.

Shortly after Christmas Baba came to visit and helped Mum sew the lace ruffles on the bassinet. After a while Sharkey appeared and settled into my room. I was moved onto a cot in the guest room with Baba, and the place was a sea of women. The Five Cent Gent's calls began.

In that era babies were born at home, a marvelous idea in every way, as from the moment of arrival the new little person was part of the family and the mother never left the nest. Everything revolved around her. There were pretty bed jackets of pink silk and lace, bouquets of flowers and potted plants, as well as all sorts of delightful cookies and cakes brought by adoring ladies of the parish.

The arrival of Bobsie was an event at which we were all virtually present, as it was in progress when we three were picked up at ten o'clock to go to the bathroom. It occurs to me now that Mum and Pop must have had very little faith in our retention powers; this ritual went on for years, simply because somebody or other wet the bed occasionally. Wetting the bed was a disgraceful affair, the kind of scandal we whispered about in school—almost as bad as wetting your pants. Anyway, this time Pop attended to us by himself and seemed in a very nervous state. As we shuffled, bleary-eyed, through the upstairs hall on our way to the Big Bathroom I noticed that the door to Mum's room was closed and from behind it came the sounds of voices, one of them a man's.

"Who's in there?" I asked Pop.

Pop said a lot of people were, and just then the door opened and Baba came out to whisper something to him. Through the crack I caught a confused vision of Sharkey and Dr. Bagg, a friend of Pop's, bending over the bed. The final clue—Mum was clearly sick in bed again. Still, in my state of abysmal ignorance even this meant nothing in particular.

The next step in the proceedings came shortly after I had fallen asleep again in my cot. The guest-room door burst open and Pop stood there in his nightshirt. Baba in her pigtail reared up in the sleigh bed; I lifted my head and peered muzzily at my parent. What now? was about the way I felt.

"You've got a little brother and he's howling like Sid!" cried Pop in his croaking emotional voice.

"Listen," said Pop. "There he is!"

A rhythmic caterwauling came from the other end of the house. Out in the hall we met the boys, who seemed irritable at being roused once more from their beds.

"What's that?" Aldie was saying. "There must be a cat in here."

"It's your new brother!" croaked Pop.

"He'll be a nuisance sometimes," said Aldie cynically and

headed back to his room. However, he was intercepted and we were once more steered toward the bathroom. This time, though, we were only permitted to peek in the door. There was Sharkey in the little rocker, and in her lap on a towel was a bright red naked baby yelling its head off. Sharkey was busy washing out its eyes with something and in a very cross voice ordered us all out.

"Well, there he was," said Pop. "His name is Robert Stewart."

All the baby paraphernalia appeared again, and the whole business of Dave's arrival was repeated. We felt like old hands, well versed in the basic facts of birth and baby culture.

When I say basic facts I mean these: that when a new baby arrived Mum was always sick in bed, Baba visiting and Sharkey in residence. I remember remarking on this curious coincidence of events to Pop and he agreed that it was interesting.

Bobsie proved to be an enchanting baby, and being all of ten years old, I was allowed to take care of him, even changing his pants. Once, when I had him during the afternoon, I put him in a peach basket and with Aldie's help pulled him up into the cherry tree. We climbed up with him and spent the afternoon in the branches. In this way his presence did not interfere with our regular tree-climbing activities.

"You're my good little helper," Mum used to say to me. "I'm so lucky to have a daughter to take care of our baby."

At this point it occurred to me that it was about time we had a girl baby. I needed a sister, and although obscure references had been made over the years to the possibility of one, she never arrived. Just boys, boys, boys. Dave and Aldie were beginning to gang up on me, and now here we were again with a third brother.

When Mum once more removed the bassinet to be reconditioned, I was completely taken in by the explanation that it needed to be cleaned up for my doll baby who had gone back to sleeping there. She was too real to be put away in a trunk. I was twelve, but in those days we were told nothing about babies ahead of time. This reticence was I suppose a hangover from the Victorian Age, when pregnancy was vaguely indecorous. (It was proof that other things had taken place.) One did not mention this delicate condition in polite society.

"Mrs. Jones isn't *going out* this year," Baba would say significantly.

Mum told me that she wasn't allowed to go to Uncle B.'s wedding because she was great with child (Aldie).

One day in February Buffy's sister invited me to spend the night at her house, a special treat. Our house was a bit congested with visitors, as both Baba and Sharkey were there again. The next morning I was returned to the nest by my hostess, who seemed in a very mysterious mood.

"Just wait and see," she said. "There's a big surprise for you at home."

As soon as I started upstairs I had a vague feeling of having done this before—grinning faces over the bannisters, Pop croaking happily at the top of the stairs, Baba smiling benignly by Mum's door. Even Aldie and Dave were hopping up and down in the hall, full of giggles.

In I went—the surprise was clearly for me alone—and there was Mum in bed, beaming joyfully, with something in her arms, hidden by the covers. Even Sharkey was smiling, almost the way she did when the Five Cent Gent called.

"Look," said Mum, and turned back the blanket. "This is your baby sister."

It was a great moment—a girl at last for me. A real sister, not a boy.

The baby's name was Margaret, and she had gold fuzz on her head like all the rest of them. When she was a few days old, Mum called me into her room and told me to sit beside her while she fed the baby. Then she talked a little bit about the mother cat in Synton's hayloft and how all those kittens had been carried around inside her before they were born.

"All mothers carry their babies inside them," she said, "and then when it's time they come out."

"How do they get out?" I asked, alarmed.

Mum told me. She said it hurt a lot but it was worth it.

"I never remember the pain," she said. "You forget all about it in the joy of having a new baby."

After this she told me how I was made inside and about the thing that would happen to me every month. This meant that I would be able to have babies myself someday.

"How do the babies get in there?" I asked.

Mum said bravely that God planted a little seed, and right away I saw a vision of a white-bearded old gentleman shuffling through a lot of Burpee's seed packets—nasturtiums, petunias, marigolds and radishes—just like Aunt K.

This part seemed to me very peculiar. I didn't want God planting any seeds in me when I wasn't looking. Mum reassured me on this point. I would know in plenty of time. Finally, she said that the things she'd told me were private, not to be talked about all over the place.

"Does Aldie know?" I asked.

"Pop will tell him," she said. "This is our secret, yours and mine. A secret just for girls."

I never worried about having babies and found the whole thing wonderful and magic. What if I'd been a boy! I'd have missed it all.

Bobsie was only two when this new sister was born, and Mum rocked them both together every night before their bedtime. She was in her element with two little ones to hug. They were beautiful babies, but somehow Dave began to call them "the Hideons" —short for Hideous Ones. Soon the name ceased to have this meaning and simply meant "the babies."

The name Margaret didn't seem to fit our sister—it was too long. Nobody knew what to call her at first, but then Dave went to a play at school where one of the characters cried, "Targets, that's all we are, targets!" When Dave returned from the play he began to call the baby Target, and then she was Targ, and so she remains to this day. Bobsie eventually became sole heir to the title of Hideon and was know as The Hideon, Hiddy or Hid. (He still is.)

We now had three birthdays quite soon after Christmas, a great strain on the pocketbook. Aldie's present usually took all our

Christmas money, and sometimes we didn't even have time to buy him a present. We just handed over the cash.

The Hideons used up all our midwinter allowance, such as it was, but on the whole, we didn't need money in winter. Coasting required no capital, and we were usually sick in bed with colds by mid-February when our stock of crayons, coloring books, clay and other necessities were renewed by Mum to keep us quiet.

9

Midwinter

After New Year's winter really got under way and became a permanent condition. We forgot all about grass and leaves, and summer was only a dream. Snow and ice were our element; we lived an arctic life in our yard like Eskimos. The snow was much deeper in those days, and the walls along the sidewalks rose way above our heads. We scaled them like mountains and made igloos out of the great piles on the corners with tunnels leading into them. Inside the igloos the light was pale blue and all sounds from the outer world were silenced. We used to hide in there eating snow but wishing we had some blubber like *The Eskimo Twins,* our Bible where igloo living was concerned.

In midwinter the icicle outside the bathroom window grew to the size of a man's leg and Pop would reach out the window with a broomstick to knock it down before it fell on somebody.

The milk froze on the back steps every morning, pushing up the cardboard bottle caps on long stalks of cream.

Every day we hoped for a blizzard, those wonders of winter, because then we'd be snowed in and not have to go to school. Luckily this often occurred, and we'd wake to a howling whiteness with snow piled halfway up our windows and the house so dark we'd have to put the lights on. The snow seemed to boil out of the ground like smoke, and great clouds of it moved across the yard like ghosts.

"A real sockdolager," Pop used to say with satisfaction. "Look at the size of those flakes." In a blizzard the flakes were small and hard like sugar. When they were big and fluffy we knew it would stop snowing soon.

I remember once it snowed for two days and two nights, and when we woke up on the last morning you couldn't hear a sound. The city had stopped dead. We were snowed in and so was everybody else. Even the milkman hadn't been able to get through. The only things moving were the tiny birds feeding in the tops of the birches—chickadees, goldfinches and the redpolls that came only after a blizzard. In among the snow-furred twigs their raspberry-pink breasts looked festive. With the goldfinches they kept up a silvery warbling like a flock of canaries. The downy woodpecker with his ruby topknot was hammering away at the suet on the cherry tree, and there was a long lineup at the bird feeder on Mum's windowsill. Pop and I watched from their room, and I could hardly wait to get out and check the feeders in the yard. When Pop made me a bird feeder for Christmas, Mum had found a book called *Wild Bird Guests* by Ernest Harold Baynes and this had opened up a whole new aspect of bird watching. Instead of struggling out into the woods to look at birds in winter you persuaded them to come to you. Ernest Harold Baynes was one of the pioneers of bird feeding and an authority on nesting boxes. There was a photograph with a chickadee eating a sunflower seed out of E.H.B.'s mouth. I decided I could do this.

Following Mr. B.'s directions I cooked up a ghastly brew of melted suet and birdseed and poured it into holes Pop had gouged in a birch log. I filled old fashioned wire soap shakers with suet. I tied hunks of suet to trees. I sat on top of a stepladder beside the suet and held sunflower seeds in my hand. After I had nearly frozen solid in this position a chickadee came and lit on my thumb. Before long I had them eating off my head and my shoulders and even picking seeds from between my lips. The boys took a dim view of this feat, but I was a girl and girls were notoriously silly. Bird feeding like bird watching was part of my private world when

I wanted to be alone. The rest of the time I joined the pack and went coasting on my new sled.

The chief business of winter, as far as we were concerned, was coasting, school being merely an irritating interruption. We had graduated from our baby sleds to Flexible Flyers, splendid things with eagles on them and steering mechanisms that were miracles of flexibility. They had appeared under the Christmas tree one year, putting us in the same sled bracket as Brew Town, whose family owned the mill called National Blank Book, and who always had the best of everything. Brew had cast aspersions on our old sleds but we could now meet him on an equal basis.

Our Flexible Flyers revolutionized our whole conception of coasting. The first time we took them out Pop delivered his usual lecture on the use and care of new equipment.

"Now remember," he said, "these are real sleds and they'll go like Jehu, so be careful. Nobody's to go beyond the corner at first. All sleds cleaned off and up on the porch when not being used. And remember, don't lick the runners!"

"Don't what?" we said.

"Lick the runners. They're metal and your tongue will stick to them."

We were barely outside the door when Aldie up-ended his sled and licked the runner. His tongue stuck and he was able to report considerable pain on removing it from the metal.

"I think I pulled out some of my taste buds," he said proudly.

Pop took coasting nearly as seriously as we did. In order to speed up our run he built us a high snow ramp at the top of the banking and iced it with the hose. We were then able to take off like rockets, shooting across the sidewalk into the street and either plunging into the opposite snowbank or turning and heading downhill to the trolley tracks, three blocks below. After a good blizzard we often made a right turn at the end of our block and coasted half a mile into the center of the business section of the town. This may give you some idea of the idyllic character of city life during those lovely winters of the twenties, when sleighbells still jingled through the white days and bobsleds or "double-rips" raced at night on one of the main thoroughfares. It was a long way down into the center of town and a long walk back dragging our sleds. If we were lucky we hooked a ride behind a farmer's sleigh, looping our clothesline towropes around the posts on the back. Good farmers sometimes let us sit on the hay inside but usually we rode on our sleds or stood on the rear runners of the sleigh.

On Saturday afternoons, when he had finished writing his sermon for the week, Pop came charging out in his arctics and thick scarf to take us sliding on his six-passenger Flexible Flyer. He'd sit in front with Dave between his knees and invite us and our friends to pile on behind, each person putting his feet in the lap of the one ahead.

"All aboard. Allons! Ready, set, GO!" Pop would shout and we'd tear lickety-split down Oak Street, careen on one runner around the corner onto the bobsled course and go racketing through the town until we ended up in front of the Public Library. Sliding with Pop was a heady business; we had to hold on around each other's waists, and all the passengers screamed the whole time. Some people complained that Pop steered us right in among the trolley cars and practically under the hoofs of giant horses, but these were timid souls.

We sometimes went up to slide on the golf course or some foreign slope covered with strangers from the other end of town. Afterward in the blue dusk Pop would hook his big sled onto the Artful Dodger's rear bumper and pull us home over trolley tracks and into puddles of brown slush, slewing and skidding in a very dangerous way. It was exciting to be down on a level with all those whickering chains and wheels, the squealing trolleys and the hoofs of cart horses that from that angle looked as big as ashcan covers. We were never afraid, though. Pop had seen to that.

We were experts on snow conditions, and the surface of Oak Street was our constant concern. The ideal surface was a hard pack, polished from the plow and lightly printed with the pattern of car chains. These parallel corrugations and the flaws of imbedded gravel, horse manure, oil and coal were what passed beneath our eyes when we went belly-floppers. Bare macadam often appeared on corners where the snow had been worn away, and the ear-splitting screech of metal runners accompanied our passage over these areas. After a long snowless period the surface of the whole street deteriorated in a marked manner, and I remember large yellow areas melted down by the milkman's horse. Horses did a lot of damage to our course, and there were a great many still around. Besides the milkman's horse there was the iceman's team, the coal man's and horses from the country, as well as huge delivery wagons that thundered along with bells chiming in a very picturesque way. Not so picturesque were the smoking piles of manure, which melted the snow and then froze, creating a hazard for runners nearly as bad as gravel. The coal wagons were disaster, as they left a lot of coal and coal dust all over our slopes. Sanding the streets was unheard of, although I believe they sometimes did this down in the center of town.

Luckily a fresh snowstorm would repair the damage, and the shining alabaster finish was renewed. Toward the end of winter there were thaws and storms of mixed sleet and freezing rain that made the street as hard as corrugated iron, incredibly fast and dangerous.

Ice storms made a creaking glass palace of our yard, for the loaded birches bent over like croquet wickets, shedding splintered crystal all over the crust and nearly blinding us with the jeweled flashes from their prisms. Unfortunately, ice storms also turned our front steps into a real death trap. They were a hazard anyway, but after an ice storm no one could get up them at all. They were like that glass mountain in the fairy story. By midwinter there was usually a kind of skating rink at their foot, a pond trapped by the walls of frozen snow on each side of the walk. Pop, once or twice a winter, used to shoot down the steps and either crack his head on the ice of the pond or go through into the freezing water beneath. One early dawn the milkman cascaded the length of the flight in a Niagara of milk and broken glass, and from then on he came up the low side of the banking, where we had made a trail for pulling up sleds.

Pop spent a lot of time carrying ashes from the furnace to spread on the steps, but the real problem was that they had no railings —simply a curved border of stone, handsome but useless. Once after an especially severe ice storm Pop had crawled up on his hands and knees and got as far as the front porch before he fell over a sled someone had left there. The crash was terrific.

"Eye Guy!" he swore, limping into the house after this fiasco. "It's all a man's life is worth trying to get into this dad-gasted house. If you don't fracture your skull on the steps you can break your neck on the porch with all those blasted sleds. How many times have I told you tykes not to leave them right in front of the door?"

It was true that the approach to our house was just one long series of hazards. The veranda in winter looked almost exactly like the outside of one of those huts built by arctic explorers—Shackleton or Scott, both heroes of Pop's whose names were familiar to us from an early age. We used to pour over photographs of these huts, with rows of bearded men standing in front of them and a lot of dog sledges, ice axes and shovels leaning up against the wall behind them. If anything, there was more snow equipment on our porch, so much that you had to kick a path through it to get to the door.

As the size of the family increased, the equipment on the porch overflowed into the hall. There was an alcove near the stairs where ordinary persons had hall tables with card trays on them. We used it as a parking space. The baby carriage spent the night here, and next to it were kiddie cars and tricycles, which the Hideons rode inside. When our Flexible Flyers were new we kept them there, and there were usually several pairs of skates and a hockey stick or two.

One of the features of the front hall was a golden oak hatrack with a mirror framed in wooden pegs where Pop hung his hats. It had a marble shelf under the mirror, a bootshelf below that and an iron scallop shell on each side for umbrellas. In winter the only visible portion of the hatrack was the mirror. Pop was unable to keep a pair of anything for very long and had an enormous collection of odd gloves, rubbers, mittens and arctics which he stored on or under the hatrack. He also had a tendency to bring home other peoples' hats and umbrellas.

The hat rack was orderly compared to the love seat, that charming Victorian piece in rosewood and green plush intended for ladies serving afternoon tea.

When we came in after coasting we would slam the front door with a thunderous boom, stamp off the worst of the snow, then head for the love seat, tearing our mittens off with our teeth. These went directly onto the huge gold radiator behind the love seat, where they began to sizzle like frying bacon and send out the inimitable odor of cooking wool. We then wrenched off our coats and hurled them on the love seat, threw our hats on top of the pile and sat down on the floor to unbuckle our arctics. These we kicked under the love seat or left wherever they fell. Leggings came off inside out and were flung on the pile, unless they were soaked through, when they were draped over some unoccupied portion of the radiator. If there wasn't any place bare, you pushed someone else's things over, and as a result by sunset the radiator was completely hidden. It was always turned full on, blistering the paint on the dismal canvas of spinach-green mountains that hung above it.

Pop said he simply could not understand why, when nobody ever put anything in the hall closet, it was always waist deep in arctics, rubbers and boots and packed solid with winter clothing. Whenever you opened the door, an avalanche of junk burst out onto the floor. Mum used to open the door a crack and fire something in, then close it quickly before it could fall out again. We did this too, tossing in footballs, skates or whatever we were told to put away.

"Whose *is* all this stuff?" I remember Pop calling out. "Now just come over here and look."

At intervals he suddenly seemed to become aware of the hall closet, and would try to mobilize his troops to deal with the problem. Mum dissolved instantly into laughter, which set us off, and pretty soon Pop would throw up his hands.

"I give up," he said once when we were all helpless with giggles in the front hall. "It's a fine thing when someone comes to see me in my study and walks into a pig pen. I'm supposed to be a minister."

"Well, why don't you start with the hatrack?" said Mum, whose usual defense was attack. "Whose are all those hats and gloves? Yours."

"That's not true," said Pop. "Some dad-gasted idiot took my hat and left me that thing up there. And I never saw that derby before in my life. Who left that here?"

I eventually developed a system for finding my own arctics. I kept them in the dinner gong that Baba had given us. As we already had a string of smaller gongs, this one was left to roll around on the floor until Pop could remember to hang it up. He never did and I found it a good storage place.

Around Valentine's Day I usually came down with a heavy cold, very convenient as it gave me a peaceful interlude in which to make my valentines.

Valentine's Day was the last milestone before Easter on the road back to spring, and this was a good time to have a cold. The five-and-ten carried what were called "valentine boxes," containing the raw materials of these entrancing items. The best boxes featured beautiful embossed folders with baroque wreaths of forget-me-nots or roses across which cupids, bluebirds and doves flew bearing love letters, red hearts, golden arrows and other tokens of affection. The most expensive of these folders were made in Germany, and the paper had a high gloss, almost like enamel. These were the foundations only, and you were supposed to build on their faces a trembling confection of paper lace, held up by springs. On top of the lace you pasted more hearts, bluebirds and cupids. The results were absolutely spectacular in our eyes and we loved making valentines, but it was a time-consuming operation and a good cold gave us the leisure to do it properly.

For some reason I always seemed to come down with colds in the middle of the night and woke up coughing and croaking like a bullfrog. My throat had a bar of soreness across it, and every time I coughed a knife seemed to stab me in the chest. Deeply gratified by these symptoms, I would hop out of bed, trail into Mum's room and give a few hoarse barks to attract attention.

"Hmmm?" someone would say from the double bed. "Whassa trouble?"

"I gotta cold. I can't stop coughing. I got knives."

After that the lovely comforting ritual would begin. First they took me into the warm bathroom, wrapped in their puff, and Pop made a cold compress by soaking a washcloth in cold water. This Mum held around my throat while Pop wound a folded linen towel around my neck and pinned it tight. After this Mum rubbed Vicks Vapo Rub on my chest and draped me over her knee while Pop put drops up my nose. I used to fight the drops; it was part of the ritual. The next step was the medicine called "Goo-men" which I now realize was paregoric. It was always administered in a souvenir spoon with a picture of Pop's church on it. A cough medicine called "Tin-Pennies" followed, and then Mum put me back in bed while Pop set up the croup kettle, a tin cylinder with a pointed snout. Soon clouds of hot steam, fragrant with eucalyptus, were pouring into my face, and I fell into an uneasy stupor, half choked by the cold compress.

The next morning I woke with the happy certainty that school was out of the question. I gave a few sepulchral barks to notify everyone that I was awake and *sick,* and soon was the center of an admiring throng. Aldie and Dave usually accused me of malingering, but I was secure in the possession of my cough, and on the first morning I was able to speak only in a deep bass voice, if at all. Pop carried me into their room, where Mum was plumping up clean pillows and preparing a nest for me. All invalids spent the day in their double bed, and no efforts were spared to make a cold a delightful experience.

I had breakfast in bed, lying back against the pillows in a flood of morning sun. After breakfast, when everybody else had gone off to work or school, Mum came up and read to me. Kack appeared to take the orders for the day's meals; Margie, the housemaid, looked in with her freckled arms piled with clean linen. Later on, Mum went downtown and bought me a valentine box, coloring books, new crayons, a new jar of Cicco paste and any other little treat she could find at the five-and-ten. While she worked at her sewing machine or mended things, I cut and pasted and colored, getting paste on the puff, scraps of red paper stuck to the pillow and crayons lost in the depths of the bedding. All the time the croup kettle blew out its resinous steam and the Vicks Vapo Rub on my chest flavored every breath I drew. We didn't have Kleenex then, so I was supplied with big clean handkerchiefs of Pop's, a great luxury. The Hideons climbed up on the bed or played on the floor. I had midmorning milk and cookies, and the bed got full of crumbs. At noon Mum put me in Pop's Morris chair in the sunny bay, threw open the bed, flapped out all the crumbs, plumped up the pillows and made everything up again, smooth and cool and neat. I climbed back and waited with folded hands for my lunch tray, while Mum brushed my hair and tied it with a fresh ribbon. At lunch I was visited by Pop, bringing some present to surprise me, and then the boys, eaten up with envy. Afterward, they all went away and I had a little nap, listening to the birds at the feeder and drowsily watching the elm branches moving against the sky outside. The telephone rang in the hall; voices and footsteps echoed through the house. It was interesting to hear what went on at home when we weren't there. Then Mum came back and read to me some more or started me off on some new project. We read a lot of Louisa May Alcott.

One of the most memorable of the projects was the making of beads out of sealing wax. The equipment for this operation consisted of a candle, a steel knitting needle and sticks of sealing wax in all colors, including gold and silver. You broke off two pieces an inch long and clamped them around the end of the knitting needle, which had been heated in the candle flame. This sandwich you turned slowly over the fire until it melted into a bead. You could drip gold and silver onto the outside and then set the bead to dry on wax paper. Later I strung them on a cord and presented them to Mum and other lucky people. This business was incredibly messy, but I did it all in bed on Pop's lapboard.

At the end of the day the shades were drawn and the whole family gathered in the room to visit, most of them sitting on the bed.

By the time the cold had run through the family and Mum and Pop were pale and drawn from lack of sleep, it was nearly spring vacation and we prepared to go back to the Point for the annual Easter visit.

❦ 10 ❦

Spring Vacation

Spring on Oak Street began in the gutter. One of the many advantages of living on a steep hill was that when the snow melted the gutters became mountain brooks in spate, and the sound of them filled the days with music. First the hollows in the sidewalk changed from scratched black skating rinks to blue wells, infinitely deep, where distant clouds moved in dreamy procession. Pop spent a lot of time digging a canal past the horse block to drain the pond at the foot of our steps, but it was a losing battle. Under the snow drifts we could hear the water trickling; it gurgled under the ice and dripped from trees, poured into the gutters and rushed downhill toward Essex Street in streams a foot deep. We all put on our rubber boots and went out to wade. The first spring sport was racing wooden matches and twigs from Miss Eaton's Corner to the drain at the end of our block. The one that went down the drain first won. Gutters were great places to play, and it was hard to understand why they had such a bad reputation.

At night everything froze up again, so people couldn't take the chains off their cars, and the sound of chains slapping the bare pavement was heard all over the city. Sometimes it snowed again and we all moaned, but according to Pop this was perfect weather for sugaring-off. In the early mornings we'd see icicles on the ends of broken maple twigs and Pop would climb up on a snowbank and break one off for us to suck.

"There," he'd say. "That's pure maple sap and up on the Old Farm they'll be sugaring-off."

Then he'd tell us about the Old Sugar Bush at the Old Farm and how he and Harry Hurd used to whittle paddles out of cedar shingles to dip in the boiling syrup and suck. When the boiling was done they made "jack-wax" by pouring the hot syrup on snow and eating it when it got chewy. One spring he and Mum found an old farm up in the hills where they had an old sugar bush, and on a sunny Saturday we drove up there to see the sugaring-off. All along the back roads were sugar maples with buckets hanging on them, and Pop stopped the car so we could taste the clear sap. At the farm Mum took the Hideons in to Mrs. Thresher's big warm kitchen, and the rest of us went up into the woods to the sugar house, where Mr. Thresher, the farmer, was almost invisible in clouds of delicious steam. Everything went off according to plan even to the cedar paddles, and at the end of our session by the pans of boiling sap we went out and sat in a snowdrift and ate jack-wax. Pop showed us how to pack down saucer-shaped circles in the snow, and then Mr. Thresher ladled some thickened syrup onto each one. It ran out in hot golden rivulets and settled in little pools, then hardened in that shape. We could pick the whole river system up by one corner and put it in our mouths. Nothing ever tasted quite as exquisite as that chewy amber, out there in the snow with the sweet steam and birchwood smoke all around us in the sunshine.

"How about that? Isn't that the taste of spring?" Pop asked us, licking his paddle.

The next step was pussy willows in the ravine by our school, and then old Miss Phelps came up our steps bringing Mum the first arbutus.

Miss Phelps was a cleaning lady who spent all day on her hands and knees scrubbing floors, wringing out mops and rags, washing toilets. She was so poor she had only an old ragged sweater over her cotton dress and a little round black hat of some strawlike substance. Her back was bowed over so she had to look up to see her way. She had a withered little apple of a face, but her eyes were blue as the spring sky, sweet and gentle. No one knew where she went for her mayflowers; she never revealed her secret place even to Mum. The shell-pink clusters she brought were perfect, with just enough rose-tipped buds to set off the starry flowers. She used to peel off all the ragged leaves and those that hid the blossoms so as to make an old-fashioned nosegay, which she held in both hands to keep it neat and round, her annual gift to Mum, whom she loved.

Mum would thank her rapturously and bury her face in the pale, frosty blossoms. Then she'd hold out the little bunch to all of us in turn. There it was again—that faint cool sweetness, the first real smell of spring.

We had our own secret places for arbutus, and after Miss Phelps came we knew it was time. The best place was out at the Senior Town House—an old farm that Mr. Town, Brew Town's uncle, had presented to Mount Holyoke College as a weekend refuge for the senior class. Pop had the key of the house, and when the seniors were not using it we went out there and had winter picnics in one of the little white-paneled rooms.

The arbutus grew in a hemlock grove behind the barn.

On some sunny April Saturday we all piled into the Artful Dodger and drove out to the farm. From the road it looked absolutely idyllic, snuggled up on the snowy slope behind its sugar maples with the sun reflected in the bubbly glass of the small paned windows. Inside, though, it was colder than a stone dungeon, and even though Pop built a fire in the fireplace and lighted the wood stove we had to eat our lunch with mittens on, our eyes smarting from the smoke that billowed out of the fireplace. Still, it was fun, and everything we cooked on the stove tasted good.

Afterward we trudged through the crunchy spring snow out to an old logging road and followed it up to the hemlock grove.

The arbutus grew in oval patches of rusty green leaves. We had to get down on our knees in the snow and hemlock needles to hunt for the flowers. Sometimes they were buried under a drift of hard old snow, and I remember pawing away the icy beads and seeing the pink clusters in full bloom underneath, their tender petals unharmed.

"Oh, smell that," Mum would say, cupping her gloved hands around them. "We can't go backward now. It's really spring." And Pop would say that winter's back was broken.

We went to another place for hepaticas, which grew in blue-eyed companies above the brown leaf carpet of winter. To see spring sunlight on petals, scattered like confetti across the wooded slope, was one of the most perfect moments of the young season. I used to lie down on the leathery oak leaves and put my face close to one of the little clumps. The flowers had no fragrance but you could smell the leaf mold and some other sweetness like honey that was spring itself—frost coming out of the ground, the pollen on the alder catkins, pussy willows—we never knew. The baby leaves of the hepaticas were covered with silver fur, and the stems were so tender we had to pinch the flowers off at the base with our fingernails. I made miniature bunches in all shades of blue, pink and white that Mum put in egg cups when we got home.

There was a marsh we visited to see the skunk cabbage horns piercing the black mud and listen to the spring peepers. Sometimes we were too early, but on an afternoon of pale primrose sunshine we'd hear them even before we stopped the car.

"There they are!" somebody would cry, and there they were, jingling their silver sleighbells in the soft air, the authentic voice of spring that meant we'd arrived. Even if it snowed now it didn't matter. Spring vacation was coming up, and we spent that at the Point packed into all Synton's extra beds. This visit was a sort of preview of coming attractions, and we could at last see summer in the distance, blue and enchanting, with its white sails and sweet airs.

Spring vacation took place right after Pop's Easter service, and the drive to the Point was an experience that only an Eskimo would have enjoyed. The Artful Dodger had no heater and the back seat was indistinguishable from a deep freeze, same size, same shape and nearly as dark, for with the side curtains on you couldn't see out. Of course, deep freezes do not, presumably, smell of dogs, and the Artful Dodger's back seat did because of the steamer rug, a thing like a horse blanket covered with dog hair, which stayed on the floor of the back seat the year round and served as a dog's bed much of the time.

The first year I remember driving to the Point for spring vacation was before Dave was born. On this trip we ended up in a blizzard and had to spend the night in the Hotel Bancroft in Worcester, Massachusetts. Our night in this caravanserai stands out in my mind as one of the most glamorous experiences of my childhood, but after the Artful Dodger's back seat a bear's lair would have seemed like paradise. As I remember, the color scheme of the Bancroft was manure-brown with touches of bile-green, and it smelled of drains and hot radiators. However, it was WARM. We all slept in the same room, and in the morning it turned out that the Easter Rabbit had hidden candy eggs and jelly beans all over the place. This was an extraordinary bonanza as we had never before been visited by the animal. We never were again, so perhaps this explains the romantic aura that surrounds the name of the Hotel Bancroft.

We spent the whole of the next day on the road churning through the blizzard, with Pop working the windshield wipers by hand and muttering under his breath. Sometime toward nightfall I woke from a stupor to find us bogged down in a drift. Pop had disappeared, and Mum said he'd gone off down a lane to find a shovel. When he came back he shoveled us out, then trudged off again to return the shovel. As he climbed into the car he said he'd sell his feet to anyone for two cents.

"Why in Sam Hill didn't we bring arctics?" he asked.

"It's supposed to be spring," said Mum.

By the time we had churned our way to the end of the lane at the Point I was almost insensible from cold and have only the vaguest recollection of the last stages of this journey. However, I do remember that the lane was unplowed.

The Artful Dodger became deeply imbedded at once, and Pop seemed happy to abandon him. Mum carried Aldie and Pop carried me and somehow they struggled through the blizzard for the last quarter mile and reeled into Synton's kitchen like two snowmen.

I'll never forget the enchanting gush of heat that met us at the door and the warm, smoky, savory fragrance from the big iron range. We stood there, smiling blissfully, while the grownups unwrapped us like packages, layer by layer. Tink, in his heavy winter clothes, stood by, beaming for joy.

After supper we were put to bed in the chilly and, it must be admitted, cheerless gloom of the upstairs bedrooms. The bathroom, with its icy linoleum, congealed our very bones, but someone lighted a cylindrical kerosene heater, which cast a wheel-shaped pattern on the ceiling that flickered in a very pleasant way.

As a result, probably, of my sojourn in the back seat, I came down with the croup. I was picked up, crowing like a rooster, and carried into the bathroom, where the kerosene stove was lighted. Here I was wrapped in a quilt and given hot flaxseed tea just like Peter Rabbit. (I know, his was camomile, but the feeling was the same.) Suddenly there was a fearful smell, and it turned out Pop had laid his bedsocks on the heater to warm and they were on fire. This was not well received by the ladies of the house, but Tink defended the culprit and from my quilted cocoon I gave him moral support.

Staying at Synton was enchanting as long as you didn't go to bed. The beds in that house had to be experienced to be believed. After the Hideons were born some of us were relegated to the servants' wing, where the small icy rooms were finished in matched boarding, and there were still washbowls and pitchers. My final resting place was the former cook's room, recently converted to a storeroom. I slept on an iron-framed cot between a dressmaker's dummy and a broken-down washstand. I complained later that the mattress was like a bag full of potatoes, but I got no sympathy from my fellow sufferers. Aldie claimed that his bed was exactly like a hammock and Dave said his was like a banana.

In the matters of lighting, heat and beds Baba practiced austerity. The really important things were open fires downstairs, pretty china, heirloom furniture, books and fresh flowers. Beds and bathrooms that were too luxurious and comfortable catered to "the body" and bodies had to be kept down. Like sugar, soft mattresses were an indulgence to be avoided.

Nothing could have been more delightful than Synton during

the day. In the sunny windows the flats of seedlings stood in rows; the canaries screamed their heads off among the gigantic plants that covered every flat surface near the windows. Baba and Aunt K. never parted with a plant and apparently never divided them either, and the maidenhair ferns were as big around as bushel baskets; the begonias on their stands were like jungle growths and there was a Christmas cactus that had finally been transferred to a washtub. Canton platters, cloisonné plates of great value and other treasures of the china cupboard were now used as plant saucers, much to Mum's horror, but the thing that drove Pop nearly to mayhem was the presence of the parakeets.

Aunt K. had made friends with a bird fancier, and after the death of Pretty-Pretty, the old canary, she bought four more—lovely daffodil-yellow beauties that lived in standard cages in the dining room. An abortive attempt was made to breed them, and I seem to remember a bedraggled female bird messing around with bits of grass and cotton, but nothing came of that.

Then the parakeets began. At first there were only two, grass green and handsome, who spent all their time on one perch billing and twittering.

"They are lovebirds," Baba said fondly, and we used to watch them at breakfast.

Soon there was a pair of turquoise-blue ones, and what with their chattering and the ear-splitting trills of the canaries it was not easy to hear what people said at meals. The final straw came one spring vacation when we found that a huge cage—a kind of bird apartment house—had been placed in the corner of the dining room under a steel engraving called "The Cricketer." It was filled with parakeets, who kept up a deafening chittering and screeching whenever anyone was in the room. Baba claimed that they only did this when Pop was present.

"Dear Robert, they know the minute he comes in," she said above the din. "When Kath and Theodore and I are alone they are quiet as mice."

Pop could hardly wait to get outside before he exploded.

"Holy Caesarea Philippi!" he said. "This is the end. They turn the place into a dad-gasted pet store and then blame me for the racket." But he wasn't really angry, only amused. He derived a certain pleasure from watching Baba adjust to some of Aunt K.'s new projects.

"Dear Kath," she used to say. "She's a genius with the dear birdies. She talks to them and they understand every word."

The proliferation of birds at Synton was not confined to the house. Out at the barn Aunt K. had simply let herself go, and the sanctity of the Victorian carriage house had been rudely violated by the introduction of a peacock named Rajah. The whole south end of the carriage house had been made into an enormous cage with a tree trunk in it where Rajah supposedly spent the night. A small door was cut in the wall so he could go out into the paddock, and when we went out to do the morning chores with Aunt K., Rajah would be sitting on the paddock fence, his jeweled tail hanging down like a lady's train. Rajah was supposed to stroll about on the front lawn like peacocks on English country estates, but he spent most of his time in the chicken yard taking dust baths or showing off to the hens. About the only place he would spread his tail was in the chicken yard, but the hens ignored him and acted like Daughters of the American Revolution in the presence of a movie star.

Aunt K. had also acquired a flock of ducks and had turned the old cow shed into a home for them, with a wire run outside. A washtub had been sunk in the ground of the pen and the whole place had been reduced to a sea of mud, but the ducks were charming creatures and laid dozens of large eggs, which Aunt K. used interchangeably with hens' eggs, goose eggs and bantam eggs. The banties, as she called them, had a little pen of their own, but the geese—a mated pair—were at large in the barnyard, as was a turkey gobbler of immense size and ferocity.

Both the geese and the turkey chased anyone who came into the barnyard, although the geese were the worst, as they ran at you flapping their wings and honking. Baba, however, said proudly that they were capital watchdogs. In the days of bootleggers and rum runners you had to be careful. A lot of horrid, rough men were about and liked to get up onto high land, where they could signal to the ships at sea.

On those spring mornings the sound of the barnyard greeting the day was enough to bring you up standing from a sound sleep.

"Eye Guy," Pop said, "it's like living next door to a loony bin."

"I thought you liked farm noises," said Mum.

"That's not a farm out there," said Pop. "It's a private zoo."

It was always amusing to watch his face at breakfast when Aunt K. brought in his boiled egg. Sometimes it would be a normal brown egg from the Rhode Island Reds or a white one from the Leghorns. Then he'd get an enormous duck egg teetering on top of his egg cup or three or four banty eggs rolling around in a bowl. Once Aunt K. scrambled him a goose egg that filled a whole plate.

Spring vacation was the traditional season for work in the woods, clearing the paths and cutting down any tree that had intruded itself into The View. Every morning after Synton's breakfast Pop went down to Snowdon with Tink and us in tow and got his axe, his saws and wedges out of the woodshed. Then we'd go into the house and look out the west windows to see which tree to attack next.

Our house out of season was all wrong. From the top of the lawn it looked almost normal except for the shades blinding its eyes and the fact that the front door was shut. In summer the door was always open, and you could see right through the living room and out the back windows to the river, with the silhouette of the kerosene lamp in the middle. Now, Pop had to unlock the door, and it creaked harshly as it swung back. A little fearfully we walked into the dead, chilly silence and the smells of mice, mildew and kerosene. The hammock and the porch chairs were piled in the dining room, and saucers of "mouse seed," a kind of poisoned birdseed, stood about among last summer's *Geographics*. There was always a chance something had gotten in during the winter, but if something had it was usually dead. By the time the Hideons were around we had real plumbing, and if someone had forgotten to drain the toilet tanks they froze and cracked. Then there was the Leak in the dining room. We always left a lot of kettles and thundermugs under the leaky places, and sometimes they had overflowed or the Leak had moved and come down on top of the mahogany table.

"This summer, dad-gast it, we'll find that leak if we have to tear the whole house down," Pop said each year, and every summer Will Brightman came and did something but the leak remained.

Mum didn't like it in the house off-season and used to go up onto the upstairs porch, where she perched in the sun and looked at The View. Finally we all ended up there. The View in early spring was spectacular. We could see through the bare twigs of the oaks all the way up to Adamsville at the head of the river and south to the sandhills and the beach. The river and ocean were as gentle a blue as they were in summer but the salt marshes were silver-blond and on the opposite shore the newly plowed fields were like brown corduroy. Everything was spare and lean, and we could see right down to the boathouse where the water of our cove glittered between the trees.

The View was intact from upstairs; it was downstairs that things were getting out of control. In order to choose which tree to eliminate Pop used to sit down in the bin, an enormous armchair of oak with leather cushions, which stood by the big window in the dining room. From the bin you could look out to the harbor entrance, the sandhills and the rocky point on the far side of the channel. Here were the roof lines of some summer cottages and the silhouette of a water tower that looked rather like the conning tower of a battleship. Unless you could see this tower, you couldn't see The View—it was the acid test. We loved it and, what's more, it was the legal residence of the Jackal, the hero of Pop and Gumpkie's serial story. Once some insensitive guest said it was too bad that ugly water tower was in the middle of our view. We looked at him pityingly. The water tower *was* The View, the focal point. If a tree got in the way of the water tower it had to go.

After we had all sat in the bin and looked out Pop would decide which tree was the worst hazard. Then we'd go down in the woods after it.

It was always a relief to get outside again into the fresh, cool air of early spring. Down in the woods the carpet of dry oak leaves rustled underfoot and the chickadees soon gathered around to make us welcome. Pop would whistle their love song to them and they'd answer. Then he'd go up to the tree he'd selected and look it over.

"We'll drop her right there," he'd say after he'd gauged the height.

First he'd clear a space around the trunk with the clippers, and soon we'd have a little room full of warm sun with a wall of brush for walls.

Pop was an excellent woodsman and loved working with his axe, which he kept bright and sharp. He insisted on strict safety measures where axes were concerned and made us all stand back well out of range. I liked to watch him take a stance, haul off and swing the axe into the tree trunk. First he'd cut down at an angle, then straight in to sever the base of the slice. The clean yellow chips were full of spring sap and smelled sweet. The slanting cut in the tree deepened, and then we'd see the top twigs quiver.

"She's going!" we'd yell.

"Not yet," Pop would say, shoving the trunk with the flat of his hand. "Stand back now!"

Then he'd give it one more cut and we'd hear a slow creaking, then a loud crack, and the tree fell forward with a great whistling sigh in exactly the slot Pop had indicated.

We used to walk up the trunk into the branches that had a moment before brushed the sky, and perch there among the swelling spring buds while Pop began limbing. Later he and Tink took opposite ends of the cross-cut saw and sawed up the trunk. Tink, galvanized by the presence of Pop, his hero, wrenched the saw back and forth like a madman.

"Hey, you son of a sea cook, Tink. Slow down!" Pop would howl, but Tink, his eyes glinting with mischief, just pulled harder than ever.

The sawdust flew, the sun poured down, gulls sailed by overhead as though summer had already come. It was always summer in the sky, and if I looked straight up I could pretend it was June.

When the tree trunk was all cut up into drums we helped Pop drag the brush up to our burning place and then we'd have a bonfire. Mum and the Hideons came to watch, and on warm days we sometimes had a noon picnic around the fire, sitting on logs, watching the sap sizzle on the ends of the green twigs and dodging the smoke. My hair always smelled smoky on these visits.

One of the traditions of spring vacation was to have picnics at the beach in a *hole.* It took quite a while to excavate a hole large enough to seat comfortably not only the seven of us but Aunt K. and Tink as well. Naturally, Baba wouldn't consider eating in any kind of a hole, but Tink was ecstatic. He helped us dig, hurling up the sand like a frenzied woodchuck. We used real shovels, of course, and when we got through we had a hole the size of a small cellar with a nice level floor and straight walls to lean against. It was so deep that not a whisper of wind could touch us, but we could see the dry sand smoking past the rim of our dugout and a lot of it managed to blow down into our lunch. Every mouthful we ate was gritty, and Pop explained that this was how the word "sandwich" originated. Sometimes, Mum simply packed bread, peanut butter, milk and fruit in a basket and made sandwiches right there in the hole. In this way, Pop said, you could be sure of getting sand not only on the outside of a sandwich but inside all over the peanut butter.

"There may be sand in the food," he said, "but I'll say one thing for this hole; there aren't any parakeets in it."

Every day we'd run down the path to the river, where the smell of rockweed and salt water was exactly like summer and the sound of waves lapping the shore was so deceptive that you could almost believe we were about to go for a swim. We peeked in the windows of the boathouse at *Dehra* and *Hawick,* our sailboats, stacked on top of each other, dismasted and forlorn. *Mandarin,* the elderly rowboat, was upside down under a tree, with eelgrass piled on her bottom to keep her from baking. Mum used to take deep breaths of the salt air and say it was only two months to June. Like sailors after a long voyage we stood on the bow of our ship and peered into the blue haze ahead for the first glimpse of land, of summer on the horizon.

When, on the final day of vacation, Pop swung the Artful Dodger out onto the main road and headed north, he said we were over the hump.

"Next time we drive down that lane, we'll sleep in our own beds."

✳ 11 ✳

The Birds and the Bees

After spring vacation the real spring swept up the Connecticut Valley in a great wave of birds and flowers. Almost overnight it turned warm. Tiny green leaves unfurled on the lilacs, robins ran on the lawns, a violet haze softened the distances and the air smelled of freshly-mown lawns. We went out with only sweaters. Pretty soon we went without those, and in the soft, dazzling sunshine we ran like captives let out of prison, drunk with freedom.

Alice Newton and I cut our clotheslines and the jump-roping season was on. Spring was in the rhythmic swipe of jump ropes on pavement, in the airy lightness of my skipping feet, winged without arctics. Sometimes we cut two whole clotheslines and with several other females set up a jump-roping operation at the only house with a cement driveway. Two people turned the rope and the rest of us ran in, one at a time, to bound up and down in those whirling circles, chanting breathlessly the ancient words:

> "Teddy Bear, Teddy Bear, turn around.
> Teddy Bear, Teddy Bear, touch the ground.
> Teddy Bear, Teddy Bear, show your shoe.
> Teddy Bear, Teddy Bear, that will DO."

Then when the two turners got tired they would call for the old classic:

"Salt, Vinegar, Mustard, Ginger, PEPPER!"

doubling the speed of the rope on "PEPPER" until the last jumper staggered gasping from the arena.

Roller skates were hunted out and we whizzed at breakneck speed around Miss Eaton's Corner and higgledy piggledy, rattlety-bang down Oak Street across tree roots, into hollows and over cracks, until we swept up Mr. Judd's concrete walk at the foot. Half the time we didn't get that far and took a toss in front of our house, where there was a bad bump in the sidewalk. Everyone on the block had scabs on his knees, and as I had to wear stockings (Baba had ruled against socks), I reduced a pair to rags almost daily.

We climbed trees; we pumped our swings high into the young leaves; we rode scooters; we rode bicycles. Mine was a Columbia. On those steep streets I could fly downhill in rubber-tired silence, with the delicious air pouring through my dress and my long hair streaming behind me like the tail of a comet.

Our yard in spring was a hive of activity. The Hideons had undermined a whole section by the side porch with their system of highways, tunnels, canals and caves. Here they played with their little iron trucks and cars and their collection of toy animals, and from the bathroom window overhead we used to eavesdrop on their dialogue. Once Dave overheard Targ squeaking, "Ha, ha, ha, ha, thought 'twas Shadow-the-Weasel!" a saying that Dave repeated so often that it became part of the family language.

Under the mulberry tree Dave made a milk wagon with the toboggan for a roof, several orange crates filled with real milk bottles, and Gillie, the old hobby horse, who was by now in a very mangy condition. Milkmen and icemen were popular heroes in those days because they drove horses. Little boys had toy milk and ice wagons of painted iron drawn by black iron horses apparently at full gallop. Dave's milk wagon was terrific, and he even had one of those bottle carriers and delivered milk to the sandbox all day long. The milk was muddy water but so convincing was Dave that he was often able to persuade a Hideon to drink it.

Spring progressed through traditional stages. At some mystic signal the boys started playing mumblety-peg and marbles on our lawn and the girls played jacks on the porch steps or bounced balls on the sidewalk, trying to get up to a thousand. Then for no apparent reason we all gathered into a group and played Hide-and-Seek, Run-Sheep-Run or Still Pond No Moving. On rainy days we played Sardines all over the Towns' big house. It was during these games that certain girls emerged as objects of male interest. There were two of them at school, both deliciously freckled, with red-gold curls. They got all the best partners in dancing school, the most valentines out of the box at school and the most May baskets. Aldie and Brew Town showed a sickening interest in these females, and there was even a rumor that one of them was willing to kiss people behind barns. The boys were getting to be periodically obnoxious, swaggering about and boasting of the relative merits of their fathers' cars or their own brand of bicycle. They had a secret clubroom upstairs in Brew Town's carriage house, and Alice Newton and I used to try to creep up and spy on this stronghold. We were pretty sure they smoked in there and talked about girls, not us, of course, for we were not considered real girls. We were good enough to use in games but not to be regarded romantically. Of course, we felt the same about them. How anyone could kiss a smelly little boy in corduroy knickers was beyond me.

May Day was one of the special milestones in the progress of spring, but in our neighborhood May baskets had no romantic significance. We hung them on the doors of anyone we liked, regardless of age or sex.

Alice and I devoted the last week in April to making May baskets, an enchanting art, now lost. We would go down to the five-and-ten and buy paper cups, crepe paper and twisted paper-covered wire for handles; then we'd spend hours at someone's dining-room table, snipping and pasting. I specialized in May baskets like flowers, daffodils, roses and peonies being my favorites. I'd cut out petals and roll the edges over a pencil, stretch the crepe paper to make the curved center and then glue the petals in layers around the paper cup. When the baskets were done we filled them with candy and flowers, and on May First the streets were busy with little flying figures hanging baskets on door knobs, then running off to hide. May baskets were always anonymous but we couldn't help revealing ourselves at the last minute. After all that trouble we wanted people to *know*.

The first week in May was also the week the warblers came through, flocking among the tiny leaves of the birches and filling our hedgerows with exciting flashes of yellow. The Big Bathroom was a superb vantage point from which to observe warblers at close range, as there were birches right outside the window. I used to go up there with my new binoculars and bird guide and study the brilliant little forms, looking for eye rings, wing bars and breast streaks.

In the early mornings Pop and I went out to an island in the Connecticut River where the warblers swarmed like bees in the greening willows.

Our cherry tree bloomed, a frozen cloud of white, stood for a few days, then snowed the grass with petals. The Persian lilac blossomed and the great syringa under the bathroom window was transformed into a tent of ivory and gold that filled our whole yard with sweetness. I remember one Saturday noon when I was washing up in the Big Bathroom and the pineapple fragrance of the syringa floated in on the blowing curtains. The soap bubbles winked in the marble basin and the sun was golden in the new birch leaves, and I felt the rapture of spring like homesickness, it was so intense.

The city celebrated spring by putting on the open trolleys and tarring the streets. On Saturday afternoons we sometimes rode the trolleys out into the country to South Hadley or Highland Park, chaperoned by some grownup to protect us from strange men who seemed to be lurking everywhere waiting to pounce.

The seats of the open trolleys were wooden ones as opposed to the hard shiny cane of the winter trolleys. The conductor collected the fares from a narrow shelf on the outside of the car, an athletic feat that we all admired. We were not allowed on the shelf, but the seats were open to the four winds and it was a heady thing to go swaying along on the singing rails between daisy fields and under arching elms. You could smell the clover and hear the birds beside the track, and all sorts of people got on and off at the stops. Out in the country you'd see an old lady hurrying down the lane from a farmhouse, and the conductor would slow down and stop at her mail box. Then he'd greet her by name and help her climb aboard. Everybody seemed to know everybody else, and the conductor was a folk hero with his blue uniform, ticket punch and money belt, where the coins were kept in a row of little silver cylinders. Boys who didn't want to be icemen or the drivers of steam-rollers often wanted to be conductors.

The iceman came the year round, but in hot weather we used to watch for his canary-yellow wagon because he gave us slivers of ice to suck.

Our iceman was known as Longpants the Hippopotamus because the large drooping seat of his pants bore a striking resemblance to the rear end of one of those animals. It was, in a way, a term of endearment, for he was a beloved figure with his beautiful team and great yellow wagon. The wagon had ICE in red letters on the side, and Longpants kept it shining clean. His team of matched bays had red ribbons braided into their manes, red pompoms on their bridles and blue and white rings on their head straps. Brass glittered like gold on their harnesses and there were bright gold knobs on top of the hames, those curved horns on their collars.

At the back of this splendid caravan, as glamorous as a gypsy's cart, was a pair of scales, the axe and tongs with which Longpants plied his trade. We used to stand around while he weighed out a block, chipped it into shape and then handed out the chips to the assembled company. Finally he swung the ice onto his back, where he wore a piece of old raincoat to protect his clothes, and toiled up our steps and around to the back of the pantry.

The man who drove the steam-roller was another hero, who appeared on those occasions when the road crews were tarring the streets. All the mothers in the area dreaded the day the tar truck came but to us the smell of tar was one of the smells of spring, all mixed up with the milky sweetness of cut grass and the perfume of the wisteria on our veranda. We used to sit on our steps and watch the street sweeper with its huge brushes, then the tar truck squirting jet-black streams from a sort of bar on the rear of the vehicle. Then there was the sand truck, followed by the steam-roller. During these operations every one of us got covered with tar; we chewed tar that congealed in thick rivulets in the gutters, the dog made tar footprints across the front porch and Pop drove the Artful Dodger right into a tarred street before he noticed what was going on. After the day of the tar truck Pop took us all out on the side porch with a can of kerosene and some rags and cleaned us up. For days afterward, though, the Hideons played steam-roller, and sometimes the steam-roller man left his elephantine steed parked by the curb, and we actually climbed up and sat in his seat under the black canopy.

A third springtime event was the circus parade, which we went downtown to watch from the lawn of Pop's church. The balloon man with his bouquet of restless candy-colored bubbles was there on the sidewalk, and the man selling whirlybirds on sticks and the popcorn man with his glass cage and popping machine. We'd hear the thumping, wheezy music of the calliope coming up Main Street and watch spellbound as the ringmaster marched past cracking his whip and the tinseled ladies postured on the white horses. Then the row of dusty elephants paced by, each holding the tail of the one in front, followed by the gold-and-scarlet cages of sad-looking beasts. The parade ended with clowns, who threw us candy and made silly jokes. I never liked clowns. When it was all over we bought balloons and whirlybirds. I always picked a blue balloon and a yellow bird. Then we walked back up Essex Street under the brooding elms and maples, our balloons jerking like live things, our whirlybirds twittering as we swept them back and forth.

School was even more unbearable in warm weather than it was in winter, but by the time I reached the top grade at Lovering, our private academy, there were only two of us in the class and I had almost ceased to do any work at all, an ideal situation. I sat on the windowsill during history class, which was only a tête-à-tête with the teacher, studied on the front steps, and generally got away with murder. We seem to have spent hours practicing the Palmer method of handwriting—doing ovals and push-and-pull. Anyone my age will know what I mean.

We no longer walked home from school but rode in a limousine driven by a magnificent chauffeur called Lynchy. This equipage belonged to my one classmate who came from West Springfield. Lynchy was a terrific driver and in winter used to divert us by charging the snowbanks. In spring he just passed every car on the road at top speed.

We were also transported here and there by the regal Fox, the chauffeur of our special friends the Greens, who lived up on Northampton Street, where the estates of the mill owners were. The Greens' was a big half-timbered house surrounded by woods and fields just like an English manor. There were a home farm and vast gardens, for up on Northampton Street most of the big houses produced a lot of their own food, and I remember cream so thick you had to spoon it from the pitcher.

The Greens were red-headed and merry, and like little English children they lived in a nursery wing with Lolla, their Welsh nanny, also red-headed, who kept us more or less in order. However, we were allowed to run wild outdoors, and in this lovely place we enjoyed all the enchanting aspects of country living as long as we attended private school.

The Greens' happy world made a deep impression on me, and that house remained in my mind as the model for every country house in literature. It was John Ridd's home in *Lorna Doone,* Tara in *Gone with the Wind,* Toad Hall in *The Wind in the Willows,* Jalna, and Robin Hill in *The Forsyte Saga,* but somehow Lorna Doone, Toad, Old Jolyon and Scarlett O'Hara were all able to use it without interfering with each other. As far as I was concerned it was the Garden of Eden. We were certainly innocent enough. The wickedest thing we ever did was persuade one of the men to let us drive the station wagon around the woods. Once we smoked a cigarette in the garage and another time Tee Green gave Aldie a dirty satin garter she'd found in the gutter, and that was considered pretty low stuff. Over that whole happy period lies an aura of sunlight on flowering fields, the smell of cut grass and watered gardens, and the nursery comforts of bread and honey, warm cookies and lemonade.

Even now I can remember the interior of those limousines and their almost soundless progress through the countryside. They had pearl-gray upholstery and little flower vases on the sides, velvet straps to hold on to and a velvet cord on the back of the front seat where the carriage robe hung. There was a sliding glass window between the front and back seats, and the owner used to give directions to the chauffeur through a little telephone. They were a far cry from the Artful Dodger, but our loyalty to that noble vehicle never wavered. One day Aldie was forced to push Brew Town down the ravine back of the school because Brew said his father's new Marmon, a silvery monster that purred like a big cat, was superior to the Artful Dodger.

Pop took a dim view of our insulated life in private school, although he couldn't help approving the wholesome country atmosphere of the Greens' domain. He was at that time acting as a sort of referee between the mill owners and the new trade unions. Both the mill owners and the union leaders were members of his parish, and he was torn in two directions. To counteract the limousine influence he used to take us to the mills to watch the workers, and on certain dreadful occasions he took us down to the slums on his visits to sick people in the tenements.

"You have to learn," he'd say as we climbed up rickety stairways through the smell of cabbage and faulty drains. "You just don't realize."

We certainly didn't, but we had reached the point of no return (Grade 7) at the Lovering School, and our days in the Garden of Eden were numbered. The next year all three of us were sent to Highland Grammar, the lair of Bissell Alderman. We were appalled at the prospect and fully expected to be torn limb from limb by our enemies. I pictured the Highland Grammar as a kind of Devil's Island full of hardened criminals, so the reality was a pleasant surprise. There were hoards of people we knew from Sunday school, and even Bissell Alderman proved to be a nice-looking blond character. The real villains, we were told, were the teachers, terrifying subhumans with fierce tempers, and the principal, who was looked on as Satan in person. To be "sent to the office" was tantamount to going to Hell. We were all in league against these tyrants, so aside from the fact that I loathed formal education I found the transition easy.

The worldliness and sophistication of my fellow scholars filled me with awe and admiration. They rode the trolley cars all over the city alone; they were familiar with corner drugstores and sat around on those little wire chairs drinking ice-cream sodas through straws; they squandered their money in candy stores, dens of vice we had been forbidden to visit. Penny candy and bubble gum were outlawed in our house; in fact, we hardly ever had candy at all except for an occasional Hershey bar or a bag of wholesome molasses taffy done up in twists of yellow waxed paper. In these candy stores you could buy some very weird sweets: candy eggs in tiny tin frying pans, poison green and pink fruit filled with a whitish substance that tasted like almonds, licorice whips, of course, all-day suckers, jelly beans in acid colors and real "candy bars" which for some reason Mum had banned from the home. These bars were enormous but my friends consumed one or more a day. They also drank bottles of arsenic green or intense orange beverages and chewed great pink balls of bubble gum, blowing gigantic bubbles and snapping them in a very expert way.

Every Saturday afternoon they went to the movies, no matter what the picture was. During these afternoons they ate boxes of crackerjacks, each of which contained a valuable metal prize. Up until this time the only movies we had seen had been *Jack and the Beanstalk, Peter Pan, Ben Hur* and Douglas Fairbanks in *The Thief of Bagdad,* which I considered the most romantic and piercingly beautiful drama of all time. We had seen some films of the Holy Land at our church and various missionary slide shows. Also Mum and Pop took us to Laurel and Hardy pictures, where we all became so hysterical that several times an usher had asked Pop to leave the theatre.

Our friends saw all these pictures, but they also saw pictures full of love and violent action with women tied to railroad tracks, villains in top hats and black moustachios and other intriguing items. I saw one of these pictures once by mistake, and although I was absolutely fascinated, I had no idea what was going on as the captions were hard to follow while you were watching the galvanic gestures and twitching faces of the actors.

Nobody I met at Highland Grammar had the slightest interest in wildflowers or birds, although there was a lot of giggling and snickering when the pigeons on the windowsills began their spring courting. The males puffed out their iridescent throats and, stuttering with love, waddled after the females, very silly to watch. Those scholars with desks near the windows were in fits of laughter and a little French girl who had taken me under her wing explained to me that it was because the pigeons were going to do it.

"Do what?" I asked.

"You know where babies come from?"

"Of course," I said stiffly.

I had begun to have some serious doubts about God and the Burpee seed packets but I hadn't been able to figure out anything better. Maybe somebody *else* planted the seeds. The idea of God doing it seemed too much like the Bible, but I didn't wish to discuss it. However, my instructors at school were determined to improve my mind, and every day at recess the little French girl and a well-developed friend of hers told me who went with whom, who had kissed whom, who loved whom and who had "gone the limit," but so primal was my innocence that this meant nothing to me.

I knew about Love, all right, but Love had nothing to do with grubby little boys like my brothers. It was the province of people like Sir Nigel in *The White Company,* John Ridd in *Lorna Doone* and Robin Hood. The amours of D'Artagnan, my other hero, were hard to understand: he had so many and most of them seemed to be already married to somebody else.

I myself had only recently fallen in love with the young man who brought the magazines every Thursday. We belonged to a magazine club whose members shared copies of *Punch,* the *London News, Country Life* and some others that were kept in stiff cardboard covers. A family called Wakelin came before Wicks, alphabetically speaking, and Jim Wakelin, the handsome son of the house, brought them to us. He was tall and brown-haired with a pleasant manner that contrasted sharply with the crude approaches of my brothers and their friends. Of course, I wasn't his sister and he was at least a senior in high school—virtually a man in my eyes.

He stepped at once into the vacant space in my heart occupied previously by Robin Hood, my favorite hero at the time. Our relationship consisted of my opening the door for him, his handing me the magazines and saying, "Hello," my saying, "Thanks" and closing the door. But that's about all I needed at the age of fourteen. My feelings for this magazine deliverer were of the purest, most romantic kind, and I used to imagine him rescuing me from robbers, who for some reason represented for me the ultimate in evil. This was, I think, the result of reading "Ali Baba and the Forty Thieves," in which people were hacked up and nailed to doors, standard procedure in so-called fairytales. I imagined dreadful bearded characters with glaring eyes creeping up the roof to my window, but exactly how my hero was to materialize in my room to protect me I never figured out. In *The Three Musketeers* D'Artagnan and the others were always getting into ladies' bedrooms and being surprised there. Once D'Artagnan was in Milady's bedroom and had to leap out the window without his breeches. Why had he taken them off, or, for that matter, what was he doing there in the first place? When I asked Pop about this he was evasive but finally said *The Three Musketeers* was about Frenchmen and they were a queer lot. Ever since he had gone to France in the war he had been disgusted with the French but would never explain why. However, he did make an attempt to warn me again about strange men. Unfortunately his references were so obscure and his embarrassment so acute that I never did figure out what he was talking about.

"You will find," he said, pottering around his study and looking under pieces of paper on his desk, "that there are a lot of people in this world who will try to—ah—who think of girls in a certain way."

"How do you mean?" I asked.

"Well, there are things your mother will tell you about that are private matters. Now that's where they belong—in the home, not in the gutter or behind the barn."

I must never speak to strange men, he said, or accept rides from them. When I pressed him for details he said there were men who offered girls things like candy or tried to get them to go with them to get ice cream.

"Never go with them," Pop said. "Run to the nearest house and ask for help."

"Why?" I asked.

"Because—ah—they're up to no good."

"What would they do?"

"They'd kidnap you," said Pop firmly. "They are kidnapers. Now let's go find your mother."

Shortly after this instructive interview Alice and I were walking down Essex Street when a car drew up and a man leaned out.

"Could you tell me where Cabot Street is?" he asked.

"Help!" I yelled. *"Kidnapers!"* and took off down the street shouting "Kidnapers!" at the top of my voice with Alice pounding along in my wake.

No further attempts were made at home to enlighten me on the Facts of Life and I went back to my fantasies of being rescued by the magazine deliverer, adding kidnapers to my list of villains.

By an odd coincidence somebody really did break into our house one May morning, arriving at five o'clock. He spent some time downstairs banging doors and falling over the furniture, then started up the back stairs, where he was met by Pop, barefoot and in a nightshirt, who bravely turned him around and marched him back downstairs. Instead of a robber, though, the invader was a one-armed drunk whose only intention was to go to bed in our house. So much for my romantic picture of rescue.

As the spring wore on the little French girl redoubled her efforts to educate me. In warm weather, she indicated, the interesting activities behind barns were almost a daily occurrence, and up behind the country club all kinds of things were going on. Would

I like to join the action? No, I said, I would not, but so dedicated was she to my welfare that I was finally forced to do my own research.

I began with the Encyclopedia Britannica but soon discovered that unless you know what you're looking up the encyclopedia is useless. I then turned my attention to that great textbook of human anatomy—the *National Geographic*. Here there were plenty of pictures of natives, virtually stark naked. Some of the women had incredible pointed bosoms; some had huge bulging stomachs, which probably contained babies. However, there was no mention of God planting seeds or, for that matter, much else. The literary style of the *Geographic* was calculated to destroy one's interest in any subject almost at once, so I gave this up and went to the Sears Roebuck catalogue.

To the children of my generation this volume was one of the dirty books. Look at the women's underwear section and you'll see what I mean. It was worse in my day as the underwear was worse —corsets, hideous undershirts, bloomers and gigantic brassières, all modeled by stylish-stout ladies with marceled hair. There was one really obscene object in the household section—an "enema bag." I had no idea what it was for, but some instinct told me it was worth exploring.

The little French girl was a source of this kind of information and instantly recognized my description of the enema bag.

"That's the thing they use to get babies," she said. "My aunt has one in her closet. If you come to play with me," she went on, "I'll show it to you and I'll show you something else, too."

She lived way outside of our territory in a foreign region of two-family houses with little porches on both levels and clotheslines out back. However, nearby was a piece of open country with fields of flowers and an apple orchard. The trees were in blossom, radiant clouds of pink and white, humming with bees. A kingbird was building a nest in one of the trees and I wanted to climb up and see it, but my friend said if I wanted to know about babies I'd have to come with her. We trudged through the buttercups and dandelions to a large cement culvert that went under the highway. My instructor led me inside, and presently we stood in an arched cave with crude drawings all over the walls. There were *graffiti* of the usual kind—"Jack loves Shirley" and so forth—but my friend passed these by and we stopped before a drawing of a character named Pomeroy, a stick figure, clearly male. Underneath was a legend describing his activity. The word was strange to me and made no sense at all, but I concealed my ignorance and we stood before Pomeroy like two art lovers in a museum.

"See, that's it," said my friend. The enema bag was not in evidence but she said it was used to get the seeds inside the mother. Learning the facts of life in the gutter—or culvert—isn't as easy as some people think.

Later on I went back alone to the orchard and investigated the kingbird's nest, which had four eggs in it—a great coup as I had never found a kingbird's nest before. I sat up among the apple blossoms for a while watching the honey bees and listening to the spring day all around me. As far as I was concerned the birds and the bees meant only this, and at that moment it was enough. I didn't even glance into the culvert.

I can't really remember when I finally figured things out. I think Aldie told me a garbled version of the facts once when we were out sailing. I have no memory of my reactions one way or another, which would certainly disappoint Freud. It seems to me I thought it was funny. Ever since the culvert incident I have been wary of people named Pomeroy but luckily only met one.

"Did you ever live in Holyoke, Massachusetts?" I asked nervously, but he said he hadn't so it was all right.

I worked on the enema-bag theory for a while but then summer drew closer and I felt a wonderful lightening of spirit. The great thing about going away for the summer was that you could let all the problems of city living drop off like winter clothes. No matter what happened in the city we forgot about it as soon as we drove across the Connecticut River and headed south to the sea. Down there were summer and freedom, blue water and boats and our own private paradise where nothing ever changed. Pomeroy, the enema bag and even the magazine deliverer faded into oblivion when summer arrived.

❧ 12 ❧

Full House

We drove to the Point along the old winding back roads that ran through farmland and every town between Springfield and Fall River. Most of the roads were in the process of reconstruction and were all torn up, so detours were a matter of course, as were hours of waiting in line for a man with a red flag to let us through the work area. We drove in clouds of dust, over ticking sticky tarred stretches and jounced and crashed over stony dug-up areas that loosened up all the luggage. We got lost, we broke down, had blow-outs, punctures, and mysterious engine troubles.

We had to stop every half hour for somebody to pee in the woods or because one of us felt carsick. The dog was always carsick, and the minute he started heaving we all screeched for Pop to stop the car. Sometimes he stopped in time, sometimes he didn't.

In the back seat we played a variety of games, fought and argued, laughed, made up limericks and sang monotonous chants of our own composition. In the front seat the Hideons squeaked and whined or knelt and looked over the seat back at us.

No matter how awful it was there was always that moment just after Providence when we smelled salt water and saw gulls. This occurred when we crossed a little tidal river and there were salt marshes, green as new peas with summer, and winding blue creeks just like ours at the Point. You could even see the windrows of dried eelgrass up on the marsh.

"Salt water!" Pop would shout, and we'd all inhale deeply, tasting the salt in the damp air.

After that it was no time at all before we were through Fall River and driving along Sanford Road looking for landmarks: the rock with "Jesus Saves" on it, the egg lady, Pettey's garage, the stone horse trough at Central Village and then the corner by Asa Allan's farm where we saw the ocean for the first time. At that corner was an old gray house with a sloping meadow and an apple tree and a haycock that had a wooden hat on it. If you looked to the right after the haycock, you could see the blue line of the sea beyond the trees. We all tried to see it first but Pop always beat us to it. One year he confessed that he had caught it off to the *left* by the islands. We were shocked.

"That's not the right place," we said, and it wasn't. The sea was off to the right where it was supposed to be.

We turned into the end of our lane about four o'clock, and the sound of the tires was muffled by the needles of the Scotch pines that made an arch over the road. We drove through stripes of sun and shadow, smelling the hot spice of the pines and sitting on the edges of our seats. At the last corner Pop began tooting the horn, so by the time we drove out onto Synton's front lawn everyone was gathered on the steps to meet us: Baba in one of her violet dresses, Aunt K. carrying something—a trowel or a kitchen spoon —and Tink in his khaki summer costume all ready for his vacation to begin.

The first night at the Point was different from all the later ones. The blankets still smelled of mothballs, the sheets of mildew. When the light was out I wriggled around until I fitted the old lumps and hollows of my ancient mattress. Then I lay still and listened to the breeze singing in the screens and the far-off murmur of surf. The cool air was heavy with the salty dampness of the sea and even my pillow felt clammy, but that was part of the magic. We were *there*.

It is my impression that we always had a baby in the house in summer, the newest one replacing the old one in the white iron crib beside Mum's bed. Still, the time did arrive when the Hideons were no longer in swaddling clothes but racing about in tiny sneakers just like real people.

Every summer for years somebody was being housebroken, and there was always a mother's helper or nursegirl imported for this duty. Buffy had so far forgotten herself as to get married, but she made up for it by asking me to be flower girl at the wedding. Her successor, Marion or "Marry," had also married, and then there was a female who carried on a feud with the cook and was not asked to return. We missed Buffy and Marry dreadfully, and none of the other nursegirls were ever half as much fun. Mum and Pop used to refer to the resident mother's helper as "the Handmaiden of the Lord," and they always called the maids "the Myrmidons" or the "Myrms." This was, I believe, a hangover from the nineteenth-century era, when the family had to present a façade of perfect decorum before the servants. "Not in front of the servants" was one of Baba's expressions. In order to refer to the servants when they were around various euphemisms were used, and "Myrmidons" was one of them. I was amazed when I found out that the real Myrmidons were some of the soldiers of Achilles in the Trojan War.

The Babies' Room had long since become the Boys' Room, where Dave and Aldie slept. After Dave was moved in there I was evicted and forced to sleep in the guest room with the Handmaiden of the Lord, whoever she might be at the time. In the beginning it had been Marry, who was a lot of fun, and I loved the guest room, which was the best bedroom in the house and faced west over the treetops to the river. Its greatest asset was a private porch that jutted out into the limitless blue space like the prow of a tall ship. The porch was private only in theory, as it was the place where everyone came to look at The View and our room was treated more or less like a corridor. Guests had barely crossed the threshold of the house when they were seized and rushed upstairs to see The View. When Marry was in there they used to knock on the door, but if it was only me nobody bothered. For the first time I felt that to be alone occasionally was important, even away from Aldie.

At all hours of the day or night the door would burst open and a gang of tourists would tramp through and out onto the porch. "Excuse us," Pop would say. "We just want to look at The View." Or it might be the sunset or a rainbow or the evening procession of blue herons flapping home to their rookery up the river. There were even times when I was roused from a sound sleep by a procession of tiptoeing figures on their way to the porch door.

"It's all right," someone would say. "We're just going out to look at the moon."

This situation never improved, but I did at last get the room to myself. As more babies arrived the juggling of bed space stepped up.

When Bobsie was born five years after Dave he spent his first summers in a crib in Mum's room a few feet from Pop's side of the bed. Every time Bobsie cried Mum took him into bed with them and if any of us had a bad dream we climbed in there too. It was not surprising that Pop developed insomnia under these conditions. His difficulties increased when the boys began traipsing through the bedroom to get to the bathroom, a modern convenience that was supposed to eliminate the slop jar duty. Their closet, the only other means of egress, opened into the maid's room so there was no alternative route.

"Eye Guy," said Pop one day at breakfast. "I might as well be sleeping in Grand Central Station. There's just a steady stream of people tramping through the dad-gasted room all night long."

"Well, what do you want us to do, wet our beds?" asked Aldie.

"If you didn't drink so much water you wouldn't have to get up all the time to pee," said Pop. "Gad, you keep pouring it in one end and out it comes the other. You're just like a pair of faucets. Then just as I start to fall asleep the baby howls and your mother gets up and gives him his bottle. The next thing I know he's yowling because his pants are wet and she gets up to change him. By that time I have to go myself. It's a fine way for a man to spend his summer vacation." When Targ was born the congestion upstairs became intolerable and Pop decided that some major remodeling of his house was necessary. He had Will Brightman and his men build on a new kitchen, thus releasing the old kitchen for a maid's room. A new guest room was built downstairs and the hand maidens slept there so I was alone at last.

Aldie was moved into the former maid's room, Bobsie went into the Boys' Room with Dave, and Targ got the crib in Mum's room. Now if one of the boys had to go to the bathroom he went through the closet and out through Aldie's room, not an ideal arrangement and one which often caused loud arguments and even physical combat when Aldie defended his privacy.

Privacy was difficult to maintain in any part of our house, and even if you shut your door people paid no attention. Grownups were always coming in to make beds or put away laundry, and I had the extra problem of the porch and The View. I had come to think of the porch as mine. It was one of the few places I could be alone to think my own thoughts, and in a way I grew up out there. I began every day by throwing open the glass door and stepping out into the morning, and that brief time of peaceful solitude gave me strength for the plunge into the maelstrom of family life downstairs. Standing with my bare feet in the dew and my head in the sun I was above the treetops, above the birdsong and the rustling leaves, up with the swallows that were hawking after gnats in the early stillness. Blue was all around and as far as the horizon, where the straight line of the ocean marked the end of the world. Some mornings there was a four-masted schooner moving dreamily across the blue field of the sea or a steamer, hull-down, only her smokestack visible.

From my perch the gulls, down on the marsh islands in the river, looked as small as white butterflies, but their clamor came up to me clearly, so quiet was it. In the stillness I could hear the bobwhites in the fields across the river and the fishermen talking in their boats as they puttered down the channel.

You could find anything you wanted in The View, and sometimes I let the wide distances go and concentrated on a warbler in the oak right beside the house. The trees were full of birds, and I kept my binoculars on my bureau, ready to examine any mysterious flash of yellow among the leaves, but usually I just stood still and breathed in the lovely air that even at that cool hour smelled of flowering fields, warm grasses and seaweed. Then Pop would snap up the shade in their room, and there he'd be in his nightshirt looking out.

"This is the day the Lord hath made!" he used to shout, and the day had begun.

Once everybody was loose in the house the porch was public property as it was the captain's walk, the watchtower, the weather station, the place everybody came to check on the tide or to see if the wind was right for sailing. Mum and Pop loved to come up there just to sit in the sun and drink in The View, which after all was why they had chosen this spot to build their house.

A six-masted schooner was enough to bring everybody up there with binoculars, and the day the New York Yacht Club went by on its annual cruise to Edgartown the porch was jammed with spectators lined up on the broad flat railing or even over on the shingles of the veranda roof, which stretched all the way around the back of the house.

The boys liked to use the porch to climb up onto the roof above, where they would show off by standing on one leg on the chimney or walking the ridgepole. Then they'd hang upside down over the gutter and look in the window at me. I liked to go up on the roof too, but sometimes I wanted to write in my private journal or read, and the boys nearly drove me crazy. They often seemed like another species. Far from wanting to be a boy, I was thankful to be a girl.

One day I complained to Mum and Pop about the problem of privacy, and they gave me the key to my room. Later I acquired a small knocker painted white with blue forget-me-nots and fancy bowknots to give it a feminine touch. I was enchanted with this knocker, and Pop fixed it on my door for me. Theoretically, anyone wishing to enter was supposed to knock and I would unlock the door. The boys, though, despised my key, the knocker and the whole idea of my being able to block the route to the porch. First, they simply kicked or banged on the door, yelling for admittance until the noise drove me to open up, if only to fight back. Then they abandoned this method and climbed out a window in Mum's room onto the veranda roof, where they could sneak around and appear on my porch *outside* the glass door. They were forbidden to do this but they did it anyway. Aldie used to materialize suddenly and make hideous faces through the glass. I could never help laughing at the boys because they were so funny, and some of the faces they had developed were outstanding. There were moments, though, as they grew older when their exhibits of masculine strength and superiority became very boring, as well as a real nuisance to any female in their path. I forget when they started flexing their muscles, but there was a summer when they were always clenching their fists and holding up their right arms to compare the size of their biceps.

"Mine's bigger than yours," one would shout.

"It is not," the other would yell, and I'd be called in to be the judge.

They sneered at the size of my muscle and my inability to throw a baseball.

"I don't want to throw baseballs," I'd say scornfully.

Then they'd hold their forearms together to see who had the best tan.

Pop took turns wrestling with them on the lawn, and sometimes he took them both on together. Tink was ecstatic when wrestling matches were in order, and would become so carried away that he'd throw himself on top of the pile, squashing the breath out of all underneath. Screams of agony would issue from Pop on the bottom, but this only encouraged Tink to further efforts. We females enjoyed this defeat of the male contingent, and used to cheer Tink on with glad cries.

The most exasperating habit the boys developed was showing their strength by joining forces and torturing people. One of them would grab me and hold my arms behind my back while the other tickled me. They even did this to Mum, who would shriek the house down. She claimed that she was a victim of claustrophobia and couldn't stand being trapped in a small place or held down. Dave especially used to make capital of this.

"How about a little claustro?" he'd say, advancing upon her.

"Oh, no, no!" she'd cry and try to escape to the kitchen or to Pop.

Once Dave and one of his horrible friends put her in a laundry bag, where she claimed she almost had a heart attack from claustro, but as she always became weak with laughter the boys never took her seriously.

"I really *do* have claustro," she said to me once, "but the boys won't believe me."

The boys were perfectly all right separately and acted just like normal human beings. I played with one or the other and had no trouble at all, but we seldom did things as a triumvirate.

When Aldie and I joined forces Dave was left out in the cold, so he'd tease the Hideons. These poor little innocents were defenseless against his methods, which were mostly psychological. Dave knew that only a blackguard would inflict physical injury on someone smaller, so he would imitate the Hideons' ways of speech or manner of locomotion. He said Bobs was a spider—looked just like one, had eyes like one and pranced around like one. As a result Bobs was called The Spider for years and if he ever capered about was accused of "spidering."

Dave said Targ was always lying around on the furniture like a sea lion. She was an enchanting little girl, round and sweet as an apple, with honey-colored pigtails and huge brown eyes. Being nicely plump and gentle she never darted around like Bobs, who was a lean, brown monkey, quick on his feet.

"Look at Targ," Dave would shout. "Stop sea-lioning."

Aldie and I combined to crush Dave at these times, but he had subtler ways of torturing Hideons. One was reading aloud to them.

"How would you like me to read to you?" he'd say and the poor trusting creatures would eagerly bring him their book and climb up, one on each arm of his chair. There was one large book they loved about twin goats called Day and Night—Day being the white one, Night, the black. Maybe they were lambs, but in any case they were baby creatures of that ilk who had a series of adventures. The one Dave always read was called *Day and Night's New Friend, Bossy.*

He would open the book to the title page and the Hideons would be wide-eyed with anticipation. Then he'd begin:

"Day and Night's new friend, Bossy; Day and Night's new friend, Bossy; Day and Night's new friend, Bossy"; etc. etc. on and on until the Hideons burst into shrieks and howls and finally floods of tears. They'd pound him with their fists, kick him, pull his hair, but he just went on relentlessly as though nothing were happening.

"Day and Night's new friend, Bossy; Day and Night's new friend, Bossy—" "STOP THAT!" Aldie would bellow if he heard this going on, and presently he'd be pounding Dave with *his* fists and Dave would race off laughing wickedly.

He had another diabolical form of Hideon torture involving a record of the Two Black Crows—a sort of early Amos'n Andy act, which we had played until the records were worn down to a mere whisper and full of scratches and nicks. This one stuck at the phrase "It's a small farm." Dave would put it on the elderly Victrola and the Hideons would cluster around, a look of apprehension on their faces. Pretty soon the needle hit the nick and went into its act—

"It's just a *small* farm, a *small* farm, a *small* farm, a *small* farm, a *small* farm—" etc. etc.

Soon the Hideons would be howling for mercy, and I remember Bobs rushing to Mum screeching, "I don't want the small farm. I hate the small farm. Dave's doing the small farm again!"

Mum would only laugh and tell Dave to stop, but we considered this far too mild a response, and I remember sitting on his stomach, holding an ear in each hand, banging his head on the floor. In no time at all, though, we were off together in the rowboat catching eels. Still, there was always the fact of my being a girl, and at any moment the boys might coalesce again into a single male unit and come after me to give horse bites, twist my arm or deliver their two brands of pinches—"a savage" and "a vicious." A "savage" was done with the thumb and forefinger only; a "vicious" was done with the fingernails. Needless to say, I would attempt to retaliate and often connected, so all summer our bare arms and legs were covered with black-and-blue pinch marks, horse bites and bruises from a thing whose name escapes me but which is done with the knuckle of the third finger into the upper arm of the victim. This was just part of the fun of living in a big family, but sometimes one tired of the noise and confusion and it was then that each of us went off alone on our private pursuits.

In this fight for privacy Pop was the one who suffered the most, as he had to have peace and quiet all morning for writing sermons. Although he had three months' summer vacation, he used every morning to study and prepare his sermons for the following year. The books he read were very difficult and he had to concentrate and take notes, then work the material into a series of sermons, each one of which could stand alone. This side of Pop was the impressive one we saw in the pulpit. He was a magnificent speaker.

In the early days he worked in a camp chair on the porch, but there were so many women around, he said, that work was impossible. Mum would call to him through the window or come out on the porch to look at The View or see whether the tide was high enough to go swimming. An added irritant of that era was Tink on the hammock below. As he swung, the hammock chain squeaked in rhythm, and Tink sang his eternal chants about the Kaiser or the iceman, whose name happened to fit the same tune. We used to join Tink on the hammock, pumping it sideways up to high speed so that it crashed into the side of the house. Pop became so incensed at the noise that he finally resorted to drastic measures. He moved the hammock around onto the long side of the porch, where no matter how hard we pumped it couldn't hit anything. This had even more disastrous results as we were now able to pump it the full length of its chains, and at the end of its swing our heads were almost touching the porch ceiling. Finally one hook gave way and we were shot out onto the floor with a sound like the delivery of a ton of coal.

"Holy Jehoshaphat, what are you doing NOW!" Pop yelled over the railing of the porch above, but we were all laughing so hard we couldn't answer.

That was the end of the upstairs porch, and Pop took his camp chair and lapboard and a briefcase full of books and papers down into the woods. He set it up beside the path to the boathouse, but every time he got really started somebody would come by on their way to swim or sail and stop to visit. One day a rabbit came right up to him, its eyes glazed with fear, and after the rabbit came a weasel that was clearly out for the kill just as in a story Pop had read to us in Dallas Lore Sharp. He drove the weasel away with stones and escorted the rabbit offstage, but the next thing he knew a red-eyed vireo came by with a worm and went into a nest on a branch nearby.

"There's too much going on down there," said Pop. "The minute I start to concentrate some dad-gasted bird comes right down and nests in my face or I'm knee deep in weasels. I can't get a thing done."

After our own boathouse was built he tried working in there but somebody was always on the dock catching crabs or banging about in the rowboat and he soon gave this up.

As a last desperate solution he took to the trees.

"There's only one way a man can get peace around here," he said, "and that's to go up in the air."

He built himself a magnificent study in the fork of a giant oak near the river. It was triangular with railings all around and benches to sit on, but Pop took his camp chair up there so he could be comfortable. The approach to his eyry was by a steep ladder, and it was quite a sight to see him struggling up it with his lapboard, briefcase, pillow and steamer rug. Kelt, the dog, would sit at the bottom of the ladder and bark until Pop drove him away with dead twigs broken off the oak and hoarse roars known as his dog voice.

"I could hear your dog voice all the way up at the house," Mum would say. "You sounded like a lunatic."

"I am a lunatic," said Pop. "Before you can say Jack Robinson, I'll be off to the bin and thrown in a padded cell. Now will somebody keep that dad-gasted dog locked up until I get out of sight?"

Mum on the other hand never wanted to be alone, and liked nothing better than living in a welter of children. Pop had taken a picture of her when Targ was a baby which he called "Mother of Five." In this picture Mum sat in a chair on the porch with Targ on her lap, Dave and Bobsie on the arms of the chair and Aldie and me leaning against her shoulders. Five years later he took it again with us all in the same positions, and the only part of Mum visible was her face peering through a small orifice in the heap of tangled limbs and crowding heads. Everybody but Mum and Pop went into a fit of laughter at this version of "Mother of Five," but they thought it was great. Being buried in children was just how Mum liked to be and Pop loved to see her that way, although he was unable to speak in the presence of the picture. He was immensely proud of his "five little towheads" as he used to call us. I thought for years that it was "toe-heads," but we were used to being called by all kinds of nicknames. They hardly ever used our real names, and our nicknames changed constantly as Mum saw something funny in the newspaper or Pop was taken by a phrase in a popular song. Just to show you, Aldie was called Ole Bull for a while, after some musician.

Pop used to make the rounds of the rooms at night, peeping in at his young, and he came to me last as the oldest.

"Every bed filled," he used to say gloatingly. "A full house."

❧ 13 ❧

Firecracker Summers

In those early years the summers had a simple pattern that hardly varied from year to year.

In June came Pop's birthday, when we had strawberry shortcake; then came the fourth of July, which in more ways than one was the starting gun. Most of the summer people had arrived by then, the boats were all in and the paths trimmed. After the Fourth there followed in rapid succession my birthday (with strawberry whip), the Methodist Church rummage sale and bazaar and the Stone Church auction. In August there was the Grange clambake. After that you were headed for Dave's birthday (lobster) and Labor Day (fish chowder).

Before the state of Massachusetts outlawed firecrackers the Fourth was celebrated with as much gunpowder and related explosives as you could afford. Pop loved the Fourth the way we did and used to lay in an enormous supply of fireworks, which were on sale everywhere. We would go up to Fall River and come back with cartons of them, long boxes of beautiful red Roman candles and thinner boxes full of sparklers in two sizes—long for us, short for the Hideons. Then there were the immense skyrocket boxes, the pinwheels and the fancy things like "Devil Among Tailors" that Pop used to buy to surprise us.

Firecrackers were the backbone of the Fourth, and we spent the whole morning setting them off on the front lawn. The action always took place around a large flat rock—far enough away from the house so as to avoid danger of fire. Each of us had about five packages of regular firecrackers, two packages of some little ones called ladyfingers and two of cannon crackers. The latter made so much noise that your ears felt funny, but they were the best for blowing up coffee cans and for sending the tin covers of cracker boxes high in the air.

All the mystery of the Orient was in those square scarlet packages. They were wrapped as neatly as Christmas presents, and on top of each one was a colored picture showing a phoenix-like bird and some flowers. Chinese characters ran down the side of the picture—very exotic. Inside the package the scarlet firecrackers were braided together by their wicks, and unless you were really reckless you unbraided them and set them off one by one. However, Aldie, who liked everything extravagant, sometimes touched off a whole string, and the fusillade of explosions was something to hear.

We lighted all fireworks with "punk"—slender slivers of bamboo coated with some brown stuff that we always thought was dried manure. Maybe it was. The smell of punk and gunpowder was powerful, and we breathed it all morning.

By ten o'clock we had tired of simple explosions and begun to improvise. Someone would light a cracker and toss it into a tree. Then Pop would go to the woodshed and get a length of pipe to make a cannon that would shoot clothespins right out of sight. Aldie would bury a firecracker in the ground all but the wick, and do some blasting. Then somebody would get a pail of water and see if they could make a firecracker go off when submerged.

The night of the Fourth was the climax of the whole business. Family and guests congregated on our front lawn, and all the little ones ran around with sparklers, each a dandelion of spitting gold. The sparks drew lines on the night, and you could wave the rods around and write your name in the air or make fiery circles that stayed in your eyes afterward. At the end, the metal rod became red hot and curled over at the tip as the last gunpowder sizzled out. Somebody always burned a finger on sparklers and I remember those white weals that later turned red and hurt like fire.

"Come on up and I'll put Unguentine on it," Mum would say.

There was a lot of Unguentine around on the Fourth, and the smell of it was part of the day.

After the sparklers it was really black-dark. Over at the harbor the skyrockets were already shooting up like golden grain, showering their colored fruit over the water without a sound. It was time for Pop to set off the big stuff. For this we all went around to the back porch, and Pop, with the express wagon full of fireworks, took his stand on the bank below us.

As an opener he set off a few pinwheels, nailing them to an oak tree, where they swished around like mad before fizzling out. Then came the Roman candles, which all of us and Tink shot off over the porch railing, playing the great brushes of sparks back and forth and sending the fireballs off over the treetops or up into the sky.

"Hold them UP!" Pop kept yelling, but Tink, carried away by the excitement, used to point them every which way, even at people.

"Tink, stop that!" we'd cry.

"Oh, p'aps I will," Tink would squeal wickedly. "P'aps I won't." Then he'd point his candle into the porch roof.

"THEODORE," Baba said, and he instantly came to order.

The skyrockets were the main feature of the evening, and every year Baba made it clear that she expected Dear Robert to set fire to the woods. Her theory was that the fire would smolder until we all went to sleep, then it would burst out, sweep through the trees, incinerating us all in our beds and reducing the entire hill to ashes.

Because of this phobia of Baba's Pop spent half the night plunging about in the underbrush, falling into holes and getting lacerated by greenbrier. The purpose of this torture was to locate the sticks of the skyrockets and pour water on them. Unfortunately some of the rockets were duds, nose-dived into the woods and swizzled around in the bushes like insane cobras. At these times Baba indicated that she felt a holocaust was inevitable, but nothing ever happened.

The launching pad for the skyrocket operation was the trough once used to conduct the dishwater from the sink out into the grass. Pop leaned it up against a juniper tree and made a little shelf in it to support the missile.

The beautiful new rocket would be placed in the trough, its blue nosecone aimed skyward, its wooden tail resting on the shelf. The pail of water was set nearby. No one breathed. Pop leaned over and lighted the fuse in dead silence. With a glorious gush of sparks the rocket roared up, arching out over the woods like a comet and boring into the deep blue night with a sound like the tearing of sheets. At the peak of its climb it popped, releasing its Christmas-tree fireballs in a brilliant shower. We all cried out in delight, and the alarmists watched to see where the stick fell.

At the end of the skyrockets Pop and the men made a final check of the woods and then everybody had hot cocoa and doughnuts.

Baba had her own Fourth of July tradition called "The Noise," a real orgy of sound that satisfied some basic urge in all of us. On their two trips around the world the family had collected an incredible number of instruments for making noises: horns of all kinds, cymbals, bells, drums, chimes, whistles—anything that a native of any foreign land used to summon sheep, hang on cows, call people to prayers, celebrate some holiday or just raise hell.

The huge Swiss cowbell used by the head of the herd was one of the louder items, and there were other cowbells that jangled and clanked from Switzerland, India and other far countries.

Switzerland had also provided an alpine horn with which the shepherds communicated with each other across valleys and from peak to peak.

The horn was six feet long, hollowed out of a single sapling and bound about with some sort of tough vine. There was a theory that water must be poured down the horn's throat in order to make it work, so this was done before The Noise began. Only a man could blow the horn, and each year Baba selected a new victim. Whoever was chosen would draw a deep breath, swell every vein in his head, turn dark purple and let go. If he was lucky, the horn emitted a low bellow or belch.

The other major instrument was the red foghorn, a magnificent thing trimmed with brass and worked by a plunger. Baba used it to summon Pop to the telephone when her megaphone had no results.

Besides these instruments there were silver cymbals, a conch shell, a peculiar bamboo instrument like a bundle of sticks, a tin whistle, Pop's sweet potato or ocarina and a large number of things like dishpans and washtubs, last-minute inspirations, all of which were welcome. Baba herself used to ring a small silver bell, the one she had used to summon servants to the table.

We'd line up on the steps of Synton's veranda; then Baba would stand up and say, "Ready, Set, GO!" and everybody went at it. Those not using their mouths to blow on something screeched at the top of their voices, belaboring their instrument with both hands. I've never heard anything so appalling.

The noise lasted as long as we could hold out; then it was over. There were no encores permitted. Afterward everyone burst out laughing and Baba cried, "Happy Fourth of July!"

We usually went sailing on the afternoon of the Fourth to get a rest, Mum said, from explosions, before starting in again at night. All was peace down at the river. There was no sound but the wash of water against stones and the cool rustle of leaves from the woods above the shore. The boats chunked up and down on the little waves, and the kingfisher rattled from his perch on *Dehra Doon's* mast. *Dehra* was a heavy old sailboat, flat-bottomed and roomy, with wide seats all around and a mildewed sail of great age. She was gaff-rigged and painted pea-green after the boat in "The Owl and the Pussy Cat." We had an enormous rowboat named *Mandarin* and a smaller sailboat called *Hawick* after a town in Scotland. The names of our boats were difficult for strangers to understand. *Dehra Doon* was named after a town in India, and Uncle B.'s sailboat, a pea-green sharpie like *Dehra,* was called *Koi-Hai*—the cry given by Englishmen in India to summon servants. You see what I mean.

My birthday came right on the heels of the Fourth and was celebrated in whatever ways God and I decided. God chose the weather, which often ruined my plans, but I chose the menu for my birthday dinner, and if God cooperated we had a picnic some-where.

Once Aunt Loraine, Uncle B.'s wife, gave me a party at their house and made an enormous cat's cradle of string with a loose end for each of us. When you had followed your string through bushes and around trees you found a present at the end. There was also a tissue-paper bag of candy up in a tree, and we were blindfolded and took turns trying to hit it with sticks. When it broke we all scrambled for the candy. The cake had a wreath of wildflowers around it, and I had a wreath of daisies to wear on my head. I've never forgotten that party. I suppose I must have been about ten.

We went to several clambakes every summer, but the Grange clambake is the one I remember the best. The Grange was a big white building up in Central Village, and they made the bake out back under a tarpaulin. The food was served in the basement of the Grange on trestle tables covered with white cloths and settings of thick white china.

We sat down in front of our empty chowder bowls and watched the families come in: people from the village, farmers, fishermen and summer boarders. There was one old man in suspenders who always brought his own napkin, which he tied around his neck, then sat like a child holding his spoon upright in one hand, his knife in the other. I remember his face was the color of good leather but his forehead was pure white where his hat had covered it, the true sign of a farmer, as was the faint breath of manure that emanated from him.

"Look at Grampa," one of his family said. "He's rarin' to go, ain't you, Grampa?"

"Ayuh, that's right," he said. "Could eat a hoss, hoofs and all. I'm that hungry."

Presently, the ladies in the flowered gingham aprons came in with the chowder kettles and ladled a generous measure into each bowl. It was the real clam chowder made with plenty of ground-up quahogs, potatoes and onions and with cubes of brown salt pork floating on top. The taste was so sublime and we were so hungry that we always had two bowls.

By then the bake was ready to open, and those who liked to watch the process rose and left the hall. Pop, who enjoyed seeing any kind of operation, took us out back and we'd stand around until the moment arrived.

"Think she's ready, George?" one of the tenders would ask.

"Ayuh, 'bout time."

Then they'd lift off the tarpaulin, and a great cloud of savory steam belched up from the pile of rockweed. After it had calmed down the men forked off the weed and laid bare the first layer of food—potatoes, sweet corn, lobsters, tripe and fish, the latter in paper packages.

Underneath were the clams, scrubbed white as snow and sending forth a fragrance that brought a moan of ecstasy from the bystanders.

Back at the table we began with the clams. The ladies brought each of us a tin bowl heaped to overflowing and planted pitchers of melted butter at intervals down the table. The clams were red hot but that didn't stop us. You pried open the shells, grabbed the clam by its snout and stripped off its black papery coating. Then you dipped the clam in the melted butter and lowered it into your mouth. Some people only ate the stomach, I ate the whole thing.

The old man with the suspenders could go through four bowls of clams without stopping. I usually managed two. We accepted all the other offerings that the ladies brought around on trays.

"Potatoes?" they'd say. "Sweet or white?"

"Fish? Corn? Tripe?"

It seems to me there was pie for dessert, but by that time we were all leaning back in our chairs too bloated to move. It was some time before anybody felt like steamed clams again, then some guest would arrive and we'd take them to Bixby's, a nice farm where they had a bake every Saturday.

There was a certain type of guest who referred to the Point as "the Cape," had never been out in a boat and was possessed to go to a clambake or eat lobster. Sometimes they proved unable to cope with steamed clams or were allergic to lobsters, but we gave them the chance. These were usually the same guests that insisted on broiling their lily-white bodies in order to get a good tan. Guests in this category were often involved in church or missionary work and were horribly devoted to Pop and Mum.

Besides the church brigade there were three other categories of guests who appeared every summer: Synton's visitors, Snowdon's regulars, who were like part of the family, and Uncle Dave.

Synton's visitors were a very superior breed of guest and dated back to my grandfather's time. This glamorous period seemed to us as far in the past as the Middle Ages, but in truth it had only come to an end a few years before my birth when Mum's father, Dr. Hall, died. Besides being president of Union Theological Seminary in New York, he had gone twice around the world giving lectures. He had traveled to England as a young man and met many famous people, including Robert Browning, and it was he who had inspired Pop to follow the ministry.

Synton's visitors were from this larger world. Some were associated with the Seminary, others were cosmopolitan figures who spoke of London and Edinburgh with familiarity and were always going abroad. There was a distinguished collection of academic ladies from Wellesley, Aunt K.'s college, and I remember Miss Pendleton, the president of the college, and a very brisk person called Miss Kendall. These ladies scared me a good deal but they seldom mingled with us or shared our primitive forms of sailing and swimming down at the river.

One very old lady with white hair and a rustling black dress came to Synton when I was quite small. She held me in her lap and told me about her collie Sigurd and later on sent me a book about him. I enjoyed the collie stories, but Baba and everyone else kept insisting that I must remember this lady because she had written a song called "America the Beautiful," which seemed to me pure gibberish. What, for instance, was the meaning of the lines "Oh, beautiful for spacious skies" or "Oh, beautiful for Pilgrim feet"?

The old lady's name was Katharine Lee Bates, and to do her justice she never referred to "America the Beautiful" and acted quite normal.

At Synton the entertainment was apt to be on a higher plane than down at our house, for Baba liked to give tea parties or garden parties to which the ladies wore hats and their pongees or Liberty silks, and the gentlemen white flannels and blazers. Pongee was a soft raw silk in its natural color, a popular summer fabric with the ladies of the hill. Baba preferred the flowered silks from Liberty's of London, and hers were, of course, in shades of violet. I used to help make the flower arrangements for these parties, combing the whole garden for blossoms in the right color and watching Baba choose the vases and put together her bouquets. At teatime I changed into one of my best dresses and passed the plates of little sandwiches and cakes, all arranged in designs on Baba's celadon or rose-medallion plates.

The guests sat around the drawing room talking or strolled up and down the paths of the garden like figures in a painting by Monet.

Down at our house guests had to work harder, but the old hands knew what they were in for. Among the old hands were regulars like Buffy and Marry—both previous mother's helpers, who had been conditioned to swimming in eelgrass and pushing boats through mud when they went aground. The correct attitude toward these activities was one of uncontrolled hilarity; the suffering was all part of the fun. On these sailing parties we entertained some guests so thoroughly that they took to their beds and doctors had to be summoned. These casualties were apt to be male members of the aforementioned church brigade, who were apparently trying to impress Mum with their capacity for enduring pain. The females were made of sterner stuff and would go through anything to be near Pop, their idol. Mum referred to these devotees as "Pop's ladies" and, far from being jealous, drove Pop nearly crazy by giving them every chance to be with him.

One of "Pop's ladies" was a tiny little person called Miss Spruce who used to talk to him about laxatives. How Miss Spruce found out that Pop had an interest in laxatives I can't imagine, for he was a very modest man. We knew his secret because Mum teased him unmercifully when he ate prunes or chewed dried figs with a loud crunching sound. Anyway, Miss Spruce had somehow learned of this weakness and made capital of it.

"Oh, Dr. Wicks," she'd say right at the breakfast table. "I must tell you about my great new discovery—senna pods. You soak them in water overnight."

"Is that so?" Pop said nervously. "Jan, would you pass Miss Spruce the marmalade please."

One time she had discovered something made out of seaweed called, she said, "agar-agar."

"It supplies gentle bulk and lubrication without medication," said Miss Spruce in rapturous tones. "I've found it very effective."

The trouble was Pop couldn't resist trying these things. There was a frightful substance made of "Psylla seeds," Miss Spruce's favorite, that looked like jellied Wheatena when the seeds had been soaked overnight. To our disgust, Pop would choke down whole glasses of the stuff.

"Gah!" he'd say, shuddering. "Worse than castor oil."

"Well, why do you drink it?" Mum said. "You and Miss Spruce!"

"Not me and Miss Spruce, dad-gast it!" Pop would cry. "It just happens that the stuff works."

The horror of it was that Miss Spruce used to try to check up on the effectiveness of her products, and Pop suffered agonies of embarrassment as she did it right in front of the whole family.

Miss Spruce loved to go berry picking and used to bring back gallons of huckleberries—the major berry on the hill. During her visits we had huckleberries in every form: huckleberry pancakes, huckleberry muffins, huckleberry pie, huckleberries raw with sugar. All of us had black tongues like chows and pled with Mum for relief, but Miss Spruce continued to pick, even going out early to get some berries for Pop's breakfast.

Whenever one of Pop's ladies was staying with us Mum used to tease him by going off and leaving him alone with her. Ignoring his pitiful cries for help, she'd rush us ahead of her up the boat-house path, her eyes snapping with mischief.

"Pop's scared out of his wits," she'd say.

Another of the lady worshipers was Miss Quinn, known privately as "Quince." Quince, besides being absolutely besotted about Pop, had an amusing failing for which she was well known. In the twenties skirts had risen to the knees and Quince seemed oblivious of the fact that whenever she sat down you could see all the way up to her waist. There wasn't anything interesting to see, as she wore thick rayon knit bloomers with elastics just above the knee, but the sight of these pink bloomers embarrassed Pop beyond words.

"Eye Guy," he complained. "A man doesn't know where to look when Quince is in the room. Doesn't the woman know enough to keep her knees together?"

Mum had no sympathy for him and just bubbled with laughter. Out in the boat Quince's bloomers were constantly visible, and Pop would have to look at the top of the mast, into the bilge or over the side, and the next thing we knew we'd be aground.

Mum was very pretty and gay, and she delighted in a handsome gallant gentleman who paid her compliments and made her laugh. However, she had no patience with some of the visiting bachelors who decided to worship her. She gave them short shrift and pushed them off on Pop.

"He's a nudger and a squeezer," she'd say. "You can have him."

"He's nothing of the kind," said Pop, who never noticed these activities. "He's a nice fella."

"He is not. He's an old lecher," she'd say, and roll her eyes at us.

Pop struggled valiantly to control his troops when some of these satellites were visiting, but it was hard going.

Uncle Dave was more than a guest, he was a natural phenomenon rather like a hurricane, which swept into our lives every July and disrupted everything. He was not a real uncle but had been a pillar of Pop's first parish and looked on himself as a kind of patron or fairy godfather presiding over Pop's career. In everyday life he was a wealthy businessman who had invented a hand soap called "Greasolvent" and thereby made his fortune. Greasolvent was a soapy pink paste full of sand and came in a yellow tin with a picture of a man in a motorman's cap on the cover. Needless to say, Uncle Dave kept us constantly supplied with his product.

Uncle Dave not only looked exactly like the late President Theodore Roosevelt, he acted like him. I've seen old movies of the famous Rough Rider shouting and waving his hands, and it could have been Uncle Dave. It was easy to imagine him bellowing "Charge!" and rushing up San Juan Hill. His hair and mustache were ginger-red and his complexion of a ruddiness bordering on the apoplectic. From the moment he came down the gangplank of the Fall River boat to the time when he waved goodbye to us over the rail of the top deck, our household was in turmoil.

We all drove up to meet him and stood on the dock waiting for the sight of that familiar straw hat and tan linen suit. It seemed to me Mum always looked apprehensive, like someone watching a ticking bomb.

Suddenly he appeared followed by a grinning porter. On sighting our little group he gave a great roar and charged down the gangplank.

"Rob!" he shouted, embracing Pop and pounding him on the back.

"Eleanor!" Mum was crushed to his chest and thoroughly smacked.

Then each of us in turn was swept up into the air and pressed to his tickly mustache, which always smelled powerfully of tobacco.

"Well, how are my little pals today?" he'd yell. "Ready for the five-and-ten?"

"Yup," we'd say with shining eyes.

Uncle Dave's first move was to give the porter a sheaf of bills and tell him to put the bags in the car. Then he'd climb into the front seat beside Pop, leaving Mum to squeeze in with us in back.

We drove into Fall River and parked. Then Uncle Dave gave us five dollars and sent us into the five-and-ten to buy anything we wanted. Mum went along with us, holding the hand of the smallest. In the beginning it was Dave, who had been named David partly after Uncle Dave but mostly after a Scottish ancestor, David Douglas.

While we wandered about the five-and-ten, filling our paper bags with loot, Uncle Dave took Pop to a hardware store and forced him to buy whatever he needed. They used to come back carrying new hoses, rakes and shovels, with Pop looking sheepish and Uncle Dave holding him around the shoulders and roaring with good fellowship.

On the way home we had to stop at a special drugstore where Uncle Dave bought us each a roll of peppermint Lifesavers. Down at the Point he put on white ducks and a sweater and looked around for something to change.

One of the best things about Uncle Dave was his understanding of Tink, who absolutely worshiped him. Uncle Dave always brought him a present, then he'd put his arm around Tink's shoulders and say, "Ready, Tink?"

"Yes, dear Unka Dave, I'm ready."

Then they'd start marching in step across the lawn while Uncle Dave bellowed out the following song.

> "LEFT, LEFT, the sergeant used to say.
> Now you got it you better keep it
> And don't you give it away."

Around and around they marched, Uncle Dave singing, Tink with a seraphic smile on his face and his arm around Uncle Dave's waist.

After this ceremony we were all hustled into the car to go down and buy fish. Uncle Dave loved seafood but had once been told that he was allergic to lobster so had abstained from it for years. Then one day at the Point he ate some and nothing happened. From then on a lobster orgy was a feature of his visit. However, this didn't happen at once. For lunch on the first day we had to have fish.

We stopped at Synton so Uncle Dave could pay his respects to Baba and Aunt K., which he did in the most courtly manner, presenting them with boxes of chocolates, which Baba never touched but accepted gracefully. She admired Uncle Dave very much.

"A perfect gentleman," she used to say. "A fine-appearing man."

Then we drove down to Whalen's at the foot of the street, where Uncle Dave was a popular figure.

Whalen's was an old gray-shingled building where you could buy work clothes, oilskins, fishing gear, marine equipment, hardware, hats, clams, fish and lobsters. We always bought new sneakers there the day after we arrived as well as the summer's supply of hats. We often bought tautog (a sea bass) for Uncle Dave's first luncheon, and these could be seen swimming around in large wooden cars that hung off the end of the wharf. Al Lees, Whalen's helper, used a long-handled net to dip out the fish, and we all leaned over to watch as he plunged it among the dark, weaving forms. The net came up full of thrashing bodies, which Al dumped into a wire basket so Pop and Uncle Dave could pick out the ones they wanted. Then Al cleaned them on a scaly old fish table right out on the wharf, with the sea gulls lining up on the pilings to get the offal.

If they had just brought in a swordfish, Al dragged out a blue-and-silver section the size of a nail keg and Uncle Dave pointed to the exact place where the cut should be made. Then Al took a knife like a machete and sliced off a thick pale pink steak, hacking through the spine with a meat cleaver.

Sometimes old Mr. Whalen would come out and tell Uncle Dave the blues were in and they had a couple of nice ones, or he might have a few stripers. Mr. Whalen had experienced Uncle Dave before and knew he was onto a good thing.

Back at the house Mum and her ladies would be shelling new peas or shucking a bushel of sweet corn—these being traditional guest offerings. For dessert there was strawberry shortcake, raspberries, blueberry pie or sliced peaches, and as likely as not a chocolate cake to fill in the gaps. To Mum a meal was not a success unless the guest took second helpings of everything and ended up in a stupor, barely able to rise from the table. Uncle Dave was an eater on a par with Henry the Eighth, so a lot of food was needed.

I've forgotten how long Uncle Dave's visits lasted. They were so intensely lived that each day seemed like a week. No one was bored, as something was always going on at full speed. In his role as fairy godfather Uncle Dave was determined that Pop's every wish be granted and even some wishes that Pop had never thought of. As I see it Uncle Dave had taken one look at the house Pop had built and instantly set about to improve it.

The first improvement was the spacious pillared veranda that he ordered Will Brightman to build across the west side. The veranda overlooked The View, and Uncle Dave went out and bought some camp chairs in which he and Pop could sit and enjoy the prospect while Uncle Dave smoked his pipe or one of his innumerable cigarettes. He was the first chain smoker I ever saw and used to fascinate us by breathing smoke out his nostrils like a dragon or producing a series of smoke rings so evenly spaced you could run a stick through them. He also teased us by saying he could make smoke come out his ears, and when we watched spellbound he'd blow a great mouthful of smoke in our faces. I can't say I liked that.

After the veranda Uncle Dave built himself a delightful guest-room on the ground floor right off the living room with a private door onto the new veranda. Pop made an attempt to control this but it was no use.

"You shouldn't let him give us so much," Mum would say over and over. "It's embarrassing. We're not paupers."

"How am I supposed to stop him?" Pop asked. "You know what he's like. Might as well try to stop an avalanche."

Shortly after the guest room was built Uncle B. converted Synton's boathouse into a summer cottage, and we had no place to put our boats.

"What we need, Rob, is a boathouse for us," said Uncle Dave firmly and summoned Will Brightman while Pop shrugged his shoulders at Mum in the background.

"You can't accept it," Mum whispered.

"What shall I do? Shoot him?" asked Pop. "He's happy. He loves giving us things. He's like the man who played God."

This was quite true, and suddenly we saw Uncle Dave as someone who was so delighted with the money he'd earned that he wanted to share it with all those he loved. It wasn't power he was after; it was the joy of giving, of seeing other people happy because of him.

His final gift each time was the lobster orgy, to which everyone at Synton was invited. In the late afternoon he and Pop with all of us in the back seat drove down to Whalen's to buy the lobsters.

"All right now, Al," Uncle Dave would say. "Let's see what you can do." And Al would take the big long-handled net and plunge it into the lobster car while we all stood on the edge of the wharf watching. The car hung in the full sweep of the current that streamed past the pilings like liquid glass, clear green, coiled into polished eddies and swirling the weed on the pilings. The water ran right through the holes in the lobster car, and we saw the lobsters milling around in a dark blue shadowy mass. Al brought up a netful, thrashing and snapping, and it wasn't easy getting them into the wire basket because they took a death grip on the net with their claws. Uncle Dave pointed to the best ones, and Al weighed them out on the scales. We took them home in two paper bags and we could hear them inside blowing bubbles and clicking around.

The lobster feast was an evening affair. Uncle Dave went up and escorted Baba down the hill. She would take his arm and look up at him with a charming toss of her head, and all of a sudden you could imagine her as a young woman, a curious idea. She was our *grandmother* and in those days grandmothers acted like grandmothers.

Baba ignored fashion. She had her own style and when skirts went up after the war hers went up only to her ankle bone. She never went out of mourning for her adored husband, but for our sake she changed from black to violet—as white was too lighthearted. With Uncle Dave she became the New York hostess again, witty and gay, and even the fact that he smoked those horrid cigarettes could be overlooked because he was a gentleman. Of course, he was also in trade but he had managed to rise above it, and one could almost believe him to be a gentleman of leisure like Baba's father.

At dinner Baba sat on Pop's right beside Uncle Dave. A scarlet pyramid of lobsters steamed on a Canton platter at Pop's end of the table, and in front of Mum was the rose-medallion platter, where ears of corn were piled under a damask napkin.

No children were allowed to partake of these delicacies because lobsters and corn were considered poisonous to the young.

In time we were each given a claw and some of the legs to suck on, but in the golden age of Uncle Dave we had the feelers, that's all. For our supper we ate something like creamed fish.

Uncle Dave's spare room made it possible for us to entertain guests all summer long. After a while he put a bathroom in one corner, thus creating what amounted to a private suite. There seemed no reason why it should ever stand empty, and as Mum was endlessly hospitable it hardly ever did. In the course of time it was the place where we stored visiting young men and girls who were being considered or were considering us for mates, but those days were far in the future.

🌣 14 🌣

Private Life

Within the pattern of family living there were certain gaps of
time when each of us went off on his own. These interludes
occurred between breakfast and swimming time in the morning,
and between lunch and sailing time in the afternoon. Such spaces
in the day were precious and gave us a chance to grow, like little
trees in a clearing from which all greenbrier and scrub have been
removed. I often watched Baba clipping and cutting around her
baby trees, giving them each a private room in the woods where
they could spread out and grow into their own shape. Our clear-
ings in the day were like that.

The first one for me was before breakfast, when by getting up
early I could steal an hour for myself. I'd wake up to the sunrise
screams of Rajah, the peacock, and lie there a minute listening to
the gulls and the sputter of fishing boats on their way down the
river. There was the old one-lunger that hiccuped and skipped a
beat at intervals like some jolly tap-dancer rejoicing in the day. No
one could lie in bed listening to that merry syncopated rhythm,
and I was up and out on my porch before the boat had reached
the harbor.

The best of these early mornings was the first one after we
arrived, when the air was lightly scented with the blossoms of the
wild grape. Only in June did you smell that perfume, and it meant

that all summer was still intact before you, not one day of it used and even this first day new and untouched. I didn't have to decide how to begin it because I always did the same thing.

I put on my old clothes as quietly as possible and, carrying my sneakers, tiptoed downstairs, using the sides of the treads to avoid the creaky places. Then I'd open the front door and step out into the sun and the fragrance of the honeysuckle vine. The chewinks were calling "Drink your tea" as I ran up the hill. There was only one place to go at that hour—Aunt K.'s kitchen.

The black-throated green warbler that nested by the path to Synton was up on the spire of his juniper buzzing his mosquitoey little song. The same tiny flowers bloomed in the grass—rabbit's-foot clover, yellow star flower, and the purple milkwort, Baba's polygala—that I always picked for her to wear in her amethyst pin. Even the big black-and-gold spider that hung her perfect web right across the path looked like the same spider.

I would have something to eat in the kitchen, go out to the barn with Aunt K. to get the eggs and then take off alone for a tour of the gardens to see what was out, hunt for peacock feathers and listen for the chirring sound that marked the location of a nest full of baby birds. In this peaceful time while most people were still asleep I could start my summer properly.

Baba had her own methods of clearing a space for each of her grandchildren. She set aside portions of every day when one of us could be up at Synton alone. The first of these was breakfast.

Breakfast at Synton was a rite Baba had initiated as soon as I was civilized enough to eat at her table. We went one at a time, in order of age, and were given the royal treatment, with all the Canton china, fresh biscuits and some special feature like kippers or lem-on-blossom marmalade. The Japanese tea ceremony was nothing compared to Baba's breakfasts.

Synton's dining room was flooded with sun at breakfast time, and I sat in a warm golden panel of light facing the conservatory so I could enjoy the green. Baba planned all these little experiences. It was, she said, important to begin the day with something beautiful in front of you and, of course, sun at breakfast was a necessity. The centerpiece on the table was also an important feature, and she gave much thought to her daily arrangements. One of a lady's main occupations was "doing the flowers."

After breakfast Baba always had something special to show me, something that would be a nice hobby for me or open a new field of interest. Every summer, she herself studied a fresh subject for her own enjoyment and for the benefit of her grandchildren, just as she had done for her children. She was teaching me all about gardens and wildflowers, and one year she decided I should learn about insects. She presented me with a book called *Sharp Eyes* by William Hamilton Gibson, a charming collection of short essays on the little miracles of the woods and fields illustrated by the author. Mr. Gibson had a butterfly net, and he used to run through a field skimming the grass tips with his net and then studying his catch—seeds, beetles, tiny flies and other residents of this filmy world of grass. Mum made me a net out of one of the wooden rings from an old sail and a piece of the mosquito netting she had used to cover the last baby's carriage. Pop fitted a bamboo handle to this and I had a butterfly net. I also had a jar containing alcohol for killing my specimens.

While Baba wrote her daily letters I would take my net and jar and run out into the hot sweet morning and into the gardens. The place for butterflies was the huge tangled mixture of flowers and vegetables that lay outside the drawing-room windows. This garden was, according to Baba, like the cottage gardens of England, where lettuce and roses, onions and sweet peas grow side by side in happy confusion. Aunt K. could be found there almost any time, crawling around on her hands and knees weeding. She did not disrupt the murmurous peace of the garden but was an integral part of it, like an earth spirit, her good sunburned hands caked with loam, her sensible cotton stockings covered with grass stains and her gingham dresses torn by thorns and spotted with berry juices. When I waded in among the crowded plants she would sit up and wipe the back of her hand across her forehead, leaving a smear of earth.

"Hell-o," she said cheerfully. "Isn't this a *day!*" She always said the same thing.

We would talk for a minute about the simple news of the Hill and then she'd go back to her weeding and I wandered off through the garden, nibbling a warm lettuce leaf, chewing a handful of parsley or pulling a baby carrot or two. I sucked the honey out of salvia blossoms, rubbed southernwood between my fingers and bent down over and over to breathe in the different scents. I loved the freshness of lavender, the honey of alyssum. Pinks had a special clove sweetness that was one of my favorites and the rugosa roses had this clove scent, too, but the old-fashioned cabbage roses were pure rose like the wild ones, the breath of early summer.

While I sniffed and nibbled I watched the butterflies, airy and aimless, and the little golden bees burrowing into the hearts of the flowers, loading up with pollen and honey. A warm, busy humming filled the air over the garden but the butterflies made no sound at all. They seemed to have no personality, as a result; they were just beautiful like the flowers. I stalked them with my net from blossom to blossom—swallowtails and fritillaries and little ones whose names I didn't know. I was charmed with the patterns on their wings—black lace over orange, pure yellow stenciled in violet and others the color of paisley shawls, with surprising blue or rose "eyes" on their underwings. It seemed a shame to catch them and put an end to their honey-drinking and all that joyous dancing in the summer air, but the collecting fever had me in its grip.

In the process of butterfly collecting I became fascinated with all kinds of insects, and from Mr. Gibson I learned to hunt down caterpillars and raise my own butterflies or moths. I remember how excited I was when I found the caterpillar of the black swallowtail munching his way through a leaf of Pop's parsley. He was a gorgeous thing—black and gold and parsley green, like some jeweler's fantasy.

The Girl of the Limberlost by Gene Stratton Porter started me off on moths, and I used to go out after dark and paint trees with molasses to attract night flyers just the way the Girl did. Once I hatched out a Luna moth, a marvelous creature of pale green velvet with antennae like ferns and a body covered with silky fur. This moth had the elegance of a lady in evening dress, and I could not bring myself to kill her. I stopped collecting after this and went back to birdnesting, a harmless pursuit that was also as exciting as a treasure hunt.

Every June I had a whole series of nests to inspect, and one of the most interesting if not the most attractive was the chimney swift's in the chimney right over Synton's drawing room.

We had never been forbidden to go up on Synton's roof because nobody had expected us to think of it. Aldie and I, though, had discovered an easy route up over the old laundry. From the laundry various ells and wings went up in shallow steps, and when you reached the top the whole world lay spread out below. I could see in a complete circle, and to the south the sea stretched from Gooseberry Neck to Sakonnet like a solid blue wall, with all the Elizabeth islands and the Vineyard plainly visible on the horizon. I saw Aunt K. down in the garden and Gyp in the paddock and the chickens fussing around their yard. I could even see people clamming out on the flats in the river.

To see the chimney swift's nest I was forced to jump up and hang over the edge of the chimney with my head down the flue. Often the mother chimney swift was clinging to the bricks just below me, staring up with eyes like jet beads. The nest was a mere bracket of black sticks glued to the side of the flue. At first there were white eggs in it and then a squirming black pile of babies, whom I observed with some revulsion.

It was peculiar hanging upside down in the chimney, as sometimes I could hear Baba and Aunt K. talking down below in the drawing room. The smell of dead ashes was not pleasant, though, so I didn't spend much time eavesdropping.

Before I went back down the hill I used to climb up to my hideout in one of Baba's twin spruces. This was a curved branch like a hammock high up in the tree, and here I used to lie rocked by the breeze that hummed in the needles with a sound like surf. The sun baked into this green nest and drew out the spicy fragrance of spruce, the heady scent of Christmas trees. I loved being alone up there, safe and secret. It was just about the only place I could be certain of privacy, for even the boys didn't know about it.

I had another special time with Baba during my read in the afternoon. Every day since we were small Baba had read aloud to Aldie and me after lunch. Other grownups took naps but Baba scorned such weakness. She used this time for her grandchildren. My read began at one-thirty, Aldie's an hour later.

When I arrived at the front door Baba would be reading the *New York Times* on her Empire sofa, her feet up on a small oriental rug to protect the pale green plush. In the afternoons the drawing room was cool and shaded by the big lindens and the veranda roof, but through the open windows came the warm southwest breeze and the fragrance of gardens and mown grass. Baba always gestured with her glasses toward the window by her desk, where the flower garden glowed in the sun like an Impressionist painting in a frame.

"See my picture today," she would say. "The shirley poppies are open. After our read I want you to go out there and look at them."

Baba sat on the sofa facing the garden window, so I sat at the other end, facing the two original Dürers—bearded saints in long sculptured robes. The maidenhair fern by the west window stirred in the soft moving air.

My feet fitted in beside Baba's; we both had pillows behind our backs. Mine was a big one covered with pale blue crewel flowers; hers was velvet.

Baba folded up her paper and reached for our book, which she kept on the lower shelf of her little table.

"Well, dear Jan," she'd say. "Where were we yesterday?" and she'd open the book and adjust her spectacles.

We had come a long way since Beatrix Potter, a long and often weary road, for Baba's choice of books was not always to my taste. The most difficult to take and, in my opinion, the most revolting books I had ever encountered were the ones she had read in her childhood. These were the books I have mentioned before, in which the main characters were children of appalling virtue, some on their deathbeds, some living in garrets or standing out in freezing rain and snow, others simpering around their homes doing good deeds. A few of these had merit—*Sara Crewe* for one—but on the whole they gave me a peculiar feeling of unreality.

There were some sad animal books that had the same dismal pattern. The good dogs or horses were always being beaten or whipped by cruel masters. In *Black Beauty* somebody put a cutting bit on one of the horses, and there were checkreins and other horrors, but the worst animal book was *Rab and His Friends*. I think it was about vivisection but I made Baba stop reading it almost at once. *Greyfriar's Bobby* was sad in another way because his master *died*. What could you do about that? Nothing. There was no way to comfort Greyfriar's Bobby or me, and even now I can't bear to think about him.

Somewhere in here we read all the Twin books, which I loved so much that I reread them myself and had a complete collection. *The Scotch Twins* was my favorite and Baba's too. She liked it because it was in Scotland, but I loved the secret hideout the twins had up on that rock, away from the nasty gamekeeper. I remember their picnics as particularly edifying.

The books Baba's children had read were a great improvement on her own juvenile collection. There were two that hardly anybody I know has ever heard of: *Davy and the Goblin* and *The Adventures of Mabel*. Then we read the delicious *Gollywog Books* and *The Wind in the Willows* and *The Adventures of a Brownie, Alice in Wonderland, Heidi* and the *Water Babies*. My favorite, though, was *The Secret Garden*. Mary, the heroine, was not good; she was *real*—adventurous, disobedient and inventive. There was a sick child in this, bedridden of course, but he wasn't good either; he was terrible, and to my delight Mary stamped into his room when he was having a tantrum and told him to shut up. The part I loved best was the discovery of the secret garden, the weeding and pruning and clearing around the spring bulbs. I loved Dickon with his pet fox and crow and the blissful picnics of new potatoes with butter and salt. Here again was the forbidden garden like Mr. McGregor's and the disobedient little adventurer who did something brave and daring like Peter Rabbit. The idea of a secret garden of my own where I could plant bulbs and weed and have gypsy picnics became my special dream.

Aldie always appeared on the dot of two-thirty, and after finishing the sentence we were on Baba closed my book, putting a bit of tartan ribbon in to mark the place. I was not allowed to listen to Aldie's books, but I did notice that they went through all of James Fenimore Cooper. After his read Aldie went out to his studio in the Cottage and painted. No one was permitted to approach the place during this time, so I have no idea what went on.

In the early afternoons the sun had moved around into the southwest, the wind had come up and the sailboats were out all over the river. I could never stay away from the water in the afternoons, and I used to run down the path to the boathouse and try to get one of the sailboats before the whole family came down. The big sailboat, *Dehra Doon*, had to be back at the dock by the time Pop and his troops arrived, but I was often able to take it out for a while alone. I've forgotten how old I was when I first went sailing by myself, but I remember wearing blue cotton bloomers and having my hair in pigtails on that historic occasion. I didn't ask permission.

The boathouse area was deserted in the early afternoon because people had naps, and it took a while to get everybody rounded up before the official sailing hour. The stony beach with its mops of bleached eelgrass slept in the sun; the boats bobbed at their moorings, ripples of light running along their pea-green sides. There was a strong smell of rockweed baking in the heat, and in the stillness I could hear the vireos preaching up in the woods.

I felt very daring as I climbed into the rowboat and cast off. As I remember the wind was fairly light and the tide was falling, but there was still plenty of water. The oars, smooth and bleached with age, were warm from the sun and so was the seat under my bloomers. When I reached *Dehra,* I shipped oars and grabbed her rail, then I inched the rowboat up to the bow and tied her painter to the proper loop in the mooring rope. So far so good.

Dehra always leaked so I had to remove the wooden floor racks and bail, using the heavy old wooden bailer. Then I began the routine: push down the centerboard; let go the sheet; uncleat the halyards and start hauling up the sail. I didn't like this part, as the boom with its blocks kept banging against my ears and the wild flapping of the canvas scared me. However, I finally got the sail up, with the peak just high enough, cleated the halyards and crawled up on the bow to cast off. The boom swung over, nearly pushing me overboard, so I climbed into the rowboat and cast off from there. I got one foot back in *Dehra* before the two boats started drifting apart, and there was a period when I was doing the split over two feet or more of water, holding *Dehra*'s painter in one hand and the mooring rope in the other.

Before my arms were wrenched from their sockets I lurched into the sailboat and with pounding heart scrambled back to the tiller and grabbed the sheet. The wind then filled the sail and we swept shoreward at a terrifying rate. I put her about just before we hit a rock and was then ready to quit, but the thought of catching the mooring was so awful that I let the sail out and ran off toward the grass flats to rest. Suddenly everything was all right. The boat flew along on a level keel, the sail curved like a shell against the blue sky and the sun was hot on my back. *Dehra*'s sail was gray with mildew and the sheet in my hand was frizzled and dark with age, but I was sailing *alone*. I can feel now the silky smoothness of *Dehra*'s tiller, the original tiller, older than I was and as silvery in color as a piece of driftwood. There was a knob carved on the end of it, and this had a polish on it from generations of hands.

Dehra had broad comfortable seats all around the stern so I could stretch out, lean back against the traveler and drive her like a person driving a horse. She tugged gently at the sheet like Gyp mouthing her bit.

The upper end of the river was drowned in pale blue haze, the little islands quivering in the heat, and the water barely ruffled by the breeze. Where the stone-walled fields met the shore cows were standing in the shallows cooling off. The channel ran like a blue lane between the shore and the grass flats, inviting me on, so I kept going with the wind behind me. It was an idyllic voyage, and as the wind grew softer I could smell the wild roses above the beach. The pair of terns who nested on a rock up there circled over me with grating cries, their white wings edged with sun. Nothing could have been more perfect. The next minute we were hard aground. I looked over the side and saw that we were in about four inches of water and long shallow waves broke nastily on each side of the boat.

When I realized that I had to let go the sheet I did, and the boom went right around to the front of the boat, pointing ahead like a bowsprit.

I walked home most of the way, holding *Dehra*'s painter in my hand and sloshing along in the warm shallows. *Dehra* followed me like a docile horse, her sail hanging limp. I had forgotten that up in that part of the river the wind was cut off by the high west shore. It was delicious out there on the mudflats with the grass on the marsh rustling gently and the flocks of sandpipers running on the bare mud nearby. An osprey that nested on one of the little islands circled over my head; blue herons stalked in the creeks. I felt like one of them, alone in the middle of the summer day with only my boat for company.

When I stepped on a quahog, as I occasionally did, I grubbed it out with one hand and sluiced it off in the water. Then I cracked it on a cleat and ate it. Probably some Indian had done the same thing in our river, pulling his canoe.

When I climbed into the boat again I could see the family all jammed up at the end of the dock waving sweaters and beckoning. I could just hear what they'd say:

"*Where* have you been?"

"It's after three."

"What's the idea of taking *Dehra?*"

Nothing they said could spoil the beauty of that sail down the bay. *Dehra* and I were friends. I always felt that boats were practically human, and I patted her warm, blistered pea-green side.

"Don't come in under full sail," bellowed Pop through cupped hands. "Bring her around on the lee side."

We hit the dock so hard that Kelt, the dog, fell off into the water, but otherwise it was a good landing.

"*Where* have you been?" they said, etc. etc.

It didn't matter. I had made my solo flight.

❦ 15 ❧

End of a Chapter

Sometime in the spring of my fifteenth year, just as we were getting into the mood for summer, Pop accepted the job of Dean of the Chapel at Princeton. It had never occurred to any of us that we would ever leave the house in Holyoke. We looked on it as a permanent thing, as unchanging as the stars in the sky or the earth under our feet. Like Snowdon at the Point it was a fixed part of our lives, the setting for those months of the year when it wasn't summer.

We were used to hearing about Pop's job offers, and the household went through a certain amount of confusion when Rochester, the Brick Church in New York or Yale proposed to him. So far he had always refused, but now, suddenly, he said yes. We were so surprised that we didn't really believe it, but it was true. We were going to Princeton down in *New Jersey,* where they were building a huge Gothic chapel.

The circumstances of our departure from 231 Oak Street had much in common with *Götterdämmerung* by Richard Wagner. Nobody actually rode a horse onto a funeral pyre, but that's about all that was missing.

Nothing was done about packing at first because it was hard to decide where to begin. All you had to do was think about the attic or the hall closet and the whole business seemed perfectly hopeless. Mum never threw anything away and Pop never knew where anything was. At that time Mum didn't feel very well, and anyway she didn't want to leave Holyoke. There was some cursory discussion of the problem of moving. Pop claimed that this was the moment to rid ourselves of surplus possessions. Certain primitive tribes, he said, made a bonfire of everything they owned at the time of the vernal equinox. They could then start the new year free and unencumbered. There was, he said, much to be said for this custom.

"Now take the front hall closet," he said. "You could burn everything in there and never know the difference. Nobody's seen the back of that place for fourteen years, and I don't think I've seen the floor since 1917. And what about that glory hole behind your desk and all those boxes of papers in the attic? Rubbish."

"No, they aren't," said Mum. "Don't you touch them. I have to see what they all are," but every time she went up into the attic she began reading old letters and nothing was done. Pop, on the contrary, was apt to throw out everything unseen.

Mum had her own system of storage, which was simple and uncomplicated. When things piled up so that they got in the way she put them in a carton and took them up into the attic. When guests were imminent she used to rush around picking up odd objects and firing them into the hall closet or behind her desk. Some articles she piled on the attic stairs, and all empty boxes were scaled up those stairs and the door quickly shut before they could fall out again. When the stairs became blocked with debris, Pop carried the stuff up and tossed it into one of the storerooms. As the attic was perfectly enormous this system worked very well, unless of course you wanted to find a specific object or you had to move out of the house. After fourteen years the attic was a sea of cartons, trunks and piles of old magazines, and on a rainy day we could spend hours up there exploring. We rooted around in boxes of treasures from India or examined someone's ancient geology collection. However, the prospect of sorting and packing all this was appalling. Here Fate intervened.

Mum had started to clear the decks for action by sending Dave and Bobs down to the Point to stay with Baba, but she had barely done so when I was stricken with measles.

I remember it had been a beastly hot day with tar melting in the streets and the leaves hanging limp on the trees. Aldie and his friends were running under the lawn sprinkler and turning the hose on each other, but I felt as though my head were an iron ball with marbles rolling around in it. Hardly had I taken to my bed with cold washcloths on my forehead when the telephone rang. It was Baba saying that Bobs had come down with measles and had been moved down to Snowdon with a nurse and cook of his own, for Tink had never had measles and could not be exposed.

This dreadful news shook the household to its foundations. Pop said he couldn't afford to maintain two establishments and we were all shattered at the thought of poor little Bobs living alone with his staff at Snowdon. Finally, they got hold of Sharkey, the nurse, to look after me, and Pop drove Mum to the Point with the dog, Targ, Aldie and Catherine, the Hideons' nursemaid. Then Pop came back to supervise the packing, a job for which he was pitifully unfit. Ordinarily Mum would sooner have expected the dog to do the packing, for Pop was so absent-minded he could not be trusted to pack even his own overnight bag. Still, in the existing crisis she had no choice.

I don't remember much of this because after Sharkey appeared I became delirious and lived in a world of nightmares with brief interludes of sanity, when I found ice bags on my head or Sharkey feeding me something with a spoon. It was dark all the time in my room, so I was never sure whether it was night or day. Once I dreamed that I opened the door of the linen closet and inside was an infernal pit full of flames with black cats yowling at the bottom. The terror of it woke me up screaming, but Sharkey was no help at all and just put a thermometer in my mouth and took my pulse with her ice-cold red fingers. I longed for Mum, who made it almost a pleasure to be sick, reading aloud for hours on end, plumping pillows and thinking up all kinds of things to do. Now I was in the hands of a real nurse, and what with everything being sterile, quiet and dark I felt very low in my mind.

Dr. Bagg came at intervals and took my pulse and temperature, and at last I was allowed to sit in a chair by the window with all the shades down to the sills. When Sharkey went downstairs I used to pull up the shade beside me and squint out at the dazzling green and gold world beyond the glass. It was our yard and our street, but it looked empty and unreal like a place in one of my nightmares. It was a little better when I opened the window, for then I could hear the robins singing and the summery rustle of leaves. Puffs of soft, warm air poured over the sill, bringing the scent of cut grass and flowers, wonderfully comforting. I felt that if I could get outside into the sun and away from the queer silence of the house I would soon recover, but there was no hope of that with Sharkey around. Her conversation consisted almost entirely of dire predictions as to the fate of my eyes if I put up the shades and anecdotes of patients with measles who had disobeyed orders and gone blind.

Pop was away most of the time winding up his church affairs, but he came back at night, and then we'd shut my door and sit in there like two conspirators. Sharkey was so polite in Pop's presence that it cast a pall over our conversation.

"Gad," said Pop, frequently, "you'd better hurry up and get well so we can clear out of here and go to the Point. Nothing's any good without your mother."

A fluttery friend of Mum's had volunteered to help him pack their personal possessions, and this nearly drove him crazy.

"She keeps asking *me* what to do with things," he told me. "How should I know what to do with all that stuff your mother has in her drawers? Anyway, I don't like poring over female undergarments in the company of a strange woman. It's very embarrassing and it isn't right to have other people poking around in our house. Do you realize that all the drawers in the bathroom cupboard are full of empty medicine bottles? Your mother never throws anything away."

Mum's friend had a tendency to give little shrieks of laughter at everything Pop said, and this made him very nervous.

The news from the Point was awful. Aldie had come down with the measles, and Targ, who was only three, had it very badly. Dave, for some reason, escaped, but things could hardly have been worse.

After a while Dr. Bagg let me get dressed, but I wasn't allowed to read, so I just wandered around through the empty rooms like a ghost visiting the scenes of its happy childhood. In my depleted state I felt very weak and sentimental, and it seemed fitting that I should go about saying farewell to the dear companions of my small years—things like the radiator in Mum's room where we had warmed our clay and melted crayons and the washstand where we had watched Pop shave.

I went down and visited the hat rack, which was not going with us, the little window seat on the stair landing where I used to sit in the sun, the polished knob on the newel post that I touched every time I went up or downstairs and the rainbow that quivered on the wall of the front hall. One of the long beveled prisms from the chandelier that made the rainbow had come off and was in the drawer of the hat rack, so I took it and sat on the stairs flashing rainbows that flew like birds all over the walls and ceilings. Then I went up to say good-bye to the Big Bathroom and the attic.

This exercise in nostalgia was very depressing, and I almost welcomed the first of the movers—large, hot men who stamped in and began rolling up rugs and pushing furniture around. The next thing I knew the orientals were gone and there were dusty bare floors, where all had been rich and cozy. What's more they had moved Pop's green chair, exposing our private hiding place behind it, the snug triangular piece of floor between the window and the library table. Somehow this seemed a dreadful thing to do, like destroying a bird's nest. It did not seem possible that anyone could take apart our *home,* that permanent arrangement of furniture, rugs and pictures where the light fell in a certain way and every object had significance because it had always been there.

Pop had finally reached the end of the road. His digestion was seriously affected by the combination of worry, packing and the rich food we ate at the farewell parties his friends gave us. Dr. Bagg had given me a clean bill of health, Sharkey had departed and nearly every night we went out to dinner. At all the big houses on Northampton Street we had their own spring chickens, their own asparagus, their own strawberries and heavenly whips and mousses, made of their own cream. Pop had indigestion all the time and ate Bell-ans by the pound.

"Let's get out of here," he said at last. "One more day in this house and I'll cut my throat. Let's get to your mother."

He said vaguely that he'd come back sometime and do something about the movers, but he'd had all the packing he could take for the moment. Also some of his lady admirers had offered to help and this scared him.

"We'll drop everything and go," he said. "The women are beginning to close in on me. Now the main problem is, will the Artful Dodger be up to the trip? When I took the others down I didn't think I'd ever get back. I had three flats and a busted fanbelt and there's a new horrendous noise in the engine, like snakes."

The Artful Dodger at thirteen was definitely on his last legs. This final drive to the Point from the horseblock at 231 Oak Street was a milestone in our lives and his. Never again would we make the classic journey through the back roads of Massachusetts. From now on we would go to the Point on the Fall River boat from New York.

Pop took the Artful down to Emil for a final checkup. On the last day I made a sentimental tour of the yard, as in the turmoil of measles nobody else had done it properly. This was a mistake: the yard was dead; empty and peculiar like the house.

Fortunately, June was the time to leave Oak Street anyway, and every cell in my body told me to get to the sea, where everything would be normal again. After all, we had the hill and Snowdon and they were eternal.

In preparation for the journey Pop put a gallon jug of water in the back seat for the Artful to drink. He opened the hood and peered in to see if the fanbelt was in sound condition. He checked all the tires and the spare. Then he told the cook and me to get aboard and went around front and cranked up the engine. The Artful gave a hollow cough then burst into loud spitting and chugging, interspersed with explosions that shook us in our seats.

"Pray!" yelled Pop and vaulted into the driver's seat. Hiccuping and backfiring we jack-rabbited up the street and, turning the corner, drove out of my childhood forever.

❦ 16 ❧

Old MacDonald Had a Farm

The summer after we left Holyoke was the longest and most beautiful we'd ever had, and it went on and on right up to the first of November. A purist might have argued that it was no longer summer after Labor Day, but for us it was summer as long as we were at the Point and free of school. We were between lives, in the place we loved best, and we gave no thought to anything but the day and the hour.

All during the real summer things had been as usual, except that Pop talked incessantly about Princeton and our new house. The place was, he said, an earthly paradise, just like Oxford, and as far as we could see we were going to live like landed gentry on a huge estate.

There had never been a Dean of the Chapel at Princeton before so a new dean's house had to be provided, one to hold five or more children. The trustees rashly told Pop that they would build him any kind of a house he wanted, but they were, I believe, somewhat taken aback when Pop said he wanted a New England farmhouse out in the country. Pop's lifelong dream had always been to live on a farm the year round, and here was his chance to do so at Princeton's expense. Mum called these dreams of Pop's "rose dreams" and didn't take them very seriously, because they often faded into thin air or he forgot all about them. But the farm rose dream had been always with us, and we had been brought up on stories of the Old Farm.

Nobody really believed that the trustees would give Pop a farm, but to our amazement they finally did. They said they would build him his New England farmhouse on the old college farm, a ninety-five-acre property above Lake Carnegie. There was a crackerbox farmhouse already on the farm, and in it were a real farmer and his family, who were at present farming the land. Pop reported ecstatically that there was a big barn containing two horses and a herd of cows as well as a chicken house full of chickens. He said he had persuaded the farmer to let Dave help with the chickens and set up a flock for us.

"I had a great talk with the old fella," he said. "He's an Englishman, a real old-timer. We're going to get all our milk from him."

"We are?" said Mum, alarmed. "Is it pasteurized?"

"Heavens, no," said Pop. "It's real fresh milk right out of the cow, just like the Old Farm when I was a boy."

"That's the way you get undulant fever and T.B.," I said, for we had had a very frightening course in hygiene at school.

"Nonsense," said Pop. "These cows are fine healthy ones."

Nobody gave Pop's milk idea much thought, and Mum said it was probably just another one of his rose dreams. It soon became clear, though, that this rose dream was not only serious but expanding every minute. Pop really had the bit in his teeth and was off to the end of the rainbow.

"We'll be practically living off the land," he said, "our own firewood, fresh milk, fresh eggs and our own vegetables. We can have a huge vegetable garden with all that manure available right in our back yard."

"Manure!" cried Mum. "You mean there's a manure pile behind our house?"

"No, no," said Pop. "It's out by the barn. You can hardly smell it at all. Just enough to remind you of the Old Farm."

The elevations of the new house really did look like a New England farmhouse, with narrow clapboards, shutters and small-paned windows. We had been in farmhouses just like it—or at least the kitchens of them—in the Connecticut Valley. In those days, though, nobody except real farmers lived in farmhouses, and they were so cold that they piled hay around the foundations and everybody lived in the kitchen in a stifling atmosphere of wood smoke, steam and manure-soaked boots. It was clear from the blueprints that the inside of Pop's farmhouse was not at all farm-like. For one thing it had a "servants' wing," five bathrooms and a greenhouse, as well as extra frills like a butler's pantry, a "game closet" and an electric dishwasher.

The original farmhouse had been picked up bodily and moved back by the barn and our house was being built in its place.

"There will be huge sugar maples right beside the house," said Pop, "and all the old fruit trees, lilacs and rose bushes. There are even two butternuts in front."

Labor Day came and went and still there was no indication that Pop's farmhouse was anything but a rose dream. Pop left the Point when the college opened but we stayed on to enjoy weeks of blue and gold weather. After a while we almost forgot we were supposed to be in school or even that we were going to Princeton at all. Suddenly, though, the axe fell. The house was done and we had to leave. Pop came back to help close up, and presently we were all crammed into the Artful Dodger: seven of us and our luggage, the maids Peg and Catherine and their luggage, the dog Kelt and his. This was the Artful Dodger's last run, his swan song, and the most appalling safari in the history of family travel. It took place in pouring rain and lasted all day and far into the evening. We drove into our new driveway in pitch darkness with a gale blowing and rain lashing the side curtains and dripping through the leaks in the canvas roof. One of the Hideons was asleep, the other crying, Kelt was whining and drooling. The rest of us were in a stupor and hardly cared whether we lived or died.

"Well, here we are," said Pop, just as a frowsy-looking cow walked into the beam of the headlights and disappeared into the night.

"What's that doing here?" Mum asked.

"Must have gotten through the fence," said Pop.

We climbed out into the rain and into what seemed to be a sea of mud, in which more cows were slipping and squelching about.

There was a powerful smell of manure in the air, and there was no question but what we were on a farm.

"Never mind the cows now," said Pop. "Come on in and see the house."

We went up a gravel path to the side porch and through a glass door into a small cozy room with a fireplace and white bookcases along one wall. Mum's desk was in there and other familiar articles of furniture from Holyoke.

"The study," said Pop, and led the way into the living room, snapping on lights as he went. Everything looked very white and clean, and the ceilings were low, just like a New England farmhouse.

In the living room was all the furniture from the living room at 231 Oak Street, so it had a dreamlike resemblance to home. Pop had laid a fire in preparation for this moment, and now he bent over and lit it. As the flames leaped up and the kindling began to snap, the room came to life. The big red-and-blue oriental rug glowed with color, and there were the rosewood sofa and Pop's green plush gentleman's chair and the fat Victorian chair known as the "Squash Green." The library table was between the windows at the far end of the room with the etching of Toledo Cathedral over it. There were more white bookcases where all the old leather-bound sets were. On top of one was the little Japanese lacquer cabinet, and on top of another was the French clock in its glass case. Flowered chintz curtains framed the windows in fresh color.

It was a lovely room, a welcoming room, and everybody sat down in one of the old chairs and stared at the fire in a sort of trance.

"Oh, this is nice," said Mum, leaning back in her little wing chair. "I never want to get up again."

"Do you really like it?" Pop asked, looking around at us all. "Do you really?"

"It's great."

"It's a ruddy mansion."

"I can't believe it's ours," we said.

The dog Kelt, who had been carsick, went around the room

digging his nose into each one of us, asking for reassurance.

"Good boy," Pop said, rubbing Kelt's ears. "You're home now."

After we had rested a while Pop gave us a guided tour of the rest of the house, and it all looked wonderful and *white*. We had lived so long with dark varnished woodwork that this whiteness seemed as festive as fresh snow or white gloves. We ran up and down the long shallow staircase with its smooth mahogany rail. We went into all the bedrooms and bathrooms and then out into the kitchen, where Peg and Catherine were shrieking with excitement over the dishwasher.

The rose dream to end all rose dreams was the combination shop and conservatory. The conservatory had a cement floor with a drain in the center, a potting bench, a hose attachment and a nice small greenhouse. The shop part had everything: benches all around, shelves, drawers and a trap door in the floor. Pop lifted this up.

"You just sweep all the sawdust and shavings down here," he said proudly. "And right outside this door is a real old-fashioned woodshed."

There it was and Pop had already accumulated a good woodpile.

That night I took a hot bath in my own private bathroom and went to bed in my new room, which had white ruffled curtains at the windows and a pretty rosebud wallpaper.

I was wakened at dawn by the honking of geese under my window. Presently I heard Pop's dog voice raised in the next room and a sound like things being hurled through space and thudding on the ground. The geese broke into angry trumpeting, and once again Pop's dog voice shattered the country silence. I climbed out of bed.

My first view of New Jersey was of fawn-colored fields stretching down to the lake, which glittered blue and silver in the November sunlight. Directly below my front windows were the geese, rolling off across an expanse of brick-red mud—our front lawn. Out my other window were cows looking over a wire fence in mild surprise. There were a lot of big trees around the house, and the road was down at the end of a long gravel drive with thorn and apple trees on each side.

There were no houses anywhere near us, and for a minute I felt unprotected. I missed the companionship of neighboring roofs and chimneys and the views into friendly yards. On Oak Street we had been tucked in between old hedges and shrubberies; here we seemed to be in the middle of a prairie.

The dining room cheered me up at once. It was a good New England room, small-paned windows, white ruffled curtains and all.

Our first breakfast in the house was an event during the course of which we had a chance to sample the fresh milk. It had a very curious taste, and at first no one could identify it, but then Aldie said it was clearly manure.

"I ate some once and this is it," he said. "Now I know what they mean by liquid manure."

"That's enough of that, boy," said Pop. "Fresh milk isn't like the city stuff you buy in a bottle."

"It sure isn't," said Aldie.

The farm was certainly unlike anything we had ever seen in New England. The barn and outbuildings seemed to lean against each other to keep from falling down; there was a lot of rusty machinery lying around, and some scrawny chickens were scratching hopelessly among the weeds. The geese advanced upon us, honking in a very hostile way, but the farmer appeared around a corner and hurled a stick at them, uttering an early English expletive in a hoarse voice. Exactly what part of England the farmer hailed from was hard to fathom but I would have said London. He looked more like a Cockney than a farmer and had just the right kind of wispy mustache, a red nose with a drop on it and small suspicious eyes. His greasy cloth cap and manure-caked boots somehow took away my appetite for milk.

Pop, though, saw everything through the rose-colored spectacles of his dream, and pretty soon he infected us with his enthusiasm. The day was mild as Spring and the sun shone right into the barn which was stuffed to the roof with hay and smelled sweet. Two big work horses were chumping grain in their battered stalls and chickens were scratching around the floor, crooning comfortably. Through the open doorway we looked over miles of blue country, dreaming in the sunlight. The tie-up where the milkers were was under the hayloft on one side and in it were several cows and a good deal of manure. Here, too, the sun poured in and it was warm and snug. Pop leaned down and squirted some milk at us in an expert way.

"Come here," he said. "You might as well learn."

He showed us how to grasp the warm rough teat at the top and squeeze down, and soon we could all send a jet of milk right into each other's faces. It was great sport, and although the cows looked curiously around at us they didn't object. When Mr. Pollett, the farmer, came in he seemed startled but said nothing at the time.

I don't think Mr. Pollett knew what had hit him. Suddenly, Pop was helping us up onto the farm horses and showing us how to ride bareback. Then he was in the hayloft teaching the Hideons how to jump off the beams and swing on the hay rope. He did a lot of milking on the side, and we all hunted around the barn and weedy patches for eggs, as the hens were always stealing nests.

On crisp November afternoons toward sunset we went down into the corn fields and helped load the wagons. The air smelled of dried cornstalks and horses. It was good to be out in the cold blue evening. Up at the top of the fields the lighted windows of our house looked like a picture of home.

"You make a house a home by coming back to it again and again," said Pop as we trudged across the fields in the moonlight. "Now we'll just grab an armload of wood in the woodshed and build your mother a nice fire."

I don't know what Mr. Pollett's role in all this was. We seem to have been out riding his horses all the time. Their names were Ned and Dick and they were big, gentle creatures who obligingly broke into a galumphing canter if you belabored their ribs long enough with your heels. They didn't appear to know what had hit them either and had no idea how to respond to signals. When you tried to change direction and pulled on a rein you simply pulled the horse's head around until he was looking backward into your eyes but he kept going straight ahead. Still, we were on horseback and it was wonderful fun. On those broad backs we learned the lay of the land and came to love the pheasant-colored fields, the tangled hedgerows, haunts of cardinals and titmice, and the spaciousness of flat country.

I'm not sure when the honeymoon with the farm ended. It may have been when we stopped buying milk from Mr. Pollett. During the winter the cows were incarcerated in a pitch-black shed, where the smell of manure was so powerful it made your eyes water. Then we found so much dirt and hair in the milk that we refused to drink it. In protest we took to undulating around the dining room, clutching our throats and giving hollow tubercular coughs.

"Undulant fever! T.B.," we'd gasp, and with much gagging and groaning collapse on the floor.

Mum was more direct.

"I'm sorry," she said, "but I'm not going to feed this milk to the children any more. You can drink it if you want to but we're switching to Walker-Gordon's."

Pop didn't fight the edict, as even after the cows were let out they got into the wild garlic and the milk was undrinkable.

Shortly after the milk order was canceled Mr. Pollett threw us out of the hayloft and refused to let us ride the horses any more. By this time, though, we had started riding at the college stables where the R.O.T.C. and polo team kept their horses. The faculty members were allowed to ride the second-string horses free, and this was one more aspect of Pop's rose dream that had come true.

Pop loved horses but on the Old Farm he had been a driver not a rider. The day he took the boys and me to the R.O.T.C. stables for the first time we were under the impression that we already knew how to ride horseback, and Pop seemed to have no qualms either. We felt like old hands but didn't look it. I wore a pair of Aldie's pants, and the others were in their regular clothes. Pop even had on his fedora hat, but then so did most of the other faculty members. We took a few turns around the tanbark ring inside and were able to watch ourselves in the huge mirrors, not an edifying sight. Eventually, we were turned loose and went off across country in several directions, all of us bouncing around on our saddles in a very alarming way. The polo ponies made wonderful mounts, instantly responsive to the touch of the reins on their necks, but after Ned and Dick this was disconcerting, for we were not prepared to turn on a dime. Pop rode a large brown cavalry horse whose back was so broad that Pop was in agony all the time. We had very little control over the horses, and at one point we were thundering down the towpath between the lake and the old canal. Pop was in the rear, banging up and down and yelling, "Help! Help!" but we kept right on going. Finally, the lead horse skidded to a stop on the edge of a highway and we all piled up against its behind like shunted freight cars.

"For the love of Mike," gasped Pop. "Why in Sam Hill couldn't you stop? I'm split right up to my chin."

At the end of that afternoon all four of us were virtually crippled, but we had become addicts. Even Mum joined us after a while and bought herself a riding habit and boots. She was nervous at first, but we put her on a plodding nag called Dinah who could hardly be made to walk. Mum had absolutely no control over Dinah and squealed helplessly as she jogged along, but we kept her sandwiched between us so she was relatively safe.

I loved everything about riding: the feel of the reins in my fingers, the creak of saddle leather, the smell of horse, and the look of the world from the saddle. The countryside around us was a network of trails, for Princeton was horse country. There was a pack—the Stony Brook Hunt—and sometimes we saw them streaming across the rolling fields on the other side of town. On crisp fall mornings the little black stable boys trit-trotted down the streets with the first-string polo ponies in their mustard-colored blankets. On the days of polo games the polo field near us was a thundering confusion of horses and waving mallets, and the smart crack of a well-driven ball became one of the sounds of our afternoons.

Pop was in his element in the saddle and became less and less of a farmer and more and more of a country squire. This was all for the best, since the farm phase of our lives was drawing to a close. As we trotted happily through the barnyard on late winter afternoons, Mr. Pollett used to spit in a marked manner and mutter under his breath in Anglo-Saxon.

Spring came in a cloud of fruit blossom. Out in the barnyard the geese led forth a string of gray goslings, and the mother hens who had hidden nests produced broods of little yellow powder puffs. The geese brought their families over to graze on our new lawn, and Pop was beside himself. Every morning the grass below his window was littered with shoes he had fired at the enemy. To top it all, a flicker used to come down and drum on the drain pipe with a noise like machine-gun fire.

"Ye gods," said Pop one day at breakfast. "You'd think on ninety-five acres of land a man could get a night's sleep. Those geese are driving me mad. I'm going to speak to Pollett."

"You're on a farm, remember?" said Aldie. "It's what you always wanted."

After Pop spoke to Mr. Pollett about the geese, things deteriorated rapidly. I think it was during the summer that the Pollett regime ended. Anyway, they were gone, and in the crackerbox house was a nice clean mailman, who had no interest in the farm at all. The barn became virtually our private property, and Pop helped Dave set up a flock of chickens, which slept in the old tie-up and had a fenced run in the barnyard. Dave rigged up a device with an alarm clock, some string and a box with a sliding bottom that opened when the alarm rang at four, dumping a pile of feed on the ground. The hens became conditioned to the bell and would rush screaming to the feeding machine at the first trill.

The hayloft was still stuffed with hay, and in May the barn swallows came back as usual and refurbished their nests on the rafters. The barn cat hid her kittens up in the mow somewhere, and I had a hideout just inside the wooden door where they pitched in the hay over the tie-up. I would take a book up there and lie back in my sun-filled nest to read and dream, safe from interruption and beautifully warm. The hay gave out the fragrance of summer grass, and from this perch I could look out over the fields to where the lake blinked between the trees.

In June the meadow larks whistled all day long from the fence posts. The fields were a tapestry of flowers in pink and gold and russet spattered all over with daisies. At the end of the polo season the ponies were put out to pasture in the big meadow next to the house and it was lovely to see them wading in grass and flowers, their haunches polished like chestnuts. When they weren't grazing they used to hang their heads over the fence and watch Pop weeding his daffodils.

"It's just like a Kentucky stud farm," said Pop proudly. The country squire had replaced the farmer, and he was delighted with his new role.

Life in Princeton had another side to it that was quite separate from our private world down by the lake. There were our new schools, the town and the university and, everywhere you looked, men, members of that powerful entity the Student Body. This whole complex we referred to as Uptown, and a large part of each day was spent trying to get up there and maneuvering to get back. Mum said she was nothing but a taxi driver, but being Mum she enjoyed every minute of it.

✺ 17 ✺

The Student Body

Princeton was an aristocratic old town with pre-Revolutionary houses of great charm and a tree-lined street of elegant small shops. The university with its Gothic towers, silvery quadrangles and green lawns filled the whole center of the town, and its playing fields extended nearly to the lake on the south side.

Miss Fine's School, where I became a member of the sophomore class, had originally been an inn.

Miss Fine, who was more beautiful and regal than Queen Mary of England, had a crown of white hair and wore charming flowered dresses and violet sweaters. At the May Day festival she carried a parasol, which may give you the idea as well as anything. She was so lovely that we all assumed she had been disappointed in love back sometime around the Civil War, but I doubt if she was that old.

Miss Fine welcomed me kindly and introduced me to some friendly girls, who soon put me at my ease. Of course, I saw at once that my ponytail was impossible, my clothes hopeless and my social graces virtually nil, but I also realized that here for the first time I was exposed to education at the highest level. The teachers, some of whom were wives of Princeton professors, were magnificent, and I was enchanted with learning. I loved racing around the hockey field in blue tunic and black stockings, but in the locker rooms I was alarmed by the constant references to members of the Princeton Student Body. These girls were experts in the art of attracting the male. Years of experience seemed to lie behind their conversation.

I gathered from these locker-room sessions that any male below a college freshman was regarded as an infant and even freshmen were almost worthless, except as raw material from which future stag lines could be fashioned. Every girl seemed to have several admirers who invited her to football games, dances and movies, but how they ever met them was beyond me. We were supposed to avoid the campus like a leper colony, and if you passed students on the street you had to act as though they were invisible. Miss Fine discussed the matter of the university once a year at assembly.

"I am in charge of you girls while you are here at school," she would say. "I trust my girls not to walk beyond the corner —question of propriety, girls, question of taste, yes, question of that. . . ."

We had our own code of ethics as well and would never have dreamed of entering the campus unescorted. Any girl who did so was welcomed with wolf whistles and shouts of "Fire!" Of course, we got this tribute even when we were with a man, but then it was all right. In fact, if no one yelled or whistled at you, you were disgraced and your escort deeply embarrassed.

Prospect Street, where the eating clubs were, was absolutely taboo, and to appear there alone was to court social ruin. To go anywhere near Prospect Street at mealtimes was comparable to soliciting in the eyes of Miss Fine's girls. Out-of-town houris sometimes parked their convertibles at the top of Prospect in hopes of an invitation to house parties or some special football game. One of these was rumored to have a case of whiskey in the trunk as bait. We despised such goings on.

Mum, being a faculty wife, was able to drive me to school up Prospect Street, so every morning I saw the upperclassmen in their tweed jackets, gray flannels and white buckskin shoes, strolling down to breakfast. In those days students *liked* to dress well, although the tweed jackets had to be old with leather patches on the elbows, the flannels not too well creased and the buckskin shoes dirty. In winter they wore polo coats and well-polished brown cordovan shoes. Hats, however, were frowned on, as were rubbers and umbrellas. Only Harvard men or Englishmen wore hats and carried umbrellas, or so I was told. All in all the breakfast procession down Prospect was a beautiful sight, but I had to keep eyes front all the way up the street, for it was improper to meet the glance of any individual member of the parade.

From Washington Road and Nassau Street I could catch glimpses through Gothic arches of ivied walls and casement windows, with young men in shirt sleeves leaning out of them. There they were, those lords of creation, around whom everything in Princeton revolved. In a way the campus was like a great Gothic zoo, where the inmates were free to wander about uncaged, separated from the spectators only by Nassau Hall's grilled iron fence or the stone walls of the quadrangles.

At intervals the inmates of the zoo got out of control, and on some still evening we'd hear a noise like lions roaring that swelled in volume as the night wore on.

"Riot," Pop would say. "I'd better go up."

After a riot we'd see cars overturned, the ticket collector's cage at the Garden Theatre lying on its side and other evidences of mayhem. Riots made me wonder somewhat about the maturity of the male sex, but it was customary to look on these affairs as endearing evidences of animal spirits.

On fall Saturdays we walked across the fields to the stadium, inhaling the exciting dust from hundreds of feet and listening to the band thumping its way into the stands. We sat in a row about halfway up on the sunny, or Princeton, side and watched the confetti-colored crowds fill the opposite rows and the puffs of blue cigarette smoke starting up all over the place as though the people were on fire. Pretty girls in fur coats, little hats and high heels teetered up the steps with their escorts; drunks and dogs rushed out onto the field and had to be retrieved. Then the team came in and the lions began to roar.

It was almost a disgrace to go to football games with your family, but the games were so glorious I didn't care. I was in love with the whole team, the entire cheering section and the band. Princeton was my college. I never felt such passionate loyalty to the institution I attended myself.

The only place where the Student Body could be observed in relative silence was Pop's chapel. Every Sunday we went to chapel, where we sat, according to Mum's custom, practically under the pulpit. Behind us we could hear the whisperings and rustlings of the restless victims of the compulsory chapel rule. In front rose the marvelous chancel, with its jeweled windows and carved oak choir stalls. Up there were Pop and the black-robed choir. During the service I was able to watch these members of the Student Body in a safe, if furtive, manner.

The thunder of the great organ and the beautiful words of the service made this hour a time of peace. I had a chance to be quiet and think my own thoughts. The whole business of competition for male attention seemed to me artificial and exhausting, with no relation to the real world. Most of the things I loved best—walking in the woods, watching birds with Pop, hunting wild flowers or reading poetry—were out as subjects of conversation. My role as a female was apparently to make myself alluring enough to earn invitations to the right football games, the proms, as many movies as possible and, as a crowning honor, house parties in May. It was a tiring prospect.

I remember the wonderful relief I felt during Christmas vacations when the Student Body went home. Then I was able to walk through the empty campus, under those Gothic arches, into ivied quadrangles and to the university store right in the center. There we did much of our Christmas shopping and emerged into the still winter sunlight with our arms full of packages. Christmas in Princeton really meant peace on earth to me. We missed the big snows of New England, the skiing and sliding and all the regal glory of a northern winter, but there was something delicious about Princeton's pale blue springlike days when we sat out on the porch in the sun and looked across the brown fields, baking in the warmth.

When the cold tightened up, the lake froze into a black mirror, and we had such skating as we had never imagined. We spent all of Christmas vacation on the ice, and so did half of Princeton. It was like Holland, with everyone out on skates and fires on the shore where you could warm yourself and buy hot dogs and coffee. When the ice was perfect we skated all day long, exploring the shoreline as far as the dam at Kingston and stopping to rest on the little islands. I used to lie on my back on the slippery brown carpet of oak leaves and watch the treetops sway against a sky as blue as Italy's. Then we'd take off again, flying free as birds through the radiant stillness of those mornings, our skates hardly touching the ice.

After New Year's the Student Body returned, and I was back in the arena.

At intervals during the academic year Miss Fine's girls were exhibited to the Student Body at carefully chaperoned teas and receptions. Seasoned veterans went to these functions like children going to a toy store at Christmas and were usually able to cut out the most attractive men and take them home to supper.

I looked on such gatherings with pure horror, and aside from the dubious honor of being stuck with a Siamese prince once, I was a failure. The Siamese prince was typical of my luck at receptions. Mrs. Dean Green, a formidable faculty wife, caught me unoccupied and brought forward a grinning oriental youth, whose head was on a level with my chest.

"This is Mr. Ned," she said. "I can't pronounce your name," she told her captive, "so you'll have to be Mr. Ned."

She then abandoned us, and for what seemed like hours I jigged about with Mr. Ned's patent-leather head bobbing about under my chin.

This episode convinced me that I would never marry. No man would look at me. It didn't occur to me that I was only fifteen and what is called a "late bloomer."

The next morning at breakfast I told the family that I never wanted to go to another dance as long as I lived. I added that I didn't care if I never saw a man again. Greta Garbo, in a movie that I had recently seen, had put it in a nutshell. "Men, men," she said in that inimitable voice. "I am so seek to death of men."

I quoted this and went on to say that if I had to go to Miss Fine's school dance I'd cut my throat, but this threat was made so often in our house that no one paid any attention.

Pop finally developed a plan that brought large sections of the Student Body to the house, not, of course, with any idea of providing me with escorts but to give them, as he said, "a taste of home." In the process he tried to explain to them why compulsory chapel was a good thing and what religion was all about, not an easy task.

Freshman suppers on Thursday nights became an institution and were eventually managed by Bruce, our black major-domo who had taken charge of us when Peg and Catherine left. Every Thursday evening at six a truck from the university ground crew deposited twenty freshmen by the front walk. Pop greeted them at the door and took them into the living room, where to break the ice he showed them his model of the whaleship *Charles W. Morgan.* Religion was never mentioned during this period.

Presently Bruce announced dinner, and they all shuffled into the dining room and were distributed around the table and the extra card tables brought in for the purpose. Here they devoured creamed chicken, mashed potatoes, peas, and gingerbread with chocolate sauce and whipped cream.

At the initial supper Pop had thought it would be nice if Mum and I helped out, so I was forced to carry in the plates while Mum sat in her place at the table. This horrible episode was the last of its kind.

"Never again," Mum said. "Never." I agreed with her.

Pop pled with us but we were adamant. From then on we all ate on a card table in the study and eavesdropped on Pop's conversations. Afterward we'd tell him where he'd made a false move or been overly sentimental about The Home or The Family.

"Now, just leave me alone," Pop would cry. "You ought to try it. What do you suggest?"

We referred to religion as "hagligion," a corruption of the word as pronounced by that famous Scot the Reverend Hugh Black, who said "hrreligion" with a thick burr.

"Don't mention hagligion at all," we'd say. "Don't go on about God. It just puts people off."

"You tend to your job. I'll tend to mine," said Pop. "Eye Guy, you and your mother think my job's a big joke."

"We're just trying to help," we said. "We're giving you a preview of what you'll be up against."

Freshmen suppers were no good to me, but Sunday suppers were very rewarding. They started when Pop began bringing home members of the chapel choir and sons of some of his friends. Mum would feed them waffles and toasted English muffins, and as we had only one waffle iron most of their time was spent waiting their turn. This gave me a chance to have speech with members of the Student Body under relatively normal conditions, although, with my brothers present, I felt constantly monitored. Most of the charter members of the Sunday-supper group were almost indistinguishable from brothers and were obsessed with sports. When they were not eating they were playing games or talking about them. At last one of them asked me to go to the movies, but the boys came along too. Somehow, it was almost impossible to go to the movies from our house without a member of my family getting into the act. Often Mum and Pop decided to join us. Nobody could believe I was old enough to go out alone with a man.

Words cannot describe how trying my male relatives were during this difficult time. If some young man did hike down to call on me in the evening, Pop would either spend the evening with us or come to the head of the stairs at nine o'clock and call, "Bedtime!"

The boys studied narrowly every man who asked me for a date and would then give a decision on his suitability. Practically every candidate was eliminated after the first trial. Sometimes, even the fact that he wore black shoes with a tweed jacket disqualified him. Anyone who didn't go out for sports was automatically scratched.

"Oh, you and your old sports," I'd cry. "Don't you ever think of anything but chasing around after a ball or a little hunk of rubber?"

What with the Student Body and the men in our house the Greta Garbo mood recurred at regular intervals. When I'd had enough, I went off alone to my secret refuge, a deserted garden we had found beyond the boundary of the farm. The garden belonged to a large Victorian house, half-buried in overgrown shrubbery and neglected roses. Enormous elms and beeches walled it in on all sides and made a dome of sunshot green overhead. When you were in the garden it was like being in a great room where the still air was warm and scented with grass and flowers. Except for the chorus of birdsong the place was uninhabited, not dead but asleep like the Sleeping Beauty's castle. I took Dave over there to reconnoiter but the house was clearly empty, and we never met a human being in all our subsequent visits. We even crawled through the rear door of the old fashioned icebox and into the house which we explored from attic to cellar, but there was no sign of life anywhere, no furniture, no pots and pans—nothing but elegant emptiness, where we met ourselves in mirrors and made footprints in the dust of Victorian parlors.

The garden of this house became my secret garden, just like the one in the book which I had always loved.

In early spring I found violet crocuses scattered under a weeping beech tree, and other bulbs pushed up their green spears in every corner. I cleared the leaves away from those that needed it and nearly every day new buds opened. The daffodils had spread in all directions, great drifts of butter-yellow filling the air with their musky scent. Violets and lily of the valley ran wild in the shrubberies and spilled over into the borders, choking the old perennials that still struggled up through the weeds. In this hidden paradise the birds too had found sanctuary; the garden was full of nests and I spent long hours searching for them.

Below the garden was a large apple orchard where bluebirds came in April, their tender calls dropping down from the pale sky as they flew in. Later they squabbled over nesting holes like great blue butterflies. Cardinals whistled in the hedgerows, and in May the orchard was teeming with warblers, probing the pink buds for insects and flashing their wings across the aisles.

I was never lonely in this garden. It was as though some happy, loving presence walked beside me down the overgrown paths or knelt with me to pick bunches of lilies-of-the-valley.

When the apple trees bloomed I used to climb up and sit among the branches watching the honey bees go from blossom to blossom, nuzzling the rosy petals and loading up with pollen. The whole orchard hummed like a plucked cello string, and the air blew sweet down the long aisles. In these moments of mindless rapture I could almost feel myself growing like the grass. I think I learned then that nobody else had the power to make you happy or unhappy. It was up to you.

❦ 18 ❦

The Great and Simple Man

On one of Pop's speaking trips he happened to sit on the train across from two old ladies. Like his father, Gumpkie, he always struck up conversations with people on trains and soon had the entire story of their lives, as indeed they had his. During the course of this particular confessional Pop had revealed his identity, and the old ladies had been bowled over, as they had often heard him preach.

"You see, my dear," one said to the other, "it's what we've often said. Great men are always simple."

Pop told us this with glee, and from then on we called him the Great and Simple Man.

It took some years for the great and simple man to accustom himself to the various aspects of his new life in Princeton. Even the house had problems that had to be tackled. It had one thing in common with a New England farmhouse—it was *cold*. It's a lucky thing it wasn't in New England or we might have frozen to death. When the north winds came roaring across those flat fields the only really warm place in the house was Mum's bathroom. I used to go in there and read because my room on the north side was so cold I had to wear a coat.

Nobody understood the heating system, nor did anyone at the college seem to feel any responsibility for it. Pop's struggles with the furnace were epic affairs, accompanied by iron crashes, curses and avalanches of coal. There was a tremendous coal bin, but the light was in the wrong place so Pop could never see the coal. The problem was further compounded by the presence of a black kitten that used the coal bin as a cat box. This kitten was, most regrettably, named the Christ Child. It had come to the back door on Christmas Eve, and when Pop tried to turn it away we told him he couldn't because it might be the Christ Child in disguise. For some reason he seemed to accept this theory, but insisted that the kitten be kept down cellar until it was housebroken. The consequences of this inhuman edict were, we said, just what Pop deserved. He always forgot the kitten was there until he slipped in a cat mess. He regularly shoveled the cat up with the coal, as it was invisible in the coal bin, and his remarks at these moments were a delight to all of us who overheard them. Once we had a very proper female guest who nearly hit the ceiling when a voice under her feet said, "All right, you dad-gasted Christ Child. Next time I'll throw you in."

"Who can that be?" she quavered.

"Oh, that's just Pop," we said calmly.

Up at the university there were other difficulties to iron out. One was the loudspeaker system in the chapel. Because of the great length of the nave loudspeakers had been affixed to the tops of columns, and there was a microphone in the pulpit right in front of the minister. For reasons hard to fathom, the controls for the system were in the basement down near the furnace.

When a visiting minister came Pop took him up to the chapel before the service and put him in the pulpit. He himself went to the back of the chapel and told the man to speak in his natural voice. He then directed the man at the controls to adjust the sound so that the minister's voice could be heard by those in the back row.

One glorious Sunday the visiting minister was a dear, gentle man named Dr. Tweedy, a friend of my grandfather's. We used to call him "Henry Hallam Tweedydeedee," as he was a D.D. and someone had once introduced him that way.

Dr. Tweedy looked, we thought, exactly like Jesus, as he had that kind of a beard. His voice was very gentle like his nature, and when Pop took him up to adjust the speakers they had to turn the thing up high. We were all in our pew that Sunday, sunk in the usual mid-service lethargy, and finally Dr. Tweedydeedee crossed the chancel in his gown, climbed the pulpit stairs and stood above us like a saint on a pedestal. We settled in for the sermon; Dr. Tweedy opened his mouth and a bellow like that of an enraged bull rattled the chandeliers and ricocheted from wall to wall, nearly rupturing our eardrums. The students sat electrified with joy, and we were absolutely spellbound. So was Mum, but Pop shot out of his carved oak stall as though a bomb had gone off under him and ran to the door with his gown billowing behind him. Dr. Tweedy thundered on and on, his eyes glazed with horror, and then suddenly he was turned off. His lips moved but there was no sound. Pop had reached the controls in the cellar.

It took Pop a long time to recover from this catastrophe, and Dr. Tweedy never came to the chapel again. We could see why but we had never enjoyed a service so much and felt privileged to have been present. As children of a minister we always hoped for things like this to happen, but until then all we'd had was a deacon who dropped a pile of collection plates up in the chancel—good, but nothing compared to Dr. Tweedy's performance.

As far as the Student Body went Pop did pretty well, considering the fact that they all resented compulsory chapel. We could tell that they liked him because in the *Gaily Printsanything*, a spoof of the *Daily Princetonian*, the college paper, they had run a composite photograph of a barroom scene with a lot of drunks lying around on the floor. They had put Pop's head on one of these figures, a rare compliment. He was delighted.

It was in his role as confidential advisor that Pop came up against problems that took him right out of his depth. He had asked to have no disciplinary powers so the boys could tell him anything, and they did. Pop could handle the traditional protests against compulsory chapel, the establishment, rules and regulations, parents, God, one's roommate and the club system. He loved a proud agnostic or a happy pagan because they were interesting and enjoyed a good argument. He could even tackle the dedicated members of Frank Buchman's Oxford Group, who wanted him to come to their house parties and tell all. The subject he fell apart on was s-x. That's how Pop thought of it—something one never mentioned. He was for it but only after people were safely married. Every now and then he'd come home from the office with his eyes starting from his head, and we'd hear him telling Mum things in a low shocked voice. Being a very innocent man he had never even heard of some of the more outré forms of human behavior, and neither had Mum. He might just as well have told us as she instantly relayed the spiciest bits to me, and I told Aldie, who shared them with Dave. Now that we had learned The Facts from the gutter and other sources, Mum had gradually shed her Victorian scruples. Baba would have been horrified. There was nothing in these confidences that you can't read today in any magazine and hear discussed openly on television, but in the thirties such matters were kept private. The only time the word "sex" was heard in our house was when Pop read aloud from Dickens. Dickens referred to women as "the Fair Sex" or simply "the Sex." This was one of the many things Aldie held against Queen Victoria and the Victorian novelists.

"They were really just a bunch of dirty old men," he said to tease Pop. "Had mistresses in red velvet lovenests."

After several years in Princeton we had come a long way.

"I won't have that kind of talk in this house," cried Pop. "And in front of your mother and sister, too."

Mum exchanged glances with us and began to laugh.

"It's not funny," said Pop angrily.

Once some dismal woman came to Mum with a piece of scandal that Mum could hardly wait to tell me. This female had a friend who was on the verge of a nervous breakdown because of her husband's outrageous demands. Every time he came home from the office he said to her, "Upstairs, Margaret." *Every day.*

We were charmed with this story and the expression "Upstairs Margaret" became part of our equipment for teasing Pop.

We referred to men like Upstairs Margaret's husband as S.C.M.'s—sex-crazed monsters—and this shocked Pop deeply.

"I don't understand it," he said to me. "In my day girls were sweet, innocent creatures."

"Yes, poor things," I said. "Went mad after the wedding night and had to be put away in loony bins."

I'm sorry to say we had a lot of wicked fun teasing Pop about sex, but, as we told him, it was for his own good.

"It's all very well to be great and simple," we said, "but you don't have to be simple-minded."

In spite of our guidance Pop was never able to discuss sex without acute embarrassment. Over the years we tried our best to educate him, but it was no use. He was always shocked that I, a young unmarried girl, knew anything at all.

"They have a whole series of lectures on it in zoology," I told him after I went to college. "We have a week off to read sex books. There are two huge charts in the classroom of the male and female—"

"STOP," cried Pop. "I'd like to get my hands on that professor —I'll bet he's a Frenchman—"

"It's a woman," I said.

"Don't tell me any more," said Pop. "I'm just a hick from off the farm. Just remember, great men are always simple. I'm a great and simple man."

❦ 19 ❦

Time Marches On

The Artful Dodger gave up the ghost soon after he delivered us all to Princeton. Like a noble war horse he had died at the front in full battle dress—duffel bags, luggage racks and all.

The Artful's successor was a secondhand Studebaker, a dreadful vehicle. The left hand front door would never stay shut so you had to keep banging it as you drove along. For a while we tied it shut with a length of clothes line. Then one day Pop backed out of the garage and ripped off both front doors, solving that problem. Eventually the Studebaker was declared unfit for the road. Pop put it out to pasture on the farm and we practiced driving in it. We used to go at fifty miles an hour over the fields, and when we hit a woodchuck hole or a rock the car would leap into the air like a bucking bronco, nearly throwing us out the window.

Pop had taught us all to drive at a very early age. First we sat in his lap and steered, and then he used to let us drive up the lane at the Point. We learned to change into second on the curve by the big laurel and practiced backing out by Baba's twin spruces, where her "service entrance" branched off. Baba didn't approve of this at all, and used to tap on the window with her thimble and shake her head.

Once when I was doing my first solo down the bumpy stretch to our house I drove right into the woods and hit a juniper tree.

However, by the time we moved to Princeton all of us but the Hideons could drive reasonably well. The bliss of having our own car and ninety-five acres to drive around was one more bonus of life on the farm. I don't know how legal it was, but Pop said he wasn't going to find out. The more practice we had before being turned loose with a license, the less terrifying it would be for him and Mum.

"If you can drive that thing over a plowed field you can handle most normal situations," he said. "But don't forget it's the Other Fella you have to watch out for."

The Other Fella became practically one of the family by the time we were licensed to drive, and he was always with us on the road. The Other Fella drank; he was reckless; he never looked where he was going; he drove an old jalopy—in fact he was utterly despicable, a monster. I pictured him crouched over the wheel of his jalopy, a drunken leer on his purple face, casting about with bloodshot eyes for someone to run down.

To replace the Studebaker Pop bought an immense Packard touring car from our doctor, a close friend who had known Mum from childhood. It was unlikely, said Pop, that such a man would cheat us, and anyway doctors were bound to be honest and reliable. In this case he was right, and the Packard was a glorious car, long and luxurious with a beautiful silver device on the radiator cap and two folding jump seats in back, making ample room for the whole family. It was cream colored—a luxurious color—and had a tan canvas roof that folded back. In fact it was exactly the kind of car for a country squire to drive. We named it Bucephalus after the horse of Alexander the Great. One of the graduate students suggested the name, and we all recognized at once that it fitted.

Pop was enchanted with Bucephalus and loved to drive around in him through the streets of Princeton. We loved Bucephalus too. He had a real personality. We had him until I went to college, and my first romantic adventures took place in his ample front seat. When in the course of time I began to go out with young men, the problem of transportation was fearful. As the students were not allowed to drive cars, anyone who asked me to go to the movies had to walk the two miles down to our house to get me. Then, we either had to hike all the way back uptown—a good half hour's work—or I had to persuade the family to let me borrow the car. If they refused Pop would drive us uptown, and after the movie we would have to walk home or call Pop. This was hardly conducive to romantic situations. Saying goodnight to a beau with Pop standing by was impossible.

Even when I was able to borrow the car, I had to drive while my escort sat sulkily beside me, and at the end of the evening I had to drop him off at the college and drive home alone, *or* he had to walk back from our house. This was not too bad in the spring or fall, but in winter with a freezing gale roaring across those fields it was an ordeal only a besotted man wished to attempt.

I remember ungodly rides sitting between Pop and a young man, with Pop making labored conversation. I remember sitting in the back seat beside a gawky student with Mum at the wheel and a Hideon staring over the front seat at us.

The problem was partly solved by my letting the student drive illegally once we got out of town.

When Aldie went away to school at Deerfield, the family circle was broken for the first time. Without his extravagant presence meals were a little more peaceful but not as funny. Nobody drew murals on bathroom walls or grotesque faces on the margins of books and magazines. Any bare space in Aldie's vicinity was to him simply a place to draw or paint something. Once, when a friend of ours was in the hospital with a broken back, Aldie drew a huge naked woman on the ceiling of the room, and it was so good the hospital didn't object. There was no doubt but what Aldie was a real artist. He even had the artistic temperament, and at this time was rebelling like mad against practically everything. Paris would perhaps have been the right place for him, but Deerfield was safer, being up in Massachusetts.

I was the next to leave home, and went to Mount Holyoke College in South Hadley, right next door to Holyoke itself. South Hadley is a small white village out in the Connecticut River Valley. At that time its only connection with civilization was a trolley line—the very trolley that we had ridden with Buffy when we lived in Holyoke. The same ads were over the windows: Wrigley's Spearmint Gum, Bromo-Seltzer, Carters Little Liver Pills and Smith Brothers' Cough Drops.

It was wonderful to be back in New England, and at first I simply wandered around looking at the white houses under the sugar maples, the steep stone-walled fields and the streets of wine-glass elms. I found an old apple orchard on a hillside above an ice pond, and here the long grass was full of windfalls, smelling of cider and buzzing with wasps. I picked a good apple from a low branch and polished it on my sleeve to eat as I walked along.

There was a path around the ice pond, bordered with white pines, birches and wet thickets of swamp azalea and red maple. Chickadees followed me along the way, tiny companions with whom I conversed by whistling their love song. The place had a curiously familiar look. Someone besides the chickadees seemed to be walking along beside me. Then I recognized it as one of the trails where Pop and I had gone in past springs when the warblers were migrating. It was like coming home, and whenever I felt slightly homesick I used to go to the ice pond for comfort.

I wasn't homesick very often, for the whole Connecticut Valley was home. Mount Tom, our old friend that we used to climb with Pop on autumn afternoons, was right across the valley from the campus. In South Hadley we lived with the mountains looking over our shoulders all the time. As the fall came on with its blue weather and flaming color we took picnics up into the hills and walked the ridge trails high above the river valley and its checkerboard of farmland. On dull Saturdays we rode the trolley to Holyoke, where there were movies and a den of vice called The Bud, an old-fashioned saloon where daring individuals could choke down an apricot brandy at three in the afternoon. The approach to that enchanted city of my youth was through the slums down by the railroad tracks and factories, and there were crude souls who referred to the place as a dump.

Once I walked alone uptown to Oak Street and stood in front of 231. It was an autumn afternoon and the birches were deep yellow, the Boston ivy on the chimney a bright lacquer red. In the air was the old incense of fall: dry leaves and the smoke from somebody's bonfire. The house looked exactly the same, but there was nothing on the front porch, not even a pair of roller skates. The sandbox and the Little House were gone and they had pruned the syringa. It gave me a queer feeling to see it.

I loved college, my new friends, the exciting courses and the place, but it seems to me I spent half my time trying to get out. I think the main problem was that, after living all my life with a houseful of males and having spent four years in Princeton, a community composed entirely of women was hard to take on a full-time basis. I missed the sound of men's voices. Large gatherings of females sounded like Aunt K.'s chicken yard. Of course, the president, Mary E. Woolley, could hardly be classed as a typical woman; she had the impact of several men and a profile like a Roman emperor. There were a few men on the faculty, and I signed up for some of their courses, but there were times when I felt that I was in a convent.

It cost a fortune to go home to Princeton, so I could only go there for the traditional vacations, but the Point was comparatively close, and I used to hop trolleys and buses down to Fall River, where Aunt K. and Tink met me. I remember the bliss of driving up the lane on a gray November afternoon and seeing Synton's windows all lit up to welcome us. The conservatory jutted out into the cold garden like a glass box full of summer, and through the jungle-green tangle I saw Baba in her violet dress setting the table.

When we came in through the kitchen she was waiting for us in the pantry door.

"Well, dear Jan," she said. "Our college girl. We want to hear all your news."

In the drawing room Baba put a fresh log on the fire. The blue dusk closed down outside, but indoors we were snug. Soon Aunt K. brought in the tea tray and we had toasted English muffins and Earl Grey tea in Baba's silver teapot.

"This is the Lansing silver," she always said, and would turn the beautiful old pieces to show me the initials of previous owners. Those of the original owner were rubbed so smooth you could hardly read them.

We used the Spode teacups in the rosebud chintz pattern, and every time I asked for a sugar lump Baba smiled tolerantly and said, "You have your father's sweet tooth."

No one in her family ever took sugar in their tea.

During these cozy times by the fire Baba inquired about my studies, and I described to her the mating of earthworms, the development of the human embryo and the appearance of guinea-pig sperm under a microscope—highlights of my zoology course.

While we were washing up the tea things in the pantry, I explained to her that the whole plot of *The Spanish Tragedy* turned on whether or not the heroine had been raped. I was proud of being a grownup person who could discuss these adult matters, but Baba did not seem very interested. When we went into the living room she took down a copy of Thoreau's *Winter*—the green Riverside edition.

"I think you will enjoy Thoreau," she said. "He loved the woods and fields as you do. These are the winter selections from his journal. I like to read them in the winter season. I will lend you this copy."

Nobody knew how to change a subject better than Baba.

The family used to spend spring vacations at the Point, but with all of us in separate institutions of learning it was sometimes impossible to match vacation schedules. Aldie preferred to visit friends (usually girls) but Dave and I would meet at the Point and stay at Synton. Here the social life was nonexistent, but we didn't care. We were there.

I used to ride down to Fall River on a bus, and I remember how the snow vanished as we drove south and the warm brown fields appeared. The woods of white pine had the silver sheen of spring, and a blue haze rose from the softened earth. I would feel the old spring rapture that blotted out everything else, pure joy, uncomplicated by love or the need for any other person.

One spring Dave met me in Fall River in a car so revolting in appearance I hesitated to get into it. It was a species of sedan, very rusted and battered, with some nameless stain down the side of the front door that instantly brought car sickness to mind. Only one of the windows opened, and that wouldn't shut. When Dave started the engine a frightful roaring and banging broke out. As soon as we moved ahead, my seat left its moorings and I ended up on my back with my legs in the air.

"Hey, this is a great car," I said when I had reassembled things. "Where on earth did you get it?"

"I rented it," said Dave. "It really goes like a bat. You wait, and listen to this." He shut off the ignition, advanced the spark, turned on the ignition, and an explosion resulted that shook the teeth in my head.

"That's terrific," I said. It was clear we were onto a good thing.

Very soon afterward we saw nailed to a tree a large wooden sign proclaiming in block letters:

"The Gift of God is Eternal Life."

Dave shinned up the tree and wrenched off the sign, and from then on we were in business. We had a regular routine. First we spotted someone walking along the side of the road, so we slowed down and drifted ahead of him. Then Dave produced a stupendous backfire, and while the person reeled away I held up the sign for him to read.

We later developed a variation on this. I knelt in the back seat; Dave passed a car full of people and backfired; I held the sign up in the rear window. It was a risky pastime, believe me. People seemed to resent being told that the gift of God was eternal life. They were, in fact, almost foaming at the mouth with rage, especially if they got the treatment more than once. I suppose it was irritating, but it was harmless enough, and we laughed so much we could hardly see to drive.

We christened the car The Gift of God but shortened this later to The Gift. The Gift was a great car, full of character and wit. We became very attached to it.

This visit to the Point was memorable for other reasons, one of which was a new horse that Aunt K. had acquired after Gyp's death. Gyp had lived so long that she seemed immortal like everything and everybody at Synton, and the truth is that she didn't really die but was put to sleep. In her place we found a strange animal who made no secret of the fact that he was a male.

"You have so enjoyed riding horseback in Princeton that Kath and I wanted you to be able to ride here," said Baba. "My father was a very good rider. He had a horse named Beauty and rode every day."

This horse, who was certainly no beauty, was a rawboned bay gelding with a sway back and a furry coat. He was an inoffensive creature and a willing mount, but we had to ride him bareback, as there was no saddle. I wore a pair of Tink's overalls as a riding habit and Dave was in L. L. Bean pants and a naval officer's cap, so all in all we presented a pretty raffish picture when we thumped past the front porch to be inspected by Baba and the rest of the household. Baba stood at the top of the veranda steps in her violet wool dress and heavy winter sweater, but she had an air like the Queen of England reviewing her troops.

"Very nice, dear Jan," she said, as I jounced by. "You have a very good seat."

Dear Dave, she said later, might have been born in the saddle.

"Very like my father," she added proudly.

This was a flight of fancy if ever there was one, as Baba's father had looked exactly like Pendennis, with mutton-chop whiskers, long wavy hair and lily-white hands.

When I returned to college and people asked me about my vacation, I said I'd been down to the sea and had done some horseback riding. They looked on me with envy.

The time arrived when the life in Princeton took on the character of a dream. I went back in May to house parties with an old beau, but the magic had gone. We parted company in what we considered a highly sophisticated manner—friendly, witty, just like something out of a Katharine Hepburn movie. I remember we were both in evening dress standing by the sundial in the Dean's garden at the graduate school. It was just right. The next day I removed his picture from my bureau and replaced it with that of a young man from the Point. I was ready for summer and real life to begin.

⁂ 20 ⁂

Blue Days at Sea

No matter what we did during the year, no matter how many things happened to us, we always ended up at the Point in summer. It never occurred to me to do anything else. On the first real spring days when the dawns were loud with robins and the warm air smelled of lilac, I began to feel the old longing for the place. Maybe birds experience this divine restlessness before they start their mysterious migrations. At college I was ready to take flight about mid-April, and in May when the apple blossoms were out I could hardly go to classes. Who cared about the plays of Molière or the mechanics of the stock market in May? I had been required to take a course called Economics 101, and it was an uphill fight all the way. Nobody could make me understand why it was a bad idea for the government to make more money when it needed it. If I could have manufactured money somehow, I would certainly have done so, but I never considered a summer job for one second. This attitude toward money had been formed at home. You could call it the grasshopper philosophy. Like the grasshopper in the fable we believed in dancing and singing the summer through, instead of wasting the lovely days storing up food for the winter like that rotten ant. These were the years of the Great Depression, and even people who wanted summer jobs couldn't get them. When June arrived most of us took three beautiful months off, and like the lilies of the field (and the grasshopper) we toiled not, neither did we spin. As for Pop, he had three months' vacation just like us. His salary as Dean of the Chapel would be spurned by a garbage collector today, but he had a longer summer vacation than the President of the United States or the head of General Motors. The Depression couldn't hurt him because he had no investments to lose.

I went back to Princeton to help celebrate the reunions and attend the graduation festivities. As soon as commencement was over, we all packed into the car and set out for the Point.

According to our new system we went to bed on the Fall River boat in New York and woke up in Fall River. Everything looked just right, even the docks. There were the first gulls hanging in the breeze, their voices sounding like the squeal of pulleys when you haul up a sail. The air smelled of saltwater.

Before the dew had dried on the hedgerows we'd be driving up the rise by the Allan farm where we saw the sea for the first time.

There it was, dreaming in the windless hush of early morning, a wedge of pale, silvery blue as enchanting as a glimpse of heaven. Better, really. We drove down toward it between the little stone-walled fields, the wine-glass elms, the white farms with their great barns, peaceful in the low sunlight. Barn swallows swept down in front of the car; meadowlarks whistled from the barways. New England! Our own country. The Point!

Only those who have been brought up in family summer places know the ecstasy of these arrivals. It was still almost a miracle to us to get there in the radiance of early morning instead of at the tail end of the afternoon. The day was so new that Baba was often out on the cairn pulling up her flag. Aunt K. would come out of the kitchen door with flour all over her hands and say she was in the middle of kneading bread. Tink, fresh and rosy in his new summer clothes, followed after her, beaming from ear to ear. We picked up right where we had left off the September before.

Down at Snowdon someone had opened all the doors and windows so the summer air had blown out the winter's mustiness. Aunt K. had put big tangled bunches of flowers around—her special bouquets, in which old-fashioned roses and daisies, sweet peas, buttercups, grass and clover were all mixed up together, just as she happened to see them in or outside of the garden.

The first thing we did was run up the creaky wooden stairs and out onto my porch to look at The View. There were the blue reaches of the river, the immemorial pattern of the salt marshes, the water tower and the sea. Next Pop and Dave went up to see how the vegetable garden was doing, and the Hideons dashed around testing the swing and unearthing last summer's homemade go-cart, which over the winter had acquired a new glamour. Aldie and I arranged our possessions in our rooms and Mum and Bruce went into conference and made lists. The two of them successfully managed all the details of the housekeeping and none of us had to lift a finger. So completely were we spoiled that I had literally never boiled an egg; Bruce didn't like people messing around his kitchen.

From the moment we arrived on the hill we were as free as birds. This gave to those summer days a special magic, and when we came home for meals the house was full of a warm hum and murmur. Rich odors of simmering stew or new-baked bread came from the kitchen. Mum might be fussing around her plants or writing letters at her desk. During the period before a meal Pop always sat in his special chair by the window with his feet up on a hassock and a book open on his knee.

"Come on in," he'd say, looking up over the top of his glasses. "Sit down and rest your neck and ears."

With all her brood around her Mum was in her element. She loved the noise and confusion of a full house, and nothing anyone did bothered her. There was always a game of some kind raging across the front lawn, and someone was constantly rattling downhill in a makeshift vehicle. Howls and shrieks filled the air, and at intervals a ball crashed through a window or one of the vehicles plunged into the barberry hedge, causing multiple wounds and lacerations to the passengers.

"Eye Guy," Pop often said. "I've read the same sentence twenty-five times and I still don't know what it's about," but his eyes glowed with pride and pleasure.

"The whole crew at home," he'd say, and then he'd gloat over our good fortune. A happy home, he declared, was the best possible gift you could give your children. And a summer home like ours was the best way to keep a family together. It was the rallying place to which we could all return, and so could our children and our children's children.

"First let me find a husband," I said, but I knew what he meant. Here was continuity, a rare treasure.

We had, not without some difficulty, persuaded Pop that it was important for us to join the beach club and meet people who weren't relatives. He finally consented to rent a bathhouse so we swam at the beach every day. One thing led to another, and almost before he knew what he was doing Pop had become the owner of a thirty-foot yawl, our beloved *Calmar*.

The purchase of the *Calmar* was a perfect example of the family's grasshopper philosophy in action. As an investment in joy it was unsurpassed but any reputable ant would have told you that a thirty-foot yawl was hardly the sort of thing Pop could afford with five children in private school and college. He was always struggling to pay off bank loans, but by a miracle of ratiocination he persuaded himself that it would be wrong not to buy the *Calmar*. The royalty check for his first book had just arrived and was burning a hole in his pocket. By an amazing coincidence the amount of the check and the price of the *Calmar* were exactly the same. You can't ignore a thing like that, not if you're a grasshopper.

"What's the use of my saving money to leave you after I'm dead?" Pop asked, as he prepared his mind for the inevitable purchase. "I should spend this check on something special we can all enjoy together while I'm alive."

"That's right," we said. "Don't wait until you're a doddering old wreck. Spend now while you can still sail a boat."

"We may end up in the poorhouse," said Pop, "but at least we'll have had fun on the way."

The *Calmar* was a sturdy, broad-beamed old boat with a snub nose and a wide flat bowsprit. She was gaff-rigged and had a centerboard, a great convenience in shoal waters. At sea she was as dry as a puffball and a beautiful sailer in any breeze. Oh, what a boat she was and how we loved her!

Calmar was Belgian for "squid." Her previous owner was a Harvard professor who had written his doctorate on the squid and somehow this seemed to Pop a guarantee of his integrity.

The *Calmar* spent her winters up in a cradle at Tripp's shipyard. She was overhauled every June, and our first weeks at the Point were spent down at the shipyard working on her. To save money we did a lot of the painting and rigging ourselves. Aldie had a job in Nonquit as tutor to some unfortunate child and was seldom present, so Pop, Dave and I did most of the work of getting the boat in shape, but we loved doing it. Every morning after breakfast we'd drive down to the shipyard where the *Calmar* stood on the ways in her high cradle. We'd climb a ladder into the cockpit and spend long, delicious hours up there sanding and varnishing the mahogany trim and polishing brass.

The shipyard at that time was a small and peaceful boat-building operation. It consisted of one big shed for the shop, a gas pump, a Coca-Cola machine and a spindly little dock, where we tied up our dinghies. The drone of the circular saw was almost the only sound, and that was no more disturbing than the buzzing of bees around a hive.

The shop was always ankle deep in blond shavings and smelled sweetly of new wood. I remember that the windows were full of blue, and that golden reflections from the water ran across the ceiling. In the center of the floor stood the beautiful skeleton of a lobster boat, her bare ribs rising in perfect curves from the keel.

Besides the *Calmar* there were only four other pleasure boats moored at the yard, and in June some of the owners were around sanding their spars or painting dinghies. There was a cozy family atmosphere about the place, and as there were usually several interfamily romances going on every day was full of interest.

Even after the *Calmar* was launched, Dave and I went down every morning and rowed out to the mooring, for there was always something to fiddle with. Dave spliced or whipped the ends of all the lines, while I mopped gull droppings off the deck. We gave the cabin a fresh coat of white enamel. We did the ceiling lying on the bunks with paint dribbling into our faces.

Everybody had something to contribute. Mum made faded blue denim covers for the bunks, and Dave and Pop built special cubbies for stowing dishes so they would not slip around at sea. Aldie designed the house flag.

The ship's clock was screwed to the bulkhead, and there was an entrancing little kerosene lamp in gimbals that we kept polished like gold. One of the most satisfying items in the cabin was the Shipmate stove, a miniature black iron coal range just like the one in Snowdon's kitchen.

"Cutest dad-gasted thing I ever saw," Pop would say, lying on his bunk with his feet up against the woodbox. The Shipmate was at the end of his bunk, the sink at the foot of the other. We had fixed a small mirror on one wall, and the charts, neatly rolled, were in a rack overhead. The Coast Pilot and Tide Tables had their own little slot. All the portholes were brass rimmed and well polished, and when you lay facing the after hatch with its square of sky and clouds you couldn't ask for anything more satisfying.

When we were out on the *Calmar* I forgot everything else. All the matters that had seemed so serious at college or in Princeton faded into thin air. Even love weighed but lightly on my mind. While we were painting the cabin or drying the sails Dave and I used to discuss various stratagems for meeting and fascinating members of the opposite sex. Dave was very helpful and gave me complete support in all my endeavors. If the man of my choice glanced at another girl, Dave condemned him as a faithless monster and told me to strike his name from the records. If I wanted to see someone, Dave asked him out on the boat. I did what I could for Dave, and the two of us used up gallons and gallons of gas patroling the countryside in the family car in order to run across people by mistake and act surprised to see them. Then we'd get them aboard the *Calmar* for the afternoon sail.

On blue afternoons when the wind was in the southwest and the sun was hot we sailed until the harbor and the beach were just a violet blur on the rim of the peacock-colored bay. To the west the sea was crumpled silver in the sun, and beyond the bow the Elizabeth Islands loomed closer and closer until we could see the little houses on Cuttyhunk and even the streaks of color on the cliffs at Gay Head on the Vineyard.

We came about at the *Hen and Chickens* lightship and then let the sail out and ran home on a quarter.

My favorite spot was the bowsprit. I stood out on the very tip, holding on to the jib stay with nothing in front of me but blue water and sky. It was almost like walking on the waves, and I rode the motion of the boat like a skier. On rough days the bowsprit described a wide arc, sweeping me high into the air one moment and plunging me up to my knees in a wave the next. When the sea was calm I used to lie along the bowsprit, watching the sun move over the sails and the shadows of the reef points dancing on the canvas.

On mornings of exceptional blueness, we'd collect a boatload and sail out to the islands for the day.

Nashawena was our favorite island, a long narrow strip of land whose gentle slopes were covered with dry golden grass and clumps of bayberry and wild roses. There were no trees or houses on our end of it—nothing but sheep trails and a few ancient stone walls. Sometimes as we came up into the wind to drop the anchor we'd see two horses watching us from above the beach. There was one cream-colored horse and one chestnut, and as soon as we approached the shore in the dinghy they'd wheel and canter off up the slope, manes and tails blowing free.

In the sheltered cove where we landed there was not a breath of wind, and the fragrance of bayberry and roses lay on the air. The whole island was steeped in sunlight; in the silence you could hear song sparrows singing, for they nested everywhere undisturbed. There was often a small flock of sheep nibbling the green turf by the old sheepfold. They'd take one look at us, bleat and bundle off with the tucked-in behinds of offended matrons.

We'd picnic in a warm hollow and then explore the island, running up and down those long hills, combing the beaches for treasure or trying to corner a sheep.

Every now and then I'd be invited by a young man to sail on one of the other boats, and we'd race the *Calmar* out to the lightship and come winging home side by side at the end of the day. The wind usually dropped before sunset, and sometimes we rode down the channel on the tide alone. At that peaceful hour the smell of grass and flowers came to us off the land. The boats drifted on level keels, and we stood up and stretched to let the sun dry our salt-soaked clothes. I'd take the wheel or tiller while my companion caught the mooring. Then we'd furl the sails, tie on the sail covers, stow the cushions and coil all the lines. The water would be gold in the sunset as we rowed in to the dock.

In the evenings of these days at sea we'd be so drugged with salt and sun that we could hardly stay awake. Pop would build a big fire of cedar logs and read aloud one of our favorite Wodehouse novels. Mum sat in her corner of the sofa with her work basket and a pile of mending beside her. The rest of us lay on the floor, the dogs stretched out beside us. The only thing that kept us awake was laughing. Sometimes Pop laughed so much he had to stop to mop his eyes. At intervals Mum would finish a pair of socks, roll it up and throw it at the owner.

"There," she'd say. "Now if you'd just given it to me earlier . . ."

Mum had an eagle eye for holes, tears, runs or missing buttons on people's clothing.

"Here," she would say, "take that off and give it to me."

Everybody gave her everything, (I'm ashamed to say we still do). In the summer she had a field day, even wresting the clothes from visitors, forcing them to give her their holey socks or sweaters for repair.

At ten o'clock someone was sure to be asleep on the floor, and Mum would put away her work basket and call, "How many for Ovaltine?"

Then she'd trot out to the kitchen and come back with a tray of steaming mugs and a plate of saltines. This marked the official end of every day. On those evenings when we were, as Pop put it, off gallivanting, we missed the Ovaltine ceremony, but we were never forgotten. There were Mum's signs.

When we came in there would be a shirt card, an old letter or box cover propped up in Mum's little fat Victorian chair.

"Turn out the lights. Quiet!" This was the basic one. There were variations.

"Jan. Dave's still out so leave the light on. quiet!"

"Check here when you come in. Last one in turn out the lights. QUIET! Pop's sleeping in the guestroom."

Sometimes the cards contained the latest newsflash.

"Guess what? Jim called and you weren't here, Jan. Now aren't you sorry you went out! QUIET. Turn out the light, etc."

When we had turned out the light and tiptoed upstairs we seldom made it to our doors before a voice spoke up from our parents' room.

"Is that you, Jan?"

They tried hard not to lie awake and check us in, but in this day of "high-powered" cars they were all too certain that we were lying somewhere dead in a ditch. Only when we were all in could they sleep.

"Good night," they'd call. "Sleep tight."

When I look back at those summers of the *Calmar,* I remember how I used to get up very early and run down to the river for a swim. At sunrise the shore and the dock were still in the shadow of the hill, and I'd swim out of the shade into the heat and glory of the sunlight. I swam without a suit, free as a seal. Later I'd rub down on the dock, looking around at the new day, savoring every sensation. In this hour of peaceful solitude I experienced a feeling of wholeness and joy hard to describe. I was not separate or alone but one with the river, the gulls sailing overhead, the roses on the shore, with the sunlight and with summer itself. Of course, I didn't think any of these things, simply existed in the moment, loving it and looking forward with delight to Bruce's bacon and eggs.

The delicate balance of these perfect days could easily be disrupted by some invasion from the larger world, and it seemed to me that there was a subtle pressure from the authorities to make me settle down. Pop tried to help me decide on a career and used to tell me that when you were given a job to do it was important to do more than was expected of you at all times. Soon people would be beating a path to your door. There was an illustration for this: a story about Booker T. Washington cleaning a cloakroom. Booker cleaned the living hell out of that cloakroom and became famous.

The alternative to the B. T. Washington route was, of course, marriage. Pop had grave doubts about the company I kept in Princeton when I was home from college on weekends. They were happy adventurers, who liked to talk about T. S. Eliot and sit around banging wine bottles on tables and saying the world was their oyster. They wrote long tragic stories in which every character ended up dead, and poetry no one could understand. Pop referred to them as Bohemians.

"Now I know that sort of thing is fun but you're a nice, wholesome girl, and you'll see that in the long run what you want is a fine chap with a sense of responsibility."

"I'm not wholesome and I don't want a fine chap," I'd cry. "Ye gods, Pop."

Mum never put forward any theories. She simply filled the house with elegible young men and hoped for the best. Her hospitality was boundless and our guest room was full all summer long. Regulars and old favorites even made reservations to be sure of getting a bed.

Any member of the old Sunday-supper group from Princeton had a standing invitation to drop in at any time and stay indefinitely. He might have to sleep in the boathouse or out on the *Calmar,* but he was welcome. These Princetonians were virtually members of the family, used our private language, played the games we had invented and called our parents Mum and Pop.

"Now there," Pop would say, "is a nice fella. He fits right in."

I knew just what he was thinking.

"Look," I said. "I don't have to marry people just because they fit in. They aren't marrying the family."

Pop couldn't understand this attitude at all, but he did his best to be patient.

Mum approved of any man who was good looking, talked our language and made her laugh. Baba, on the other hand, was going to see to it that I made the right choice. Her ideals were extremely high, and the young man had to be of good family and, above all, a gentleman.

Everybody who came to stay with us had to be presented at Baba's, after which she would hand down her verdict. Sometimes she was able to do this from a photograph only.

"Not quite the gentleman," she said once, examining a picture of a young man.

"How can you tell?" I asked.

"One can always tell," said Baba quietly.

Finally she picked out the proper man for me. After I had taken a guest to be presented Baba called me aside.

"Very suitable," she said. "A delightful young man and a perfect gentleman. So handsome, too."

Aunt K. and Tink heartily concurred; in fact Tink, the eternal eavesdropper, decided to help the work along and proposed to the poor man for me.

"You want to marry dear Jan?" he inquired, patting the victim's sleeve.

"Theodore," said Baba in a terrible voice.

"Will everybody please stop trying to marry me off?" I said at the table when this client had departed. "It just happens that I don't feel like marrying anybody right now. It's summer and I want to enjoy my vacation."

I sometimes felt that if I could just combine several men and come up with a husband who looked like Ronald Colman I'd be willing to settle down. He'd have to teach so we could go to the Point for three months every summer, and he'd have to love the sea, Dickens, *The Wind in the Willows,* the poetry of Archibald MacLeish and the music of Handel. Unless he considered Laurel and Hardy and P. G. Wodehouse funny he was ineligible. There was a long list of other necessary qualifications that made my quest almost hopeless.

When at last I met the man of my heart I forgot all about my list and knew only that he was the one. We became engaged in a canoe in the middle of Lake Carnegie because he was a fresh-water man and had always planned to get engaged in a canoe. There was a dense fog that night, and I had a heavy cold, but we went out anyway. After we were engaged he told me that in the summers he went to the most beautiful place in the world.

"Where's thad?" I asked thickly.

"It's an island in Georgian Bay in Canada."

We were married and lived happily for thirty years, and as he was a teacher at Exeter Academy, we had three months' summer vacation and could stay at the island a long time. In June and September I managed to get home to the Point for brief periods, but I went down whenever the clan rallied. In Christmas and Spring vacations and on special weekends I'd pack our four children into the car and drive from our home in New Hampshire to the Point for a quick visit. As I was the only member of the family who hadn't married a Point addict I would find the clan assembled and it was as though I'd never been away.

At the end of the evening the Ovaltine was circulated, and any wanderer coming in late would find Mum's sign with its ancient message slightly amended.

"Turn out lights. QUIET, or you'll wake up the babies."

As a matter of fact it's all still going on, only now the babies are Mum's great-grandchildren.